The Eagle Hunts

Phantom IIs, Death Defied, Hanoi's Hell,
Lost Faith Found, and Return With Honor

By
Col. John W. Clark
United States Air Force (Retired)
10 Jan 2021

The Eagle Hunts

Phantom IIs, Death Defied, Hanoi's Hell, Lost Faith Found, and Return With Honor

By
Col. John W. Clark
United States Air Force (Retired)
10 Jan 2021

Water color painting of a flight of two RF-4Cs flying in close trail formation low over the mountains and ridges of North Vietnam. The lead aircraft in the flight bears the tail number (50677) of the RF-4C that was being flown by Captain Ed Goodrich and Captain John Clark when they were shot down on 12 March 1967.

Original painting by Kerm Dyer. Not to be used without expressed written permission of Colonel John W. Clark, USAF (Ret).

Copyright © 2022 College of the Ozarks

All rights reserved. This book, or any portion thereof, may not be reproduced or used in any manner whatsoever without the express written consent of the publisher, except for the use of brief quotations in a book review.

Printed in the United States of America by the students and staff at the Hyer Press, College of the Ozarks.

Original painting for cover art by Kerm Dyer. Cover images not to be used without expressed written permission of Colonel John W. Clark, USAF (Ret).

First Printing, 2022

For additional copies of this book, or for information about College of the Ozarks, contact:

Development Office
College of the Ozarks
P. O. Box 17
Point Lookout, Missouri 65726
417-690-2209

To purchase additional copies of this book, please visit store.cofo.edu.

Dedicated to

**Lt. Colonel Thomas G. Storey,
U.S. Air Force (Retired),**
*whose valuable lessons in life and faith in God
would inspire me to refuse death
as an alternative to the hellish uncertain future
in a North Vietnamese prison.*

The proceeds from this book will go to
The William S. Knight Center for Patriotic Education
at College of the Ozarks.

The William S. Knight Center for Patriotic Education serves as a hub for patriotic education, which permeates the institution. All students take two courses in Patriotic Education, including military science, American history, American economic system (capitalism), ethics, civics, and government. A Patriotic Education Travel Program (PETP) sends students and veterans back to battlefields to learn about the honor, sacrifice, and contributions of the nation's military. The E. Bruce Heilman CitizenTrip® sends students to Washington, D.C., for an educational visit.

PREFACE

Although the subject of prisoner of war experiences in Vietnam is well covered, each story is different. They are individual stories told in different ways and of each man's survival, mentally and physically; of personal reflections, tests of faith, personal stories of tortured minds and bodies and their recoveries or deaths. All of them told by those who lived it, but they are not my story. My story is now to be told.

Growing up and attending school in Columbia, Missouri, I spent summers in the hills of northern Missouri on my dad's farm, learning life isn't always good, but it's always worth living.

There is a drifting faith in God that becomes lost and is reborn in the quest for strength and survival. Stories, about which I could not speak for many years, are told in the detail they were lived.

The reader will understand the value of overcoming hardship and challenges to life, see living as an American in a new context, and examine strength in faith in God and unity. All of this is told with a touch of self-deprecation, humor and a rollercoaster of moods and experiences.

Younger audiences are intrigued by the covert aspects, the action and the shootdown. More mature audiences ponder the mental processes of survival under the stresses of torture and deprivation. Could "I have survived that?" they ask themselves, while the most mature of my audiences whose life experiences may themselves involve the times, pose questions about what they hear me say that confirms or contradicts that which was told to them or they experienced during their youthful, perhaps anti-war, life.

My story is written for everyone, even vets, for there is no better audience for a war story than another veteran. There is no hero here, only an American warrior who survived and *came home with honor*.

INTRODUCTION

From the opening chapter to the last, I describe, in detail, the thoughts flashing through my mind as I escaped death's repeated attempts on my life. These thoughts, some might call instincts, kept me alive again and again from one crisis after another, beginning with a tractor. The Air Force Reserve Officers Training course saved me from yet another youthful disaster and sent me off to Air Force pilot training. Gone was the immature naïve geek, replaced by an Air Force officer, jet pilot, husband, father, escape and evasion artist and possessor of highly classified survival training. High marks in flying skills at first launched me into "mercy" flying before I discovered my love of speed, performance, formation, low and swashbuckling in the RF-4C Phantom II. It's a hulking beast with state-of-the-art technology, a beast I flew 13 miles into the atmosphere at two times the speed of sound. It took me to war in Southeast Asia where it was shot down, ejecting me at 600 miles per hour, only four seconds before becoming a huge fireball.

Being a Prisoner of War in the infamous Hanoi Hilton revealed a lost faith in God. I struggled with survival and regaining my faith but was rewarded in ways that are explained only through faith itself. Moving from camp to camp and forced to endure harsh conditions, including torture, I contracted a sickness that caused a dramatic struggle with death. But when I turned my life over to the Almighty, my physical strength improved without explanation, and HE sustained me throughout the remainder of my ordeal.

At Son Tay, a rural prison in North Vietnam, I and 61 other POWs were moved just prior to a raid intended to rescue us, but when we learned of the attempt our spirits soared because we knew we had not been forgotten by our nation. Survival included mental games, the creation of a "tap code" to communicate with fellow POWs and participating in a variety of educational pursuits such as learning French, history, and musical composition. When the full fury of American airpower turned Hanoi into rubble, our release came within a few months, but not before our captors threatened 20 of us, myself included, to be made to "disappear forever" within the vast hell of the North Vietnamese prison system.

You, the reader, may be astounded, annoyed, in disbelief, tearful, turn to God, and yes, even chuckle while reading *The Eagle Hunts*.

ACKNOWLEDGEMENTS

Over the several years this book was being written many people deserve recognition in bringing it to fruition:

My wife whose continued encouragement never let the book be forgotten, but never read it saying simply "I just can't do it."

My sister Vevonna, who established the grounds for accuracy by pointing out "John it's your story-it's how you lived it, no one else's, so tell your story." And the great amount of time she spent on the magnificent painting she did with me in the cell, the light ray, and the cross.

My brother-in-law, Dr. Robert Kennedy who has lived a life of renown in international relations and is himself published said upon reading the first draft "John, this book needs to be read."

My granddaughter Elly, who said after a period of letting the book stagnate, "Pa Pa when are you going to finish your book."

All of the many friends and audiences, to whom I have spoken that have asked "have you written a book?"

Dr. Jerry C. Davis, president of the College of the Ozarks, who has authored several books documenting the amazing history of that small college steeped in morality, patriotism, hard work and achievement. His last book being *Vietnam 101, a Class Like No Other* was published in 2021 by Hyer Press of the College of the Ozarks. It's a must-read, especially for all who think their liberties just come free with being American. Dr. Davis also decided the The *Eagle Hunts* was a book to be read and the College of the Ozarks press would print it.

All of the faculty and staff of the College of the Ozarks who have contributed to making this book a reality; Mr. Craig Cogdill, Hyer Press Manager and his staff with Sammie Blackwell, Graphic Design Supervisor and Don Codillo, Imaging Supervisor; Dr. David Dalton,

Professor of History, who so artfully edited the final proof; Sarah Franks, who took the book in its publishing infancy and injected enormous energy in starting the publishing process; Brian Cizek who continues to provide administrative support; Prof. Mark Young MGA, Theater Director, who produced a play by the College of the Ozarks, which played through the fall of 2021 entitled *A Flight to Faith, The Story of a Vietnam POW*, which was inspired by this book and Dr. Davis's book *Vietnam 101, A Class Like No Other*.

And to those who proofed the first drafts of *The Eagle Hunts*; Kurt Storey, Mary Carnahan, Debbie Worn, Vevonna Kennedy, and Robert Kennedy.

Thank you and God Bless you each for your wonderful considerations.

Table of Contents

Chapter 1
A Life 1

Chapter 2
University Of Missouri And ROTC 7

Chapter 3
Pilot Training And Survival School 11

Chapter 4
McGuire AFB 15

Chapter 5
Shaw, Combat Crew Training and the Phantom II 21

Chapter 6
Alconbury 29

Chapter 7
Ramstein and Europe 35

Chapter 8
The War in Southeast Asia 45

Chapter 9
Dodging SAMS 55

Chapter 10
Lucky or Not? 61

Chapter 11
On to Hoa Lo 79

Chapter 12
The Knobby Room 83

Chapter 13
Heartbreak Hotel 97

Chapter 14
Little Vegas and the Tap Code 117

Chapter 15
Uncle Tom and Faith 137

Chapter 16
Baby Ruth and Berkshires 143

Chapter 17	
The Power Plant	149

Chapter 18	
Return to Hoa Lo	159

Chapter 19	
Sickness	167

Chapter 20	
The Witch Doctor	173

Chapter 21	
Son Tay	177

Chapter 22	
Hot or Cold War	189

Chapter 23	
Big Cells	195

Chapter 24	
Back to School	203

Chapter 25	
Onward Christian Soldiers	213

Chapter 26	
Cell Mates, Sex, and Scalawags	221

Chapter 27	
Cold Nights	229

Chapter 28	
Linebacker II	231

Chapter 29	
The Proclamation	239

Chapter 30	
Refusing to Go Home	243

Epilogue	249
About the Author	253

CHAPTER 1

A LIFE

    The front wheels of the red 1951 Farmall C tractor with its powerful little 4-cylinder engine bounced on the steep firm incline leading from the muck and mud of the ditch. Its new sharp lugged tires dug into the solid buried ledge at the edge of the muddy ditch, then catching traction they held onto the ledge of firm soil and the front of the tractor reared up in the air. The back of the tractor seat began to sink into the muck behind. The nose of the tractor approached straight up while the 11 or 12-year-old boy sitting in the seat grasped the steering wheel pointed straight at his chest. His genes had blessed him with uncommon ability to assess a situation and react quickly. So far, only about three seconds have transpired, and seeing the tractor coming over backwards on top of him, he released the wheel and rolled off of the seat into the muck on his hands and knees. Knowing that the tractor was coming over backwards and would drop on anything under it, he clawed his way through the muck and mire on his hands and knees toward the eight-inch trunk of a tree growing on the opposite bank of the ditch. He knew by the sound of the engine that it was falling and he didn't have time to stand up or even stop his crawl and look up at it. His only thought was getting to that tree trunk which would hopefully afford some protection. He reasoned it was doubtful that the tractor would fall straight over but would most likely rotate one direction or the other while it was vertical and therefore crawling 90 degrees away from where he started was no assurance that it would miss him. In fact, it did not fall straight over, but rotated about 45 degrees while in the air. Just as he reached the tree and was about to scramble around to the other side of the trunk,

The Eagle Hunts

there was a huge "splush"* as the tractor landed completely upside down in the ditch splattering muck and mud all over him.

Knowing the event was over, he looked up to see that the new red tractor only missed him by a couple of feet. He watched as the nose wheel slowly rotated to a halt while steam boiled out from the radiator through the muck into the air. The engine was dead, and as he looked directly under the smashed seat and steering wheel of the tractor, mostly buried in the muck, he noticed the two marks of where his knees first landed as he rolled off the tractor. Good idea not wasting time trying to stand up or turning around and looking up; also heading for the tree was the right direction to go, he thought. Following that thought he supposed, I should walk over the hill and tell Irmal, the hired man, as dad was not around the farm today.

Irmal, hearing the news, disconnected the corn planter while the young boy stepped on the drawbar of the green and yellow John Deere B and they traveled two miles back to his grandparent's house where a call was made on the hand cranked party phone and a message was left for dad.

Later that day, dad arrived and they traveled back to the accident site. His dad also noticed the knee prints and said, "Son you were lucky, now, just like you've got to get back on a horse when it throws you, we've got to get you back on another tractor so you don't become afraid of one."

So, John ended the day on the green and yellow John Deere B pulling the eight foot tandem disk with which I started across the ditch.

It was my second escape from the clutches of death, which I have experienced with uncommon regularity over my many years on this earth. More at least, than the nine allotted to cats, of which my lovely wife, Anne, reminds me, as it seems she has been part of at least a few.

It all started in the early hours of January 1, 1940 in Columbia, Mo. I was to be the first baby of the new decade in Boone County Missouri. I was entered into 1st grade a year early because it was thought that I would be able to keep up with the older kids. Well, I

---

* "Splash" is the sound a Farmall C makes when it turns over in water, but "splush" is the sound it makes when it turns over in muck and mud.

Chapter 1 | A Life

don't know about that, but that year did cost me an edge in athletics in high school and made me wait for another year after all my classmates to start "legally" driving. But I made up for it by cramming my four-year college engineering program into five years.

I attended Ulysses S. Grant grade school which was a large, imposing red brick structure built on a hill in the highest and oldest part of Columbia, MO. There was a huge portrait of Ulysses S. Grant adorning the hall of the main entryway, and so no one would forget how divided Missouri was during the Civil War, there was also a Robert E. Lee grade school in Columbia, which was a likewise imposing structure for a young grade-schooler.

At recess, which would end the most undesirable part of school, spelling, I raced around the playground with my arms outspread swooping and diving and making the sounds of an aircraft engine by blowing breath through my fluttering lips. Mom used to say if I kept on doing that my lips would get fat. I don't know if she was really worried about her tall, blue-eyed son having fat lips or making a fool of himself and bringing discredit upon anyone with whom he associated. My sister, Kathryn, could sit down at a piano and play any song she had just heard for the first time and my younger sister, Vevonna, proved in life that she had all the rest of the family talent including song, art, sculpture, music, language and anything else she damn well wanted to do. I, on the other hand, concentrated on my "creative" pictures of American fighters diving on German planes hopelessly attempting to escape their blazing guns. There were, of course, chunks of the doomed German aircraft being shot off everywhere.

I didn't like spelling and much preferred drawing pictures of German planes being shot down. I discovered that if I did not make eye contact with the teacher, I probably would not have to spell the word that was assigned as homework, which I did not do. By that I mean, I had a red Radio Flyer wagon with a large wooden cask placed on the back and a liver and white colored retriever pup that needed to be coaxed into it so we could begin the afternoon's exploratory venture. Thus, started a very bad practice of ignoring homework. I was, however, awarded a very impressive document that said I was certified a member of the first School Boy Patrol in Columbia. Eventually in spite of my spelling grades, I was sent on to Jefferson Junior High School.

I had my first wreck when I smashed my bike into the side of a car at a downtown intersection while speeding home from Jeff Junior HS. I thought I was pretty much free from hazards of traffic with my new rear tire that I had purchased for my "high speed" bike. I had reasoned it would stop my bike much quicker than did my old tire. One could tell my bike was high speed because it had no front fender. There I was, headed down Broadway hill, imbued with stopping confidence, passing through a green light and picking up speed. About halfway down the block I realized I had not made the next green light and there was this little old lady slowly pulling into the intersection with her big all steel Oldsmobile. I hit the brakes and laid back on the rear wheel and we (the rear wheel and I) slid and slid and smashed head on into the driver's door. "T-boning" they call it today. It knocked me silly, bent up my fender-less front wheel, twisted my handlebars, and made a huge dent in her driver's door. I'm not sure what made the dent but most likely my head followed by the rest of my lanky body. She was very upset that I must be hurt, got out of the car, was extremely apologetic and wanted to rush me to the hospital, the very same hospital in which I was born. She seemed to think it was her fault. Although I didn't see it that way, forgiving her seemed the best way out and so I did. Then I proved I had nothing broken, had at least some of my mental facilities intact, and could proceed with a skinned elbow and knee home so mom could put some iodine on them. Off I went, no police, no ambulance, no fire trucks, no paramedics, wobbling down Broadway hill with my crooked handlebars and bent front wheel somewhat less confident in my super tire's stopping ability. Life then made one responsible for their own actions and the repercussions was theirs to accept like it or not. Life's lessons begin early, heed them.

Spending all of my summers working on dad's farm in north Missouri I became familiar with hard work, long hours and peer isolation. I was known to drive one of our tractors four miles to the small town of Milan to go to the drive-in movie. Meanwhile, back in Columbia I played some football and was voted to have the best

Chapter 1 | A Life

posture in English class at Jefferson Junior High School. It turns out, that was the only thing in English at which I ever excelled. In school choir, I was told to just mouth the words because apparently staying on key was not a talent with which I was blessed. I think girls started to like me, but they scared me. Down one car, one tractor, bad at spelling and English, and beginning my youthful adult life as a social misfit, I was passed on to the 10th grade at David H. Hickman High School as the second youngest in a class of about 250. High School suited me better. I played football all three years and lettered my last, not because I was that good but because of tenacity and guts. In track I ran the high and low hurdles, dashes and relays and lettered my junior and senior years. I won the class-A Mid Missouri State Championship in the high hurdles, was awarded All-State, tied the Hickman record also in the high hurdles and was chosen Co-Captain of the track team my senior year.

On the academic side, despite not being able to spell, I usually made the honor roll and was a member of The National Honor Society. Socially, I still spent all summer on the farm and missed all of the social activities taking place at home. Nevertheless, I liked looking at the girls, but from a distance. My best friend Lon, set me up on a date with a cute and bold one named Judy and we had lots of fun together but mostly as friends. It wouldn't be until my sophomore year at the University of Missouri when I pledged Phi Delta Theta fraternity, with Lon as my Big Brother, that I received the proper tutorage in the ways of these girl things that so mystified me.

The Eagle Hunts

CHAPTER 2

UNIVERSITY OF MISSOURI AND ROTC

As I became older, my passion for flying became less obvious but no less real. Some time between my outstretched arms and fluttering lips and Air Force Reserve Officers Training Corps (ROTC) at the University of Missouri I remember reading a newspaper comic strip, which by the way is still my most favorite part of the paper, about one of my superheroes. Steve Canyon was saving the world by flying a secret brand new very fast and very good American jet fighter. Two huge jet engines that pushed it faster than twice the speed of sound; so fast even a bullet couldn't catch it and so high that a person's blood would boil if they were not protected by its pressurized cockpit. That aircraft and I would have a later encounter, which would catapult me into a completely different life of flying than I had started following my future graduation from pilot training.

I did well as an ROTC student at the University of Missouri, advancing to the position of Cadet Corps Commander my senior year. While the disciplined life of the military seemed to suit me very well, the study involved in making good grades in my academic major of Mechanical Engineering did not enamor me. Hence, I spent a lot of time "spinning wheels," chasing girls, which came to me late in my youthful life, drinking and basically majoring in "home town" antics and fraternity. However I excelled in ROTC, and with that came my choice of pilot training bases after the Air Force Academy graduates got their pick, an immediate entry into pilot training rather than waiting for several months as some others did, and a "Regular Air Force Commission" which was a significant honor. Only the Air Force Academy Graduates received a Regular Commission unless you were one of the very few Air Force Reserve Officer Training graduates that distinguished themselves enough to be selected as a candidate and awarded the prized commission.

On the other hand, I had recently married, and rather hastily I might add. Living with my youthful pregnant wife in an 8 by 41-foot house trailer in the Vagabond Mobil Home Park, I was recovering from infectious mononucleosis and had to quit my part-time job because my recovery was slow. In addition, I encountered another one of those life lessons that my glib academic attitude brought upon me.

I had not enjoyed those electrical engineering courses because I usually had to do homework, the motivation for which I was still "challenged." So, I managed to put the most difficult one off until my last semester and being ever so clever I had obtained a commitment for tutorage from a high school friend, Wayne Riggens, who was a major in Electrical Engineering and did his homework. With that major asset on which to fall back, I stumbled along with minimal grades doing my own work. Then as we approached finals week, I requested his assistance to show me how to work all the problems I had not done during the semester. To my surprise Wayne wanted to study for his finals also, how inconsiderate. Things were serious; I was supposed to graduate, be commissioned an Air Force Officer, and move with a pregnant wife in a trailer to Lubbock, Texas, reporting into my already assigned pilot training class in a month. It was all predicated on graduation, and this Electrical Engineering course was required for graduation. I could not even imagine the impact that not passing this course would have on a very promising start to life in the Air Force. Why this realization had not occurred to me previously, I am at a loss to explain.

I humbly sought out the course instructor and explained the dire consequences of my academic indiscretions and threw myself at his mercy. He regarded me with an emotionless expression and his eyes said, "Why should this kid be special, why should I allow him that which I won't others?" But he did allow me to turn in the homework

Chapter 2 | University Of Missouri And ROTC

I had ignored for some grade improvement and told me everything would hinge on the final exam. As I departed, his emotionless expression had not changed. What else could I do but get to work? The homework was hard and my notes were weak at best. I went into the final with little sleep, hyped on coffee and weak in the knees. The test could have been written in Latin for all I knew. I had no choice but to make the best effort I could and not give up without giving it my all. After the test, I had a bad feeling but, there were other tests on which I then needed to concentrate. On the day the Electrical Engineering test scores were to be posted, I approached the display board in the hall outside of my instructor's locked and unoccupied office with considerable consternation and looked for my student number. Grades were posted by student numbers so that others wouldn't know who did poorly or perhaps failed. To my dismay there were a lot more failures than I expected from a junior and senior level course. Suddenly I just wanted to know the final grade. My fate had already been decided and I would have to live with it, whatever it might be. "D minus, holy crap I passed." To this day, I believe that was a gift. One's blessings can come from the most unexpected places, as you will see.

The Eagle Hunts

CHAPTER 3

PILOT TRAINING AND SURVIVAL SCHOOL

United States Air Force, Air Training Command, Reese Air Force Base, Lubbock, Texas, and pilot training; one of eight such bases scattered about the southern United States where, I was convinced, the Air Force put 2nd Lieutenants for a year so the rest of the Air Force wouldn't have to put up with them. My status as a real United States Air Force officer had not quite been sorted out yet when I needed to go to the flight line fire station to gather some information for an assignment. The fire station was a very important part of flying and the firemen, rescue helicopters with their pilots and para rescue men, crash trucks, and crash crews stood constant alert when any one of us were in the air. They were rightfully, very prideful and very highly respected.

With the gold bars on my shoulders shinning in all their newness in the afternoon sun, I rounded the corner of the large hanger with wide open doors, and positioned, polished, and ready fire and rescue trucks. The "spit and polished" crews were readily available but otherwise occupied with various activities. Now I thought, I need to find someone who looks in charge. Suddenly, I heard a large booming command "Fire Station Ahhhh-tennn-hut!!" Quickly looking about to see what that was all about, I realized the whole fire station was standing at attention looking at me and from the side came this very polished senior enlisted sergeant. I knew that because of lots of stripes on his sleeve. Halting in front of me he gave a crisp salute which I returned and he said "SIR, what may we help you with today." Quickly gaining the composure at which I had excelled during my ROTC training I authoritatively responded, "Sergeant please give your men carry on" and returned a crisp "order arms." The First Sergeant invited me to tour the facility while he answered my questions and after having met several of his airmen and sergeants, we returned to the hanger entry and he said, "Lt. Clark if there is anything else please let me know, and if not come back and see us anyway." He called the fire station to attention, gave me a salute which I returned and as I rounded the hanger corner on the way out, I heard him give his men a "carry on." "WOW," I thought, I really am an Air Force Officer and if I am ever on final* with a broken aircraft, those are the guys I want to see parked beside the runway in their red fire trucks with their fire suits on and beacons flashing. It was then in this young officer's life, that I began to realize just how many very capable and dedicated people it took to put an aircraft and its pilot(s) and crew into the air.

Pilot Training was intensive. It was a course of instruction intended to eliminate those who were there for the glory, money, sex appeal, or had a weak stomach for being upside down, and any physical imparity that would disqualify them from being a superhero. After one close encounter with some insecurity, I received some encouragement from a T-37 flight commander and proceeded to graduate a Distinguished Flying Graduate, ranked second only behind the student who graduated at the top of all the classes from all eight pilot training bases. We graduated only 27 from a starting class of 55 and I was awarded the honor of standing at the head of the entire student wing as Parade Commander for our graduation ceremonies.

Domestically my new wife Bonnie and I lived in our black and silver trailer in a small trailer park along the Levelland highway which ran from Lubbock, passing the base a few miles to the west, and then off into the oblivion of west Texas. There were cotton fields all around us and one barbwire fence between us and the dust storms that swept in from the west with such intensity that all activity stopped until

---

* Final is short for the final part of an approach to landing. It is the most critical part of a flight, especially if you are having an emergency.

Chapter 3 | Pilot Training And Survival School

they passed, leaving rows of dust even on the inside sills of tightly closed windows. Though living simply, I had a regular paycheck and a little money to spend but just as little time to spend it so all was working out. I was blessed by the arrival of a beautiful baby girl a few months later and a wife who fit right into the social structure of my classmates and their spouses. Life was intense but good.

After the thirteen months and graduation we packed up the trailer, gave it to the Air Force to ship to McGuire Air Force Base (AFB) just outside Trenton, New Jersey and I headed to survival school at the now closed Stead AFB at Reno, Nevada. Bonnie went with our new dark haired, dark eyed daughter to stay with her grandparents in Chicago.

My task was to learn how to survive in the mountains after ejection or bailout, escape and evade the enemy, contact friendly forces and be returned to fight again. Also, there was a capture and interrogation phase that was to prepare us for being a prisoner of war should the eventuality occur. This was an especially undesirable phase of the whole curriculum because it involved practice torture which was a bit like practice bleeding—it hurt. There was this very little black box, much too little for a child to fit into, but into which I found I could be made to fit. From a very young age at which I am told I almost suffocated by entwining myself in the sheet of my crib, I was somewhat claustrophobic. By what blessing I don't know, but there was a mere pinhole in the door of this black box that let in a small spot of light. I concentrated on this pin hole of light as my connection to the outside. I heard the other "prisoners" and classmates begging not to be put into the boxes, screaming to get out, and spilling their guts when they did. It was terrible because even a graduate of pilot training could not fly in the U.S. Air Force without graduating from survival school. We had already washed out half of our starting pilot training class and we were still dropping like flies. How could we have any pilots left to fly if everyone was giving up because of the "little black box?" I surprised myself by getting through the ordeal with no panic but physically I retained the dimensions of "the box" for some minutes after rolling out onto the dirt when the box was finally opened. After being thrown back together with my fellow survival students we discussed our various reactions to the treatment and arrived at the conclusion that all of the begging and cowing racket from the weaker men came from some rather well practiced instructors who did a superb job of acting. I was delighted to find that we were a stronger group that it had appeared, and we were all still there.

After three weeks of an often sleepless, starving, sick, cold, painful, harrowing experience I was specially selected to receive orders to attend an advanced survival course also held at Stead. A half dozen or so of us were chosen to attend a highly-classified classroom course that would be held in a mysterious and guarded barbed wire enclosure on the base.

2nd Lt. Clark in an official Air Force photograph most likely taken shortly after reporting to McGuire Air Force Base, New Jersey to begin flying with the 12th Aero Medical Evacuation Squadron.

CHAPTER 4

MCGUIRE AFB

McGuire AFB in New Jersey was a small piece of a large sprawling army base known as Fort Dix. It was an old base with its history dating to 1917, and also encompassed Lakehurst naval facility of Hindenburg fame. It had been a jumping off point for troops heading overseas in WWI and WWII. Fort Dix was still a very active training base with tanks roaring around through the woods and machine guns rattling throughout the surrounding forests and ranges, not a place one would desire to casually sojourn up and down the numerous dirt roads and trails on a beautiful fall day. I know this because I found a lovely small trailer park in which to set up our mobile home after I arrived at McGuire, armed with more survival skills than any man should ever hope to need. The little trailer park was perfect, not far from the base, nestled back in the woods, well kept, and quiet. After a couple of days of setting up our old home in a new place and sending word that the "cabin" was ready to be occupied by my family, I spent my first night there. The following morning I awoke to a lovely bright sunny fall day. I had no duty because it was Sunday. I could see the fall oak leaves shinning iridescently outside the small sliding glass bedroom window. I could see all this so well because I was bloody wide ass awake due to the roaring engines, clanking of tracks, exploding cannon, and rattling machine guns just over the barbed wire fence about 20 feet from the side of the trailer. The fence had a small Department of Defense sign that said "no trespassing – U.S. Army exercise area" or something like that. I was somewhat assured by the fact that in my investigations of the area neighboring the trailer site I had not seen any tank tracks, shot up trees, or blown up trailers. The commotion didn't go on for long, and I chose not to mention this to Bonnie because I assumed we could always move if it became necessary. There were very few occasions that this reoccurred during our year and a half stay there, which was nice because it was a very comfortable sylvan site, if one could tolerate an 8ft by 41ft trailer home.

McGuire AFB itself was a large spread-out base with wide and long runways, an extensive concrete aircraft parking area called in the trade as "a ramp," and numerous cavernous Quonset Hut like aircraft hangers in which entire large aircraft could be given complete and thorough inspections and noted deficiencies corrected. I had been flying with the 12th Aeromedical Transport Squadron based at McGuire for over a year and was well qualified in the C-131 Convair that we were flying. I found the leadership and squadron members to be of the first order and I was proud to be a member. On a trip to Kelly AFB at San Antonio I was flying with Aircraft Commander Captain Lee Mollet. Lee was a favorite of mine and was an old F-100 fighter pilot who had flown during the occupation of Germany after WWII. He had separated from active duty to fly with the airlines and after having been furloughed from the airlines decided to come back on active duty. He was a good fit in the mission due to his airline experience. Lee and I spent lots of good times flying, drinking, and telling war stories about flying fighters, he telling, and me listening in rapt enthusiasm. This trip was no different and he had plenty of time to tell exaggerated tales and I had plenty of time to brag about how good of a formation pilot I was. But it was times like this I realized, although I was gaining valuable experience flying with the very best in the business, I was not spending enough time upside down and hurling my body at the ground. This thought was on my mind as we taxied the twin-engine propeller driven transport aircraft with the large Red Cross on the tail to our position on the ramp at Kelly and shut it down beside the blue Air Force hospital busses awaiting our arrival. When the shutdown checklist was complete and I had time to allow my gaze to wander around the ramp and into one of the open maintenance hangers nearby there was an ugly silhouetted form that had some distinctive characteristics I had only seen in pictures; a tail with the horizontal stabilizer that bent down, wings with the ends

Chapter 4 | McGuire AFB

turned up, a stubby drooped nose, two cockpits with one behind the other, and two huge jet engines with afterburners so big one could crawl inside on their hands and knees. Great Scott! It was the F-4C Phantom II, Steve Canyon's secret fighter newly operational with the U.S. Navy and Air Force. No one was around (and it would not have mattered if they had been), so I decided to look at that magnificent bird, all 29 tons of it. As I approached, I became aware of how large it was. I had flown the T-33 in pilot training which was just an old F-80 Shooting Star that was flown in the Korean War with the gun ports in the nose patched over. It seemed big, but this Phantom II dwarfed it. This was clearly a no-nonsense supersonic jet fighter and I absolutely had to fly it.

There was a stigma attached to flying propeller type aircraft that I did not know about when I graduated from pilot training and selected the choice assignment I now had. It seemed that those who flew jets assumed that those who did not, should not. It also meant that me switching back to jets was unlikely, but I decided to give it a go anyway. After all, I did get a D minus in that electrical engineering course and I was a "hot stick" in formation. Of course, there was that "dictates of the Air Force" thing. Maybe the Air Force would want me to fly C-131s more than they did F-4s. It was apparent I needed to give someone a good convincing!

Langley AFB was the headquarters of Tactical Air Command (TAC) to which all of the air-to-ground fighter units belonged. If you wore a flight suit with a "TAC" patch on it, you had bragging rights and could swagger. In pilot training, we were instructed never to wear your flight suit with unzipped pockets. However, as I later learned in the real world of aviation, if you wore a "TAC" patch on your flight suit the lower leg pockets could be unzipped because in the left one you would have your flight map on a knee clipboard, well worn, and dinged up from being banged about, and in the right pocket your worn leather flight gloves with the tops hanging out and flopped over. After all, you were a "fighter pilot."

Langley was a beautiful base located at Arlington, Virginia and a place that we often stopped on our return from San Antonio. Because it was a headquarters base, we would often pick up some

The Eagle Hunts

VIPs traveling to Andrews AFB, Washington, DC, which served the Pentagon. We had a large comfortable airplane and flew a very predictable schedule so we were a desired mode of transportation for VIPs. On one trip a Major General who was the Operations Officer for TAC boarded our aircraft and after takeoff joined us in the cockpit for a good BS session in route to Andrews. The Operations Officer of any command is very influential and is in charge of numerous flying programs that affect the command and its flying personnel. Lee knew this, and I was still learning. He began to brag about my flying achievements to the General, then switched the conversation to how the F-4 conversion was going with TAC. (TAC was just starting a training program for new pilots in the RF-4C). The General explained that within the next few weeks Headquarters, Tactical Air Command would come out with requests for volunteers to join a new training program for the RF-4C. They were replacing the RB-66s which were being phased out of the Air Force and TAC would be training rear seat pilots to complete the two-pilot crew for the new airplanes. Then the back-seaters would be upgraded to the front seat as the current front-seaters completed their tours and rotated. The location of the assignment had not yet been determined. He suggested that jet pilot training instructors and existing pilots of jet fighter type aircraft were the general category of pilot which they desired. However, other commands like Material Air Transport Command, to which all three of the aero-medical evacuation squadrons belonged, might receive the volunteer statements for a couple of training slots. The message was clear enough; be watching and react quickly if the opportunity presented itself. He also had a distinct twinkle in his very senior, and very much in charge eyes, as he explained that his staff would be reviewing the applicants and then HE would personally make a final review and approve them. He jotted down John Clark, 1st Lieutenant, and my service number, 70474A, on a scrap of paper and departed the cockpit for a seat in the back as we began our approach for a landing at Andrews. I'm certain his business that day at the Pentagon would involve TAC forces, and their involvement in the small but seemingly more and more involved conflict in a faraway place called Vietnam. Wasn't Dien Bien Phu in Vietnam? Wasn't that

Chapter 4 | McGuire AFB

where the French were just defeated by a ragtag army of Communist guerillas? I might be well served to study up on this area of the world, its geopolitics, and military history.

Winter flying up and down the east coast could be dastardly with lots of heavy thick unpredictable fog, snow, rain and drizzle, freezing rain and ice. Jets got to zoom up through it and fly above it whereas C-131s had to fly through it. Sometimes the temperatures were so cold at Loring AFB, the remote B-52 bomber base in northern Maine, the seals on our aircraft landing gear would start to leak. Our flight engineer would watch with considerable consternation while the aircraft sat on the bitter cold ramp waiting for the wrapped up ambulatory patients to walk on board and the medical staff to transfer those on litters from the large blue hospital busses with big red crosses, to the silver and white airplane with the very obvious red cross on its tail, and the dripping landing gear.

Still, it was very gratifying, and it came with a good feeling, knowing you were taking these people to some place that would give them hope for a quick recovery. It was not uncommon to be told by the medical crew on board that a critical patient we were transporting had their vital signs stabilize and improve upon takeoff and climb out. It was assurance that they were on their way to the best care our country had to offer. But if anyone was going anywhere, we had to get off the ground and get the gear folded up in the wings before we lost too much hydraulic fluid. We always made it though, sometimes nursing the next landing or two onto the runway just to make sure we had plenty of hydraulic fluid in the gear.

As we began the day at McGuire, it was one of those mornings, cold, misty and wet which forecast a mission with lots Instrument Flight Rules (IFR) flying and ice control. Sitting in the first pilot seat, flipping switches and running through the pre-flight checklist I noticed the squadron First Sergeant walking briskly to the loading aircraft with that "I'm in charge, and I don't care what your rank is" walk, holding aloft a sheet of paper. We were waiting for the aircraft doors to be closed and locked as he climbed the steps into the aircraft and stuck his head into the cockpit saying "Lieutenant Clark here is a volunteer statement for an RF-4C combat crew training slot I thought you might want to see. It looks like you might need to make up your mind quickly and it seems to be an assignment to Alconbury Royal AFB, England after training. If you are interested, I can fill out all the information and transfer any records they need today if you sign here." I did, he did, and a few weeks later I received orders to report to Shaw AFB at Sumter, South Carolina for three months of RF-4C combat crew training with end assignment to Alconbury Royal AFB, England. There was going to be lots of going fast, flying low, hurling my body at the ground, formation, a TAC patch and swaggering. It was early 1965; I had just turned 25 and things couldn't be better.

The first operational aircraft 2nd Lt. Clark flew with U.S. Air Force Aeromedical Evacuation system except the actual 'aero-evac' aircraft had a large cargo door on the side and a big red cross on the tail.

CHAPTER 5

SHAW, COMBAT CREW TRAINING AND THE PHANTOM II

Shaw was a typical Air Force Base, not large but with a dedicated mission of training Air Force tactical reconnaissance pilots. There are two words that the military applies to a mission to define its role and scope and which become particularly appropriate when it comes to defining the type of flying and training in which I was about to become engaged. An army will fight its wars and conflicts in two arenas, one in the country itself (at home) where the army draws it soldiers, where they are trained and equipped and where the military equipment, guns, ammunition, tanks, trucks, planes and all other accruements of combat and war are built or derived and two, the battle front or front lines where the actual combat takes place. The distance between the two becomes the supply lines and can be short as when a country first attacks its neighbor and is first moving its army out of its own territory or, long as when the U.S. became involved in the wars in Europe and was required to move its troops and supply them over great distances. Aerial combat or activities that take place in the first arena or "rear" are referred to as "strategic" and those at the front "tactical." During WWII, when our B-17s and B-24s flew deep into Germany to bomb the factories manufacturing ball bearings or refineries which supplied fuel to the German war effort, they were flying high altitude long range "strategic" bombardment missions. When our fighters flew up and down the front lines bombing and strafing the Germans in direct support of our troops engaged in combat on the ground, the missions were low level short range and "tactical." Just about everything else is a support function, such as supply and training, hence "Tactical Air Command" or TAC, "Strategic Air Command" or SAC, "Material Air Transport Service" or MATS, "Air Training Command" or ATC and so on. These were current titles and acronyms at the time, but have been long since changed, and in later conflicts the front lines and enemies have become less well defined. We were tactical.

Now there was a new boy in town, the F4-C Phantom II had its tactical reconnaissance version, the brand new highly sophisticated RF-4C that would begin to replace the RB-66 and the RF-101. The "RF-4" as we called it, was so new that the ground radar system being developed for it was not even finished. Some of its sensor systems were classified and had to be covered up so they could not be photographed or viewed at public displays of the new aircraft. Infrared sensors could see a tank completely covered up inside a haystack, or an old WWII runway currently being plowed up for row crops, or side looking radar that could detect ships and structures miles to the side from altitudes that were also miles high, and a high speed low altitude panoramic camera that could photograph a blade of grass with amazing clarity in the top of a fence post while flying over it at 500 mph and 50 feet.

Several of the new RF-4's sat on the flight line at Shaw AFB just outside of the combat crew training squadron operations building. They were perfectly in line, canopies open, beckoning those who would dare, and appearing as hulking warriors awaiting a command. They were glistening silver with some tarnished areas and the large black letters "U.S. Air Force." It was the tarnished areas that I particularly noticed for I knew the tarnished look came from the titanium that was used on the skin of the aircraft to withstand the enormous heat that would build up during high-speed flight. It was also found around the afterburners of the two huge J-79 General Electric jet engines with after-burners that when engaged would melt normal steel. Formidable seems a wholly inadequate description.

Chapter 5 | Shaw, Combat Crew Training and the Phantom II

I regret to say in those youthful years my attitude had been very egocentric and focused on flying. Now it was focused on flying the RF-4 and my family was in the role of camp followers. I was going to be here, whether Bonnie was or not. Fortunately for marital harmony she had lived in the close confines of our trailer quite long enough and looked forward to going with me for the short period in South Carolina. Bonnie was much happier when we left our trailer behind in New Jersey and rented a duplex in Sumter. The duplex was small and furnished but so much larger than the trailer that it seemed quite spacious. Bonnie knew we had said goodbye to the trailer for good because we had already decided to rent a house off of the base at Alconbury. It was a busy time for her taking care of our young daughter, Renée, and getting acquainted with the rest of the wives and families of my class with whom we would be stationed in England. The duplex stayed rather austere because we were to be there only three or four months and we wanted to save what we could to buy furnishings in England.

There was a short period of academic drudgery and learning how to radar navigate so that we could utilize the new radar system not yet installed in the aircraft. We were learning on an old system used by navigators and flying in the T-29 which is just another set of numbers used for the aircraft I had been flying at McGuire. I could not help but realize the irony.

My anticipation was increasing considerably as I stood in the squadron personal equipment room waiting for the fitting and issue of a new state of the art helmet with oxygen mask and parachute harness that would attach to the parachute (chute) built into the Martin Baker ejection seat. Watching the instructors and the former RB-66 pilots from Alconbury that were converting to the new RF-4s, and who would be our front seat crew members and sponsors, slog in from the flight line with sweat soaked flight suits and wet helmet matted hair, speak excitedly about maneuvers and aircraft performance only enhanced the anticipation. It was obvious that flying this bad bird was demanding and hot in the southern heat that was already in season. They were wearing the recently developed anti-gravity suits (G suits) which gave the bottom half of their flight suits a real fighter pilot's appearance being tightly laced to their legs and abdomen and for which I was yet to be fitted. These G suits, I noticed, covered up the flight suit pockets that I had planned to keep unzipped. But all was not lost because they also had pockets and that was even better; one could leave the bottom of G suit leggings unzipped and swagger around looking like you were wearing chaps, which you sort of were. This, it seems, my older compatriots had already figured out, and I was more than happy to include myself in the act of vanity. Besides, it was very hot out there and they were tight and hot and wet with sweat. What would anyone else have us to do after a mission in the Phantom II?

The G suit would be put on before flight and plugged in to the aircraft anti-gravity system that would blow pressurized air into bladders around the waste, thighs, and calves squeezing them tightly to keep the blood from going into that part of the body and away from the head and more particularly the brain, eyes and ears during high-G maneuvers. There was no doubt this airplane could do high-G maneuvers with a 7.4 maximum G-loading and with over 8-G's often seen in more extreme circumstances like combat.

When someone sits in a comfortable chair watching TV, they are experiencing a G-loading of 1 and let us say they weigh 200 lbs. Most of us have been in a carnival ride or on a roller coaster that slings you around or over and have felt the action cause you to feel heavier or your stomach to sink. That is the effect of additional G-loading due to the centrifugal force of slinging about. In an aircraft, if it were making a turn that would cause its wings to tip 60 degrees, they would experience a G-loading of 2 or weigh 400 lbs. Everything, their head, hands, cheeks, arms, blood, everything would weigh twice as much and their blood, which is liquid, would be looking for a lower place to go. Since young blood vessels are tough and stretchable the blood shoves its way into the blood vessels in your lower body and legs by stretching them, thus leaving one's upper body and head without much blood. As the blood leaves your head the brain and eyes become starved for oxygen and your vision starts to gray out, you become light headed and eventually pass out. This is not good when you are flying a high-performance jet fighter. The RF-4 can make you feel eight times heavier than you actually are. That's why RF-4 pilots fly with G suits. It's so they can stay conscious while hurling themselves toward the earth, or escaping a pursuing Mikoyan-Gurevich 21 Russian fighter aircraft (MIG-21), or surface to air missiles. These G suits for which we were being fitted portended the need to be able to withstand lots of hurling and high-G flight. This was exciting and although I was aware someday it might actually involve some escaping from MIGS and surface to air missiles (SAMs) that was not even close to my near horizon of flying the RF-4.

Mach 1 is the speed of sound and is pronounced "mock one" by those who find it necessary to occasionally exceed the speed of sound which varies with the temperature and atmospheric pressure and is approximately 760 miles per hour at sea level and 59 degrees Fahrenheit. During my time at Combat Crew Training School in the RF-4C one of the instruction periods was a flight where the instructor and I flew a high altitude, high speed profile where we would maximize the power-to-drag ratio of the aircraft and allow it to achieve its maximum speed. The airplane had a lot of power but also a lot of drag, or air friction to support its weight and "ugliness." On this flight, we reduced its weight then all of its power could be used to accelerate to a higher speed. Thus, the profile involved a climb to an intermediate altitude of 35,000 feet, about the altitude the average airliner flies, and accelerate through the Mach (speed of sound) picking up approximately Mach 1.5, then pulling up and holding that Mach in full burner, I started a 0-G or weightlessness pushover. The goal was to top out around 60,000 feet and Mach 2. What seemed like a big heavy powerful fighter at low level felt like a sports car in this higher Mach environment, with lots of power, smooth positive control response, and pure exhilaration for the human in control. As I flew over the top of the arch the airspeed indicator reported Mach 2.2, 1260 knots, 1451 miles per hour or over twice the speed of a bullet fired from a 45-caliber pistol. The altimeter indicated 68,000 feet. The rocket I was riding seemed perfectly comfortable with itself but had we been lower in the atmosphere we would soon be seeing a "skin temperature" warning light that would have told us the skin of our bird was heating up to the point of losing its strength because of the air friction against it. The altitude was above the boiling point of human blood and without pressure suits, if we lost cabin pressure, our blood would boil in our bodies and we would literally explode from within. We did not have on pressure suits, and so it briefly occurred to me that flying this beast was to "play for all the marbles." The thought was fleeting for there was far too much joy in living than to waste time thinking about ways to die.

Lt. Clark is back row center with arms crossed. This picture is of an RF-4C Phantom II with the combat crew training class at Shaw AFB, Sumter, South Carolina, circa 1965.

Through a clear beautiful sky, the horizon appeared with a slight curvature as it disappeared into the dark blue hue of our atmosphere, most of which was now below us. There were shimmering shock waves standing off the nose and the engine intakes but everything else seemed motionless and still, with not so much as a quiver and in that moment, I recalled the last few stanzas of the poem "High Flight" by John Gillespie Magee, Jr;

"Up, up the long delirious, burning blue,
I've topped the wind-swept heights with easy grace,

Where never lark, or even eagle, flew;
And, while with silent lifting mind I've trod
The high untrespassed sanctity of space,
Put out my hand, and touched the face of God."

And they actually pay me to do this.

The Eagle Hunts

CHAPTER 6

ALCONBURY

The house was a lovely old early century brick two story building with tall white wooden framed windows, and an ornate white wooden front door. The center steps up to the door were casually adorned with dark green ivy that seemed to have been there forever, and the yard, or garden as the English called it, was well trimmed and lush green. It was very fitting for a cloudy, slightly misty morning. The flight from McGuire AFB to London Heathrow Airport was long and uneventful. We were met when we left the customs area at Heathrow by Captain Lee Littel, with whom I had been crewed at Shaw, and who was to be my front seat pilot and squadron sponsor. The ride up to Alconbury was full of curiosity, what with driving on the wrong side of the road with a car that had the steering wheel on the wrong side and things that the traffic whipped around called "round-abouts." Lee told me that he would be loaning us his second car, a small red Austin Mini, with which to get around until we were able to take delivery on the new red Volkswagen "bug" (1964 model 1300) we had ordered before we left the states. The Mini was perfect for the time and place. It was small and simple with sliding glass windows—that's correct, no window cranks, a little cable to pull down to open the door from the inside—yes, that's also correct, no door handle on the inside either. It was powered with the cutest little four-cylinder engine which sat sideways over the front wheels. I think if I had been able to acquire one of those little engines when I was growing up, I would have mounted it on my red Radio Flyer wagon. But it was nevertheless wonderfully adapted to parking half on and half off the sidewalks of the small cobblestone streets of Hemingford Gray where we eventually found our rental home.

Lee had brought us to this charming, very English place where we would be the guest of a pleasant lady who well remembered the sacrifices made by the English people during WWII and the aid and assistance given by the Americans. It was a period of my life that ended when I was five and which was of no relevance to anything in which I was involved. Ah, how self-absorbed and naïve is youth.

Our housing would be temporary until we could rent a home off the base or "on the economy," as the base finance office called it. There was only a limited number of small duplexes on the base to house the officers and pilots and since the number of pilots was being doubled with the upgrade to the RF-4, there were more of us new guys and families than there were places to live on base. We would, however, be getting extra pay for housing, which suited us just fine.

Alconbury was a small obscure Royal AFB the English had allowed the Americans to use for a reconnaissance wing, which was part of the North Atlantic Treaty Organization (NATO) forces protecting Western Europe from the threat of Communist invasion from Eastern Germany or the Soviet Union. Lee had said when we first met at Shaw that England and its people, though English speaking and very similar in demographic to Americans, definitely had their own way of approaching life. He philosophized that if one wanted to enjoy their tour of duty in England one would be best served to accept the English customs and ways, although it might offer a few frustrations in the beginning. On the other hand, one could insist on keeping our own demanding habits, and harried way of doing things which would most certainly cause disdain for the English, and since we were outnumbered, one would most certainly be smashing one's head against the wall with unpleasant regularity. With that advice, we decided right off to do it the English way. It was a great decision based on excellent counsel, for we grew to enjoy our stay very much and developed a great affection and respect for the "Brits." Lee also advised me that his name was pronounced "Li-tell." Although spelled Littel it was easily confused with "little" of which I suspect his sturdy 5'8" stature may have had a part. But he and his wife Gene were very

Chapter 6 | Alconbury

likeable and we enjoyed our relationship with them a great deal. We certainly enjoyed their offer of the little red Mini and on those narrow winding roads about the English countryside it was just as much fun to drive as my little red Radio Flyer several years earlier.

Our house was small by American standards, a bungalow we might have called it, but very nice. It was a brick two level with a "sort of attached" single car garage that barely held our brand new bright red VW 1300 "bug." The house was heated by a single coal fireplace that would have fit into a corner of an American wood fireplace. I don't mean this as a slight to the Brits, but it was just a surprise. They had long since realized that they did not have enough trees if they committed to heating homes by wood and so resorted to coal and peat. If we were burning coal in one of our large wood fireplaces it would look like a Pittsburg steel blast furnace because coal burns much hotter than wood without as much flame. Our hot water was heated by coils at the back of the fireplace so we had to wait for a fire in the evening to heat the water before we could bathe, that is if you wanted to bathe at all, because there was no central heat, only the fireplace. Heat from the fireplace rose the staircase to the upper level, that is if you left the doors to the staircase open. There was even weather stripping around the interior doors of the house so that different rooms could be closed off if you didn't wish to heat them. This was a bit hard to understand until we started paying for coal and electricity for space heaters, then it became clear. One of the luxuries of this small home was standby electric heat for the hot water, but someone was required to go up the steps into the bathroom, open a cabinet door and turn on an electric switch. However, when you received the electric bill you realized that this luxury came at a noticeable cost.

There were several luxuries about this very nice and homey place on a quiet street in the small village of Hemingford Gray. It was owned by an English banker who had been sent to Kenya for a couple of years and was renting it out while gone. A small walled in garden, yard we would call it, in the back had a few plants and shrubs, and an odd weed called Burdock. It looked somewhat like Rhubarb but had no desirable qualities at all; the cattle would not even eat it, and it stunk. I left it alone because maybe English bankers had a thing

The Eagle Hunts

for Burdock and would be disappointed if upon his return it were gone. Future growth and closer inspection, such as sniffing, revealed to me that it was not Burdock but was in fact Rhubarb, and I liked Rhubarb cobbler. I had never watched very closely when grandma or mom made a Rhubarb cobbler, just hung around the oven until it came out. Bonnie was not about to try to make one, so I did. I cut some stalks, cleaned them, cut them up, boiled them, added lots of sugar and some thickening, put the mixture in a pie shell, which I made with some confidence, and put it in the oven for a while. It was surprisingly good, if I might say so, and proved that anything will be good if you add enough sugar.

Bonnie was happy with our new home, became quick friends with the English neighbors, walked to the nearby village center frequently for provisions and easily fell into the English life. Lee and I were flying a lot and melding into a good combat crew and he was very understanding about the fact I was a pilot, but relegated to the back seat. He frequently offered me the opportunity to fly the plane. It wasn't long before he had enough confidence in my flying that on many missions he would just go outboard with the throttles on takeoff roll so I could light the afterburners and then the rest of the mission was mine until we taxied in and parked and I called for him to go outboard with the throttles again to shut the beast down. It was great flying, I loved it, and I was good at it.

The war in Vietnam was heating up and even though I was only six months or so into a three-year tour in England and felt secure that any involvement with Vietnam was very improbable, I did feel a professional obligation to become somewhat informed on the Southeast Asian part of the world. And so, I studied some of its history and something of the notable leaders who had defeated the Nationalist Chinese and the French in a place called Indochina. Mao Tse-tung, the great Chinese Communist leader had written a book on guerrilla warfare and we seemed to be engaged in a guerilla war in South Vietnam. Also, there were some books written on the fall of the large French garrison in the far Northwest corner of North Vietnam at Dien Bien Phu. The famous North Vietnamese Communist Leader Ho Chi Minh and the North Vietnamese General Vo Nguyen Giap

Chapter 6 | Alconbury

were both very prominent in these historical recounts. I became more and more familiar with the part of the globe that was demanding an increasing amount of our military resources and attention. Our awesome national might was not squashing these ragtag insurgents nearly as easily as our leaders seemed to think it should. The more I read and studied I began to realize maybe we did not understand the nature of our involvement, nor those with whom we were engaged in this military skirmish, which neither our president or Congress called a "war."

There were no bases that could ground service the RF-4 in the European theater of operations except Ramstein Air Base in Germany. That was significant because it meant there were no bases suitable for cross country training. At this time in our training, it was not particularly relevant because we could fly across the English Channel, around Germany, and return without refueling. We were, however, capable of air refueling and did on occasion practice it. As our reconnaissance role was to gather intelligence on the movement and positions of Soviet and East German forces should they move into Western Germany, we often flew missions over the German countryside. Flying at two or three thousand feet afforded one a great view of the lovely forests, small quaint villages, and great rivers. Some of the most memorable scenes and often photographed sites were the great castles scattered about. But cruising at one or two thousand feet was not a luxury we often enjoyed and it was not nearly as exciting as the low-level missions we most generally flew when training to avoid enemy radar and the inevitable Soviet anti-aircraft surface to air missiles (SAMS). There were lots of these missiles and radar looking our direction as we flew missions over western Germany, and occasionally there would be a flight of MIGS that followed us along their side of the border should we be within close proximity of the East German border. The year before I arrived at Alconbury there had been an American unarmed RB-66 shot down over the border by East German MIGS when the crew strayed from their designated flight plan and either flew over or strayed too close to the border. We were unarmed also and didn't really care for it, but those who claimed to be smarter than we, thought it prudent. Their logic went something like this: if we give those young zealots guns or rockets, then they are going to be looking for a fight and will most likely find one. That is not good because they will have an aircraft full of valuable battlefield and target data, including low-level photos, infrared, electronic and radar and it will do no one any good if they get shot down. Therefore, we must make professional cowards out of them to get them back home with the information they were sent out for. Our logic went something like this: since we had all this valuable intelligence that our battlefield commander urgently needed then we should be able to protect ourselves to ensure that we returned safely with it, and if some sorry East German MIG happened to cross our path in doing so, then rather than stealthily executing a rapid and evasive maneuver we might blast through guns blazing and rid the conflict of one such MIG. Oh well, maybe they had a point.

The buffer zone was a 30-mile-wide strip that ran the length of the East German border and required special clearance and procedures to enter and was intended to make sure NATO aircraft were under special control if they were to be operating close to the border. It was always a bit more exciting to be flying in the buffer zone. It was like thumbing your nose or "flipping off" the East Germans flying the MIGS on the other side of the Iron Curtain to make sure we didn't intrude.

CHAPTER 7

RAMSTEIN AND EUROPE

Lee and I had become a great team and our strengths seem to be very complementary; Lee and his experience in flying around Europe and in reconnaissance and mine in what I'm not sure. But since I did spend a lot of time flying up and down the east coast of the United States in disgusting weather it was perhaps, flight planning, air traffic control, radio procedures and flying in less than desirable weather. Our flight this day was to Ramstein Airbase, Germany where we would make an instrument approach and then without landing make a low approach and began our low-level segment flying under visual flight rules (VFR) or out of the clouds, then return to Ramstein, climb out on an instrument departure or in the clouds if necessary, returning to Alconbury. Whether the weather was good or bad we would have used the instrument arrival and departure at Ramstein due to the heavy flying traffic in and out of the base and Rein Main International Airport at Frankfurt, Germany, which was in close proximity and one of the busiest airports in the world. In this manner, air traffic control could keep better control of us and fit us into the very heavy air traffic in the area. There was a low overcast hanging over Europe and our approach to Ramstein was in solid clouds and we broke out of them much lower than the weather briefing we had received on departure told us to expect. The clouds hung low and ragged over the airbase and almost on top of the ridge of hills to the south. Lee, realizing that the weather was too bad to fly our low-level portion chose to abort the mission and make a departure back to Alconbury. He called Ramstein tower, to whom we were talking at the time, and asked for an instrument departure as he snuck our jet between the ragged overcast and the tops of the ridge to the south all the while maintaining VFR so we could avoid any other airplanes flying in the area. Ramstein tower replied that we were not in radar contact and they could not issue a departure. They continued looking for us on radar with no success while we made a couple of unapproved passes down the runway then circling over the hills to the south. The tower became very concerned because here was this RF-4C appearing from nowhere and making random low passes down the active runway while not being cleared to do so! The tower commenced using "guard channel," which was a channel reserved for emergencies only, and which transmitted to all aircraft in the area. Things were getting tense, and I knew what the problems were with air traffic control, and how to solve it, so I decided to assist Lee by taking over the radios while Lee, who was getting stressed and a bit flustered, could concentrate on flying the fighter and staying under the overcast while not flying into the hills. On our next pass down the ridge, the tower called for the Phantom flying down the runway to identify itself and report the nature of its emergency. Before Lee could respond I said "I have it," meaning the radio calls, but Lee said "you have it" and shook the stick which meant I had the whole aircraft, both the radios and flying. Holy cow! Okay, I'll give this a go and let Lee take a break; it may take all we both have to offer to get us out of this predicament.

Quickly depressing the mike button, I responded to Ramstein tower:

"Roger Ramstein this is Phantom one one on left downwind maintaining VFR over the ridge but too low to be seen on your radar, expecting the approach end of runway two seven in two minutes at three five, request a departure and climb on course to Alconbury."

Ramstein control tower, being relieved and delighted that they now had communications with the mystery jet fighter that was buzzing the airport, after a brief pause quickly responded:

"Roger Phantom one one cleared to Alconbury via Ramstein-5 departure, climb on course."

The problem here was we had no departure plan or information on the Ramstein-5 departure with us in the confined cockpit of that jet. I followed their transmission with:

Chapter 7 | Ramstein and Europe

"Roger Ramstein, understand cleared to Alconbury via the Ramstein-5 departure climb on course---be advised Sir, we do not have the Ramstein-5 departure on board--standing by to copy."

The tower read the moderately complex departure involving altitude, course changes, and ground radio navigation radial interceptions, all of which I copied in my shorthand developed over the last couple of years flying Air-Evac missions. During all of this I also flew the jet to the approach end of the runway replying:

"Roger understand," and proceeded to read back the copied departure.

"Read back correct, call departing one thousand five hundred" was the towers immediate response.

I flew the length of the runway while staying VFR under the clouds and sitting up the navigation radios and communications frequencies, and at the departure end smoothly brought in full power gradually pulled the nose up and starting to climb while disappearing quickly into the rain, mist and thick clouds. I began my turn onto the first course of the departure while maintaining a near perfect "tech order climb." On nothing but instruments now and while working the trim button on the stick until my jet was right on the climb speed and flying steady, I pressed the mike button on the throttle and called Ramstein tower saying:

"Phantom one one departing one thousand five hundred"
to which the tower replied:
"Roger contact Ramstein departure 283.6."
My final contact with Ramstein tower was:
"Roger Ramstein 283.6, thanks, and sorry for the confusion," hoping no violation would be filed against us which would not be a pleasant thing to explain to our seniors at Alconbury who would be reviewing it. Instantly I heard two clicks of the mike from Ramstein tower, that indicated acknowledgement and at least some level of forgiveness, which was a good sign. Now I just needed to fly the departure correctly. I knew Lee, though quiet, was watching and would mention any needed corrections. But none were needed and it was a textbook departure. Turning on the final course to Alconbury I leveled on our final altitude above a glistening white blanket of clouds

that stretched as far beneath us as we could see. Very pleased with my performance I suddenly realized because of a communication failure between us, Lee had just been along for the ride thinking I had usurped his position as aircraft commander, presumably because I thought he did not know what to do and could not make the departure, which I guess was mutinous. I thought about clarifying it, and since Lee had been absolutely silent the whole time I just said:

"You have it" and shook the stick.

"I have it," Lee replied.

Then until now, nothing has ever been mentioned about the event and Lee and I continued to enjoy a great crew relationship.

Time passed quickly. Jack Gray and Al Milligan, two pilots in my RF-4 Combat Crew Training Class at Shaw had been pilot training instructors and were the first to upgrade to the front seat. That was taken as a good sign. Any indication that our leadership was interested in upgrading us new "back seaters" to the front seat was very encouraging. We were, after all, pilots and did not like being relegated to a cockpit that was generally assumed to be for a navigator, or a weapons system officer. Admittedly the rear cockpit for the Air Force RF-4s were fully outfitted for flight and we knew we would be assigned to the rear cockpit when we volunteered for the assignment, but most of us who had previous flying experience hoped that upgrade would come soon. Jack and Al had the most experience in fighter type aircraft and their experience as previous pilot training instructors made them the most obvious first candidates. Both Jack and Al had come from Reese AFB and had been instructors for my pilot training class so we knew each other and although I was assumed, as a student, to be a lower life form, everything now was "fighter jockey to fighter jockey" or "jock to jock." I hoped that their remembrances of me as a student were complimentary because as respected new RF-4 front seat pilots their advice might be sought out in the selection of the next upgrades. Looking back, I can see that I was quick to show my talent and enthusiasm for flying tactical or fighter type jet aircraft.

Tom Storey was a stocky square jawed man of his early thirties with a gruff manner about him who had been sent with us to Alconbury to be our resident RF-4 flight instructor, check pilot, and

Chapter 7 | Ramstein and Europe

standardization pilot. He had come from MacDill AFB in Florida where he had been flying new F-4's and had a considerable amount of experience in fighter aircraft, much of it with the Illinois Air National Guard flying P-51's. Tom was "God" and had an office somewhere on base in wing headquarters. He could be seen frequently in either the 30th Tactical Reconnaissance Squadron (TRS) building or in ours, the 1st TRS helping both the front seaters and formally RB-66 pilots and us new back seaters become more capable and sophisticated in the operation of this new Air Force weapons system. And so, it would pass that I was scheduled for a flight with Tom. I don't remember if it was a check ride or not but Tom was good about flying with all of us just to give us hints and break bad habits. Since both front seaters and rear seaters in the RF-4 were pilots, those who flew in the rear cockpits needed lots of flying time, "stick time" we called it. The front seaters were good about sharing the stick time and Tom was especially good about it because he wanted to see how well we flew. This flight was no exception as I flew most of it. It was a good flight to Germany with some low-level and as I entered the overhead pattern* at Ramstein Air Base on our return I knew we would both take the opportunity to practice some landings. We called them "touch and go's," which is pretty much self-explanatory. I was anxious to put forward a good finish to the flight.

I flew initially at 1500 feet above the ground, just right, then a nice tight pitch to the right holding my 1500 feet right on, gear, flaps, gear check, roll off the perch to final, line up with the runway perfectly with no jockeying around, back in with a bit of power to hold the glide slope, perfect airspeed and angle of attack and finally a slight burst of power to gently touch the monster down. Okay, who could not be impressed with that? But I would have the opportunity to show Tom that I just didn't luck out so I was to make a go-around pull up into a closed pattern and do it all over again. I kept the nose gear from touching the runway which showed I had a flair for feeling this jet, added full power, and that's a lot of power, and executed

---

* An overhead pattern is a term that is used to describe a type of approach to landing that is flown on a clear day that allows the aircraft (usually tactical type) to fly over the end of the runway at 1500 feet over ground and make an oblong circle, the last part of which is steep and descending to land on the runway, all while staying close to the end of the runway.

the go-around. A closed pattern is a great opportunity to "shine one's ass." It can be steep and tight with lots of power or much more conservative with less bank and set further out from the runway resulting in a wider, gentler turn to final approach. The latter is much easier to control and end up at exactly the correct altitude, airspeed and distance from the runway to execute a nice easily controllable final approach leading to the most likely opportunity for a good landing in the correct place on the runway. It seemed a good time to exhibit a bit of aggressiveness to "God" and this Captain known for his flying skills. So, lots of power, keeping the climb out to the end of the runway shallow for lots of speed, an aggressive, tight, steep pull up, lots of aircraft shaking and quivering, demonstrating I was flying her right on the edge of the performance envelope, rolling out on the perch on altitude, airspeed and in tight, proving once again, my skill as a tactical pilot, or so I thought. After an equally satisfying touchdown as the first one I waited for the accolades from the front cockpit, which up to now had been quiet. There was a low rumbling "hummm" and Tom said "here let me have it" and shook the stick. I shook the stick in response, said "you have it," sat back, looked around a bit, and waited for Tom to get in a landing or two assuming the accolades would have to wait for the after-flight debriefing. Tom's approach to the pull-up for the closed was much the same, a really steep tight pull-up, but no shaking and no buffeting. That big jet just gracefully slid into the closed pattern perfectly on altitude and airspeed and so close to the runway that it would almost take a "split S" to make the landing. A split S is the second half of a loop, one rolls upside down from straight and level flight and pulls the jet through the bottom of the loop going the other direction and is usually done with several thousand feet between you and the ground. It is the stuff air shows are made of but when you do it to a landing it's gutsy at the least. Tom executed a near split S to landing without so much as the slightest glitch. There was no doubt who was impressed by whom on this flight. On the last go-around, Tom gave me the airplane and said:

"Don't be so rough, treat her like a fine lady, not necessary to yank and bank, treat her gently, let her know what you want her to

Chapter 7 | Ramstein and Europe

do, nurse her into it and then be as firm as you want, but be steady and you will get more than you could ever realize."

What a great lesson and not the last I would receive from Tom which would not only improve my flying but benefit me as a person and an officer.

Germany is a beautiful country. Flying low over the lovely green sylvan hills, up the twisting river valleys and popping over an imposing hill one is very likely to come upon a large gray stone castle, its walls and parapets in various forms of ruin but nevertheless a poignant reminder of the kingdoms that ruled and the knights that defended this countryside centuries long ago. It was almost impossible not to hit the camera button and take a picture as you roll over the top enjoying the sight of the castle slipping past your upside-down canopy. It slips by quickly because at 480 knots it takes less than eight seconds to travel a mile and about three seconds to pass through the castle field of view. Also at our height above the ground one could only see about a half of a mile, so we had only two or three seconds to make a decision as to whether a correction to course was needed. Consequently, there was not much opportunity to divide our attention and so our enjoyment of such discoveries was fleeting but no less pleasurable. There was enough fuel on board the aircraft that we could fly a high-low-high mission to Germany and return to Alconbury without refueling. A high-low-high mission started out with the aircraft climbing to a high altitude of around 30,000 feet then descending to a low level of less than 1000 feet to run the reconnaissance mission and then returning to high altitude for the return to base.

On occasion, we would deploy to Ramstein, which was near the German city of Frankfort, to engage in exercises with the Army as it practiced maneuvers with the other NATO forces. Our missions were all during daylight and flown by looking outside the aircraft and following our course with checkpoints on the ground, a manner of flying called "day visual flight rules" or "day VFR," previously mentioned and highly revered as the most fun way to fly. However, we knew about and had been trained at Shaw for the brand new very high-powered navigational radar that was to be installed in the aircraft, which would permit us to fly at night and on instruments only. Flying at night on instruments during a cross country at altitude was one thing and flying at 500 feet above the ground at 480 knots with only radar and instruments to tell you when to climb and dive in order to avoid hills and other hard things was yet another, and frankly, somewhat unnerving to even the most self-assured fighter pilot. But this was to be our future and it was something that only the U.S. Air Force could do with its RF-4C and we were getting ready. We couldn't help but notice the war in Southeast Asia getting closer and closer. The RF-101s were already deployed there and were getting shot down much too frequently. The word was that they would soon be replaced with the RF-4Cs from Mountain Home AFB, in Idaho. However, we knew that Mountain Home was not nearly as advanced as we were because they had started training after us.

1st Lt. Gary Cherry was a guy that looked the part of a perfect fighter pilot. Young, tall, slender, lots of dark hair, quick alert eyes and intelligent. He stood confidently on the ladder hanging off of the front cockpit of the RF-4 parked in the open hanger on a cloudy, cool Alconbury morning. Gary was observing my every move from over the canopy rail as I sat in the front cockpit with a blindfold on, touching and moving switches as he called them out. His intense scrutiny was to make certain each switch was the one he called out and was moved to the correct position without hesitation or fumbling about. There could be no room for error for if he was to be my new rear seat pilot then we both could accept nothing less than being certain I knew instantly and absolutely where every single switch, button and circuit breaker was in the front cockpit without having to look at it. Mistakes could not be made when switches needed to be selected and moved to certain positions without taking your eyes off the fast-moving situation outside. Gary was good at his job as a rear seat pilot and it was in both our interests to ensure that I was to become just as good in my new job as his front seat pilot.

Tom Storey gave me my front seat check ride and I passed with flying colors. Then it was time for Gary and me to complete our combat training as a crew. Both of us were combat crew qualified

Chapter 7 | Ramstein and Europe

in the back seat, so it was only necessary for me to become combat qualified in the front seat and take a check ride with Gary in the rear cockpit. Tom would be flying on our wing as our evaluator, and that would fulfill my qualifications to become a fully combat ready front seater. Gary and I would also become a qualified combat crew, the highest crew qualification. When we were ready to take our check ride, most of the 1st Tactical Reconnaissance Squadron had received orders to deploy to Udorn Royal Thai Airbase, Thailand to replace the RF-101s which had been badly depleted due to combat losses over Vietnam. Bonnie had just become pregnant and I could have claimed some kind of deferral until our son Keith was born except I chose not to. The tour in Thailand was a one-year unaccompanied tour that would probably be completed in close to six months due to the maximum number of 100 combat missions being completed in that period of time. Lee, with whom I was still combat crew qualified, was married to the daughter of the Commander of the 7th Air Force, Headquartered at Ramstein, and he would not be accompanying us to Thailand. It was decided that I would be crewed up with Captain Ed Goodrich and return to the back seat since I was a "new" front seater and a well-qualified and experienced back seater. This was a real blow to my ego as I was slated to become the first First Lieutenant F-4 front seater in NATO, and it was only one ride away. Our deployment to Southeast Asia (SEA) would take us back to the states and to wherever we were to settle our families, then to Mountain Home Air Force Base where we were to pick up RF-4s and fly them to Thailand via Hawaii and Guam. The ones at Alconbury would stay there for the new crews to train on.

Ed and I were not picked to fly one of the RF-4s across the Pacific so we made the trip with some other crews aboard one of the C-141s that carried support equipment and personnel. It was our task to act as backup crews should any of the RF-4 crews get sick or injured. It was an easy but boring flight and I was able to visit with my Aunt Susie and Uncle Chet as we passed through Hawaii. Bonnie and Renee settled in Columbia to be close to my parents while Ed's wife Pat and two daughters went to live in Georgia. Both of our wives were pleased that Ed and I were crewed together. Ed was the Wing Flying Safety Officer and one of the best qualified front seaters in the wing as was I qualified in the rear seat. It pleased us also as we looked forward to flying together, even if it was in war.

Lt. Clark at Alconbury Royal Air Base England with RF-4C Phantom II, 1965.

CHAPTER 8

THE WAR IN SOUTHEAST ASIA

It was October 1966 and we were riding the crest of the technology wave by flying the RF-4C and utilizing the latest developments in sensors, communications, radar and inertial navigation, all which were integrated into the flight instrumentation of the aircraft giving us automated day, night and all-weather flight capabilities. But technologies which we take for common today had not been developed or even conceived at that time. There was no satellite navigation, communication or imagery, no internet, no laptops, no Apple, and no pilotless drones except in crude versions which were not very dependable. Intelligence was gathered by seeing it, or taking images of it, be they photographic, infrared or radar and then delivering the images to the intelligence facility on a base that viewed and interpreted them. It was the thought of our seniors, who developed the format of air operations, that because the RF-4C carried two pilots it would not be necessary to fly two ship formations as the RF-101s were. The RF-101s that we were replacing at Udorn were single seaters and the second aircraft added an additional set of eyes and another aircraft to provide information and assistance should the first be shot down or damaged during a mission. All that seemed to have some logic until our RF-4s started not returning to base, with no information as to why or where the aircraft and its crew had been lost. That second set of eyes, it seems, needed to be in another aircraft that would escape being shot down. That was only one of the several lessons which we learned as we flung ourselves into this "conflict" that our government would not call a war, or declare it so. I remember thinking of the war in South Vietnam like the war in South Korea. Our friends in South Vietnam were being infiltrated by insurgents incited and supplied by the Communist North Vietnamese. That turned out to be a very nearsighted view of the conflict. Without going into a history of the politics of Southeast Asia reaching back before WWII, suffice it to say that the entirety of the nations of North Vietnam, South Vietnam, Laos, Cambodia, Thailand and parts of China, and Burma were embroiled in armed conflict. Even though Laos, Cambodia and Burma declared neutrality, they were involved. Laos, through which ran the well-known Ho Chi Minh Trail, was the most heavily involved. Cambodia, at the south end of the Ho Chi Minh Trail, was also a sanctuary for the Vietnamese insurgents called Viet Cong, and regular North Vietnamese troops. It had its own brutal Communist sympathizing dictator, Pol Pot, who was later to be infamous for the "Killing Fields" of Cambodia. Both China and Russia supplied North Vietnam with advisors, airplanes, pilots, guns, tanks, missiles and lots of other equipment and personnel; China, through rail and roads from southern China into northern Vietnam, and Russia through the large harbor at Haiphong and Gia Lam, the airfield at Hanoi. I was embarrassed at my naivety and disgusted at the government and the news media for misleading the American public into believing that we were just helping our victimized friends in South Vietnam resist the expansionist aspirations of the Communists to the north who were espousing a reunification doctrine. What seemed to make it even more unnerving was our arrogance and grand superiority complex which led us to a strategy of "measured response." We just did not want to look like the big bad bully picking on poor little destitute North Vietnam. We went about the war almost as if it were an exercise but with real bullets and bombs.

"Let's bomb them a little bit and then wait to see if they give up." "No? Well then, maybe a little bit more this time and surely that will work." "No, still not?" "Okay, they are really asking for it, let's surprise them." Whoever thought up that strategy needed to do a better job of studying their enemy and talking to the French.

Chapter 8 | The War in Southeast Asia

Tacked on the walls of the small operations section of the squadron building were various clippings, jokes, and pictures that would most likely be offensive to many of the fine young female pilots we have today. Since we were a "recon" squadron there were also pictures of some of the more spectacular missions we had flown. One I recall so well was a picture categorized as "bridge over water" with some classification of secrecy which I don't remember. The picture clearly showed the structure spanning the water still in perfect condition with total destruction all around it for many feet. The jungle was nothing but a moonscape of bomb craters. The intelligence report printed on the photo described something like, two flights of four F-105s delivering their total bomb loads on the target (bomb loads for F-105s were worthy of note, see page 164.) and "damage to target – none, damage to surrounding area – considerable." The target photo taken by our guys with our super sophisticated RF-4s clearly showed a log, probably one foot in diameter lying across a stream of water, maybe two to four feet wide. Yep, you could have hopped across it without getting your feet wet. Was it a joke? No, we didn't joke about dropping bombs from F-105s. In some disturbing way, it seemed to be an outrageous example of how this "sorta" war was being fought.

I loved the smell of teak. While Bonnie had been at Alconbury we had ordered and taken delivery on some teak furniture from Sweden and I just adored the smell of it. So, when I arrived at Udorn and discovered that the Officers Club was constructed almost entirely of teak, which grew in the jungles of Southeast Asia like our oaks did in the forests at home, it just polished off the mystique of being stationed at a small wartime base on the eastern lowlands of Thailand. Our quarters were also of teak with very austere rooms for two crewmembers. The ceiling and roof were plain corrugated steel but kept the rain out well enough. My memory is that of a base almost entirely of red sandy soil, including the roads. Scattered around were foreboding bunkers of sandbags that were to be used as shelters in the event of a mortar attack. I never investigated, nor needed one of these structures, and I'm not certain I wouldn't have rather taken my chances with the mortar shells than the snakes that surely were enjoying the dark coolness within the bunkers. We were not unique

The Eagle Hunts

as an active Royal Thai Airbase which had American flying units in Thailand. Nakhom Phanom was located to the east of us and close to the Mekong River which was the border between Thailand and Laos. Just a few miles further to the east of the Mekong lay the infamous Ho Chi Minh trail, a labyrinth of small trails and roads leading from North Vietnam to Cambodia. Nakhom Phanom had pierced steel planking for a runway and a special operations and air rescue mission. To our south were other fighter bases. Ubon, which was home to Robin Olds and Chappie James of the famous F-4 555 "Triple Nickel Squadron," the others, Takhli and Korat, were bases from where the F-105 Thunderchiefs flew. Further south were the Strategic Air Command (SAC) bases of U-Tapao and Don Muang, from which flew the B-52s and KC-135s.

One day an old boxy twin engine C-119 taxied in past the newly camouflage painted RF-4Cs and shut down with a certain confidence that we did not yet demonstrate due to our just arrived status. The cockpit windows slid open and the young Anglo-Saxon pilots pulled off their headsets and prepared to deplane while another opened the large rear door to take on cargo. Printed on the side of this antique prop driven cargo plane was "Air America" with few other markings. Who was Air America? Also, I couldn't help but notice taxing in, the flight of two low winged, tandem cockpit, single propeller engine fighter type aircraft of Korean War pilot training vintage, but they had guns in their wing roots and bomb racks on the underside of the wings. They were T-28s and each had a white skinned and a dark-skinned pilot. The planes carried the colors of Laos but we were in Thailand, and the Laotian colors were inserted into a small slide rack on each side of the aircraft so that it could be slid out and another national color inserted. Thai, Cambodian, South Vietnamese, who knew. We, however, were cranking up for a flight into Laos which was neutral.

There were lots of interesting things going on at Udorn, some of which we knew about and some of which remained mysterious. It turns out that Air America was an airline operated by the CIA to ferry supplies and personnel into and out of Laos and perhaps other places it wasn't supposed to. The Laotian T-28s flew combat missions out of

Chapter 8 | The War in Southeast Asia

Udorn to support the friendly mountain tribes who were resisting the Pathet Lao, who were the indigenous Communist guerrillas that were supplied and supported by the North Vietnamese as they extended their tentacles into Laos.

I began to learn that this "non-war" was not just a conflict in South Vietnam but one whose combatants could be engaged in South Vietnam, North Vietnam, Laos, Cambodia, Thailand and other places about which were not often spoken. It comprised an area called Indo-China during WWII and the days of French occupation. Not only were the American people being sold short on the extent of the conflict by our government, but the press was grossly mischaracterizing the nature and outcomes of battles of the war, intentionally fanning the flames of discontent among Americans and, by the way, selling papers and magazines.

At first, our missions were daytime flights over lightly or non-defended targets to give us a feel for the area and tactics. The tactics that we employed were similar to the ones we practiced in Europe, low level to evade radar and surface to air missiles. However, in Southeast Asia, we generally flew over 3500 feet over the target area because the "gooks"* had a bad habit of just shooting everything they had up into the air and hoping we would run into a bullet, which was entirely possible. It was called "barrage fire" and the answer to it was to cross the target area above 3500 feet over the ground, which was about the highest that an AK-47, pistol, and other small arms could reach. If you were unlucky enough to encounter barrage fire it looked like a wall of tracers being shot straight up in the air and if that wasn't enough, for each tracer there were several bullets that you could not see. I will say that at night it was a rather impressive display of fireworks, but as we were not in the frame of mind to enjoy it, it went unappreciated, unless of course we were able to wake them up at night. Then we had the pleasure of seeing it behind us and you couldn't help but wonder how many soiled pants there were and how many gooks shot themselves as they scrambled to cock their weapons and fire them up into the black of night after having being shocked

---

* Politically incorrect name to show contempt and disrespect for Asians we did not like because they wanted to kill us.

into consciousness by the horrendous roar of our reconnaissance jet flashing unseen only a few feet overhead.

At the speeds we flew they could not hear us coming and when they did hear us, we were gone. If there were some anti-aircraft artillery (AAA) involved, usually 37mm (little yellow/orange balls) or 57mm (bigger white balls) then a greater height was advisable, but that put you up in the surface to air missile (SAM) environment and they had a hell of a lot of those damn things, especially over their important targets. Generally, we flew through that stuff, which surprisingly enough, there was a good probability we could do because of the slower rate of fire of that type of AAA and the speed of our jets. Keep in mind it was only a probability, and after a while you began to wonder if you were not beginning to wear out your good luck, even if statistically it was not supposed to matter. So, we had fast jets they could not hear coming, cameras, which we called sensors because they were not all optical, that could see at night, or day, or in clouds, very high or very low. It would seem like an uneven fight but the communist adversary had their own strengths, which too often our arrogance prevented us from recognizing or too quickly dismissing. The technologically inept, very unsophisticated enemy, was also very creative.

Not having radar good enough or well distributed over the vastness of the jungle terrain to counter our low-level high-speed flights, they reverted to a very crude system that worked better than one might think. Listening posts on many of the hilltops would report the sound of passing aircraft, "jet South, headed East" at a particular time. Another post to the South would report the sound to the "North headed East," so the aircraft was between them, the relative distant from them based on sound. That gave them an airplane at a point headed east. A moment later two more reports from different listening posts of aircraft sounds between them but more to the North and timed so that an approximate speed was indicated. Point two was determined so they could draw a line between them and extend it in the direction of flight. There were numerous listening posts throughout the jungle mountains and the more that reported the sounds of aircraft the more accurate the approximations. When the course being flown looked like it was going to pass over a defended

Chapter 8 | The War in Southeast Asia

area or suspected target, with the approximate time and direction from which to expect the attack, the suspected target defenders would not be very surprised. At the least, they could throw lots of lead into the sky.

It was quickly realized by those of us who saw the war first hand that it was not just a Vietnam war against an oppressive communist regime, but a war against a people who believed in their cause and who were resourceful and cunning. Unfortunately, our leadership did not understand this and it seemed that the higher up the chain of command, the less it was understood.

There was a mission competition going on between the Air Force and the Navy to see who could fly the most missions because, after all, war funding was based on demand and the more missions the more need or demand for money. We had a jet that could fly 30 miles and take a continuous strip of high speed high-resolution photos and yet we were sent out to fly a five-mile section of a road, so that six more jets from our squadron would get to fly on that target and increase the sortie count. Do you not think that after the first couple of RF-4 jets blew over, the gooks might have figured out what the target was, and that there might be a few more coming and be ready? Yes, it got pretty hot for that last jet. Six jets with twelve pilots exposed to the risks and realities of combat when one jet could have run a 30 mile stretch of road in four minutes if they were just moseying along, three minutes if they were in a hurry.

The National Command Authority, which was the President or those appointed to represent him, Secretary of Defense or those appointed to represent him, and including the Joint Chiefs of Staff and other advising high-ranking groups were seemingly unable to understand the nature of the conflict and our involvement. The concept that this was a conflict wherein the expansion of Communism into the south and then potentially spreading from there not only to the rest of Southeast Asia but the South Pacific as well was generally understood. Whether it was as generally accepted can be debated. How to strategically and tactically prevent this expansion seemed to completely escape the pinnacle of our governmental and military strategists. Between them they derived and/or supported the policy of "measured response." It was based on the precept that the United States was such an overwhelming power that it would be unfair for us to apply all our resources and strength to fighting a war against a small, backward, and poor nation like North Vietnam. Therefore, to keep it a fair fight, so the rest of the world would not view the U.S. as an international bully, we would gently increase our military pressure until the Communist Vietnamese realized how futile it would be to resist such a technologically advanced and powerful war machine, and quietly fade back into the jungle and leave South Vietnam, Laos, and Cambodia alone. A FAIR WAR, WHAT THE HELL!!! Needless to say, the result of that arrogance is history.

The fact that this "conflict" was not actually a declared war was a detail that did not seem to bother the leadership of our nation. Our Congress seemed too weak and noncommittal to declare war. Maybe it was because they didn't want to recognize the benefits that might eventually inure to those who had to fight it, or maybe it was because they didn't think the people of the United States wanted a "war" in Southeast Asia. So, let's do it, but don't declare it, maybe no one will notice. However, let's seize upon a relatively inconsequential event that is today considered questionable called the "Gulf of Tonkin Incident" to grant the president power to commit the nation to "armed conflict" in the interest of urgency. In that manner Congress would be able to avoid the tacky discussion of, and act of, declaring a war that Americans did not want. Individual representatives and senators could always blame the president whose administration was all too anxious to usurp the constitutional powers given only to Congress to declare war. The Gulf of Tonkin Resolution, as it is known, was "to permit the maintenance of peace and security in Southeast Asia." It was NOT a declaration of war, just as Congress did not declare war in either Iraq or Afghanistan, yet we have still expended vast amounts of financial, material, and human resources in lands far away in the interest of foreign policy. We are so quick to call a program intended to alleviate some social ill a "war" against that issue; "a war against drugs," "a war against terrorism," "a war against poverty," etc., but it's not a war when 58,000 of our men and women are told to sacrifice their lives fighting it.

Chapter 8 | The War in Southeast Asia

As one might detect there was then, and is still today, a bit of displeasure with our involvement in Vietnam. I was certainly not alone in my disdain. The more we saw of it, the more we saw our friends fly off and not return, the more we realized that this was deadly and that we were indeed mortal. Then the more we realized our resources and capabilities were being wasted, the more we wondered why we should be committed to a war, a long way from home, when we wouldn't call it a war. This attitude played a role in the later captivity and seemingly unerring support of an administration that was difficult to believe in. Irrespective of this, it was my professional and patriotic duty to perform my duty as best as I could and that I did. We all did!

Lt. Clark at the American Consulate in Udorn, Thailand.

I was 26, young and fit, tanned and sporting a handlebar mustache. Flying at war was fun because of the things we were able to do such as temporary duty (TDY) at Clark Air Base at Manila in the Philippines to attend Jungle Survival School for a week or two or rest and recreation (R&R) trips to Tokyo via Saigon and Taipei or perhaps to Bangkok and Pattaya Beach on the Bay of Thailand. Yes, the war was fun, that is except for the getting shot at, friends who took off and never came back, finally realizing that we were "playing for all the marbles," getting burned up or blown up with your jet, getting killed, dying slowly in the jungle or worse, captured. There weren't many rules that we had to attend at war. All those flying things that prudence and regulations said you should not do while flying in peacetime were overlooked and became less of an issue, especially upon returning from a mission where barrage fire was flown through, SAMs were dodged and MIGS might have been encountered. There was a bit of a swashbuckling, a "they didn't get us this time, but tomorrow we may die attitude." At first, we drank quite a bit after missions but then the reality of it all began to set in, and we realized that if we wanted to complete our 100 missions and go home, we had better be very sober and rested when the next mission came around and that could be in just a few hours. Many of us bought guitars, and Al Tichner who was one of us, and had been with us at Alconbury, set out to teach us something of playing the guitar. We wrote letters, we read books, studied and further developed air tactics.

I had the most unpleasant squadron extra duty of writing letters for the commander to sign and mail to the families of those squadron mates who did not return. They were classified as "missing in action" (MIA). If they were seen to crash with their jet and no corpse was observed, they were classified as "missing in action presumed killed." When the corpse was seen, the classification was "killed in action" (KIA). It was not a pleasant job for most were guys with young families I had known at Alconbury. Sadly, I don't remember any; I suppose one blocks out things like that at a time of an "undeclared fun war."

CHAPTER 9

DODGING SAMS

I was approaching 80 "counters," or missions "up north." It seemed I would easily make the go home goal of 100 within the six-month arbitrary target that had been established for returning back stateside. As veterans of combat in Southeast Asia, we were given some priority in selecting our next assignment after we completed our combat tour of duty. Unfortunately for the back seaters, of which I was considered, remember I had not yet been given my combat crew check ride for the front cockpit, the dictates of the Air Force took a higher priority than sending them to a front cockpit assignment. Instead, we were all sent to pilot instructor training to become future T-38 pilot training instructors. Many of the current pilot training instructors were being sent to combat crew training school and needed to be replaced. However, there were two of us that received assignments to F-4C fighters. We were to go to the F-4C combat crew training school and get a stateside assignment flying the gun, rocket, and "bomb-toten" version of the jet I was now flying. It would be front seat with a navigator/weapons system officer in the rear cockpit. My spirits could not have been higher and I basked in the jealousy of my compatriots.

The weather had been cloudy and overcast with fog and rain over much of the flying area including Thailand, Laos, and Vietnam for a couple of weeks and had slowed down the number of daily missions being flown. As the winter monsoon season drew to a close, the days began to have more and larger breaks in the overcast skies with fewer clouds. The fighter guys at Ubon and Takhli were getting impatient to start dropping bombs and shooting up those who would not understand the futility in resisting us. Early each morning among the reconnaissance mission tasks would be one or two weather reconnaissance flights. These were considered "milk runs" because their only mission was to look at the weather over the targets planned by the fighters that day, and since the weather over any particular area could be viewed from a distance, flying over the specific target area was not necessary, hence avoiding enemy air defenses. Having been advised of the weather which we would report, the command center would then decide whether or not to commit to the bombing missions for the day. It would involve a large contingent of fighters and support aircraft, which would include airborne radar surveillance and control, airborne refueling tankers, fighter cap that would be one or more flights of air to air fighters flying a "cap" above the bomber force to intercept the MIGS and prevent them from interfering with the bomber force, Wild Weasels which would suppress surface to air missile and anti-aircraft fire, electronic surveillance and jamming aircraft that would search for and jam enemy radar, and lastly and perhaps most importantly, the rescue A1E "Sandy" prop driven fighters and CH-43 "Jolly Green Giant" helicopters. The Sandys and the Jolly Greens were the task force search and rescue team to pick up downed airman. These strike missions were frequently followed up with a bomb damage assessment recon flight. These were not pleasant flights, for the hornets' nest would really be stirred up. So, the first mission to just look at where the clouds were and which would not be specifically flown over the target area to keep from telegraphing it to the enemy was one of the least stressful missions that would be flown among the attack force that day, with the possible minor detail that all that previously described airborne support was still on the ground and we were all by ourselves; "Alone unarmed and unafraid" as the moto went. The MIGS loved to cruise around just waiting for us to predictably show up "be-bopping" along all by ourselves. Easy kill, but oddly enough we had no record of anyone being shot down by MIGS. Oh wait, maybe some of those flights that just never returned, perhaps, who knew?

    One day, we were assigned one of those "weather recce[*]" missions. We were to look at the Red River Valley in the vicinity of Hanoi. That alone would suggest that the targets for that day would be Hanoi and

---

[*] Recce is short for reconnaissance.

CHAPTER 9 | Dodging SAMS

vicinity. We did not generally know the specific targets on a weather recce because we were concerned about the weather for all of the task force which would cover a considerable area around the target as well as routes into and out of the target area.

Captain Clark and Captain Goodrich on takeoff roll in an RF-4C Phantom II, afterburners lit, Udorn Royal Air Force Base, Udorn, Thailand, circa 1967.

In northern Laos, on a steep karst mountain easily definable on our ground mapping radar, was a secret "tactical air navigation" (TACAN) site manned by the CIA, and a small force of Laotian Montagnards*. It was invaluable as a navigation site to all of the aircraft flying missions out of Thailand into North Vietnam and it was called "channel 97" by the aviators who knew little about what all went on there to make it possible for us to just "dial it in" as we blasted northward from Udorn and other Thai airbases. It was known in the classified vernacular as Lima Site 85 and now unclassified it has a sad but interesting story in the history of the air war in SEA. Flying toward it then turning eastward on a radial from there would give us a course into the Red River valley. There was the prize, Hanoi, with its key bridges traversing the Red River, its vital road and rail system, Gia Lam air base from whence flew the MIGS, and which, except for Moscow, had the

---

* A French term meaning "mountain dwellers."

strongest air defenses in the world. That day we took the familiar route dropping down low, very low, after heading east to avoid the always searching radar. Streaking past the southern edge of the Black River as it snaked its way south through the jungle, then turned back northeast to join the Red River, we turned inbound toward Hanoi. Hitting the burners and accelerating to around 600 knots* we began a very steep climb that pressed us down into our seats with the weight of an 800-pound man and we started looking around at the weather as the earth rapidly fell away beneath us. As the different enemy radar sites spotted us and started "ranging" and going into launch and fire modes the lights on our Radar Acquisition and Warning (RAW) gear lit up and the scope displayed radials of different lengths depicting the direction and strength of the radar signal. A "three-ringer" with a launch light was not a good thing but it did give us an idea where to look, unless of course, there were clouds below, then you waited for it to pop through the clouds. Hopefully you would be looking at the right spot and have time to out maneuver it. If there were very many SAMS launching at the same time it could get kind of busy. Then there was the loud buzz in our helmet headset letting us know things had turned to shit, as if the yellow and red lights on the RAW gear did not get our attention. As we approached 15,000 to 20,000 feet, we started a roll upside down which would give us a better view of the airspace below by looking down through the canopy while keeping us planted in our seats as we pulled the nose back down to the ground disappearing into the "ground clutter"** from whence we had just appeared. We would very likely be supersonic much to the aggravation of the Peoples Air Defense Forces who no longer had a target for their launched missiles and which were now wandering helter-skelter about the sky before crashing back to earth, who knows where, hopefully downtown Hanoi, or better, the launch site from where they were fired.

    On one mission, which was not a weather recce we had to stay at altitude until we completed the photo run, I took a picture of a missile passing between us and the lead aircraft. Their crew was inexperienced

---

*   Nautical miles per hour or about 690 statute miles per hour.
**   Ground clutter is the radar return when the radar is aimed low and picks up all of the terrain and buildings in a big ill defined echo.

CHAPTER 9 | Dodging SAMS

at the full intensity of the air war over Hanoi and I was, therefore, assisting in avoidance maneuvers by telling them where the missiles were coming from and how to lead them astray. Then, once the missile was committed, how to break inside it and to force it to lose them as a target and go wild, hopefully not toward us who were similarly jinking*. That was one reason the most experienced crew was assigned to fly the wing position. Believe it or not, the wing man could usually see more and could clear better, by looking through the lead and thus, could not only fly off of lead, but scan the skies and ground beyond.

---

* A basic fighter maneuver when the aircraft suddenly changes speed, direction, and altitude.

The Eagle Hunts

CHAPTER 10

LUCKY OR NOT?

The ridges were low, jungle covered, and ran almost parallel northwest to southeast for a distance along this portion of the ill-defined border between the "neutral" country of Laos and Communist North Vietnam. Between the ridges were small flat valleys, clean, cultivated and planted with maize (corn to Midwesterners). The maize, which was about 12 inches tall in weed free loose soil, was unnoticed as we streaked low over the ridges clearing them by no more than 100 or 200 feet. There were some small agricultural villages, mostly hidden by the jungle trees, along the valley edges. Our aircraft, painted in jungle camouflage to make them less visible to the higher flying MIGS, were positioned in a line-abreast formation, a formation we had chosen to fly off of the lead aircraft giving us tactical separation but still allowing a low profile. As no threat had been identified by squadron intelligence in this area and our Radar Advanced Warning (RAW) gear was quiet, everything seemed peaceful, but it was war and there was no relaxation in the situational awareness among any of us. The two external wing tanks had not yet been jettisoned as it was prudent to retain them and any fuel they might contain for as long as possible. Doing so increased the likelihood when we flew into the "hot" zone we would have full internal fuel tanks allowing us to use full throttle and the afterburners to execute high-speed and high-G maneuvers to avoid surface to air missiles, North Vietnamese fighter aircraft, and anti-aircraft artillery (AAA). They would most certainly be encountered. They always engaged us in the Red River Valley around Hanoi.

While dividing my time between watching the lead aircraft off our left-wing, clearing the sky for threats and closely monitoring our time and checkpoints, a shower of orange balls of light suddenly started flashing all around us while seeming to come from nowhere. I had come to recognize orange balls as 37 mm AAA. If those balls of light were white then it would likely be the larger 57 mm AAA or larger. These balls flashing by were both orange and white indicating a combined site of 57 and 37 mm AAA. The most hazardous for low-flying aircraft were the quad mounted 14.7 ZPUs. They were a Soviet-made single gun mount with four fast firing 14.7 mm machine guns. I can't say that I remember exactly what they looked like coming at me, however, it looked like an almost solid stream of fire if they were shooting at someone else. The gun site that engaged us was not using radar and so our RAW gear had picked up no radar search or ranging signal, but their visual aiming was spot on target… that was us. Ed saw it the moment I did and asked where it was coming from while punching the throttles full forward. When I responded "10 o'clock" he broke up and to the right. The profile of the aircraft straight on is just the small nose, canopy area, and the leading edge of the wings, but when we pulled up and rolled away from the guns, it put our belly and the bottom of our wings up as a full belly target. I felt a sudden "thud" and the jet did a couple of Dutch rolls* as if a boxer was staggering under the impact of an opponent's heavy blow. Then our jet departed from controlled flight, rolling and tumbling end over end. In my years of flying tactical fighter jets, I had been in lots of different, and sometimes violent, attitudes. Some slammed my helmet against the canopy as its many marks and scratches would attest. Some pinned me in my ejection seat with the force of eight gravities (Gs), or the equivalent of about 1600 pounds for a 200-pound man. Some pressed me against my harness and straps with negative gravity forces, but never before had I not known exactly what that flying machine to which I was strapped was doing. At this moment, I did not. I instantly knew we were out of control and being flung through the sky like a tumbling stone, a stone being acted on by the basic force of nature called gravity. We had shot ourselves upward,

---

* This is when the aircraft wobbles back and forth, left and right.

Chapter 10 | Lucky or Not?

but now we were no longer flying and were falling back to earth while also being hurled forward with a velocity of over 600 miles per hour. Even in my twirling disorientation, I realized we were destined to impact the onrushing low ridge very shortly. The ejection seat used a 40-mm cannon shell to blow it and the occupant out of the aircraft cockpit a bit like a human cannonball, except you were strapped in a seat. Consider for a moment if the aircraft were very low and upside down, it would simply blast me into the ground. My options seemed to be indeterminable. I knew we were going very fast, just marginally within the survival envelope of the ejection seat capability. I knew we were very low and getting lower and I knew I had virtually no chance to survive unless the seat shot upward. And I had no idea if we were up or down or somewhere in between. It was a moment in my life where my future was in the hands of Lady Luck and the good Lord. Delaying action meant very quickly crashing with tons of howling,

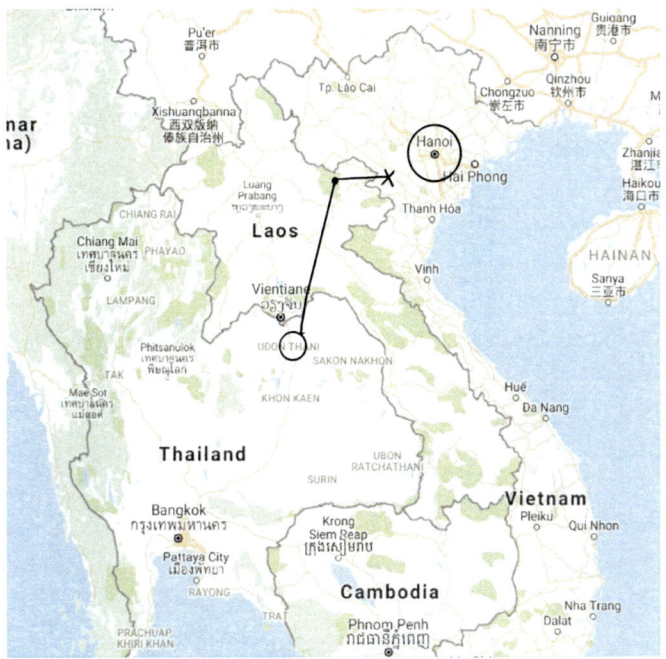

Flight path of Capt. Clark on 12 March 1967. He and Captain Goodrich took off at small circle, turned at dot, shot down at 'X' with the target at Hanoi (big circle).

flailing, tearing metal, and exploding fuel, historically not a desirable situation for an aviator hoping for a long life. Life looked tentative at this point but I did not have time to ponder the philosophy any further. I opted for whatever probability of survival immediacy gave me and took the chance that I was pointed up. The decision being made in the blink of an eye, I went for the handles on the face curtain installed in the back of the ejection seat above my helmet. But I could not raise my arms for the G forces were so strong that no matter how hard I tried, I could not lift my hands to grasp the handles. Those handles would pull the canvas curtain down over the front of my helmet, protecting it and my face and head from the onrushing blast of air as it fired the seat and slammed me into the 600 mile per hour airstream outside. The designers of the English Martin Baker seat had given due consideration to this conundrum and placed a handle between the pilot's legs that would be accessible should the handles on the face curtain not be reachable. As I could not lift my hands off of my thighs, I gave the job of pulling the ejection handle between my legs to the first hand that got there. I slid them both forward; the right-hand won. But I quickly realized the same G forces that kept me from lifting my hands to grasp the handles above my helmet were keeping me from pulling the handle up. If I could not raise my arm how was I going to pull a handle up? So, I grasped the handle and rolled my wrist over my thigh. The handle moved only slightly, but it was a positive movement like the ones I had felt during checkout at Shaw a couple of years earlier, **but the seat did not fire!** Then I recalled our ejection seat trainer had said, even though it would only take one-fourth of one second for the seat to fire after the handle was pulled, the time compression would be so severe in such a circumstance it would seem like it was not firing, and to keep pulling. Since I was out of options, I held on and kept pulling. The blast of air was mind-numbing. My vision went gray, my left arm which had lost the race to the handle was all by itself flailing in the wind like an empty shirt sleeve stuck out of the window of a speeding car. My unrestrained helmet and head flung from side-to-side disrespecting entirely my ineffectual effort to keep it firmly planted in the center of the seat headrest.

Chapter 10 | Lucky or Not?

The Martin Baker seat was a very reliable, though complex, piece of engineering and design worthy of the now disabled RF-4C, itself a masterpiece of aeronautical engineering and construction. The Martin Baker seat's best aspect was once it had been fired, all of the numerous actions required to eject the pilot from the jet were fully automatic. Twenty-seven different pyrotechnic cartridges fired together or in sequence to perform actions like: pulling your legs back to the seat to keep your knees and legs from hitting the canopy rail and being broken or ripped off as you were shot out of the cockpit, snapping your harness tight and locking it, firing the canopy off, firing the seat out of the cockpit, holding the occupant and the seat in a tight bundle to minimize flailing, deploying a small drogue chute to stabilize the seat and its occupant, determining when the seat and occupant package had slowed down so the harness could then be blown loose separating the pilot from the seat, and deploying the main chute. All of it was done automatically. All of it was performed in less than four seconds, but also depending on the time it took the seat-pilot package to slow down to a safe chute-opening speed. Failure of any one of these sequences could mean disabling injury or death. For example, at those speeds if the main chute deployed before the hurling ejected pilot had slowed down there would be enough opening force to shred the parachute rendering it useless, or it might rip the harness off the pilot's body regardless of the legs and the shoulders holding it on. Either of these or a combination was considered undesirable.

Almost as quickly as I had been hurled into semiconsciousness by the enormous wind blast, I felt the jerk of the parachute harness when the drogue chute and then the main chute opened. The tug seemed like nothing more than a carnival ride. What was not like a carnival ride was the huge ball of fire a couple of hundred yards in front of me with a small chute floating to the ground just before it which meant Ed had ejected but almost too late. My observation was no more than a blink because the crashing jet was almost level with me hanging in the chute, which told me I had work to do and fast. I looked up to check the chute canopy and saw there were no tangled risers, or risers looped over the canopy that needed to be cut loose to prevent it from diminishing the lift of the billowing parachute canopy. I also took note of the size of the surprisingly small chute that was supposed to gently lower my 200-pound body adorned with a wide array of flight and survival gear to the earth below. Another part of this instantaneous sight frame was the tops of the valley trees. I was looking up at them! But at this point any air between me and the ground at all was welcomed. I could not possibly have worked as fast as Martin Baker had done to accomplish the task of getting me out of that jet hurling at over 600 miles an hour while slowing me down and getting rid of the seat and everything that tied me to it. Then properly opening the chute all in four and a quarter seconds. Later when I had a moment, in fact six years of moments, I realized that four and a quarter seconds was only how long it took the rocketing RF-4 to turn into a huge fireball at the edge of the jungle. Four and one quarter seconds from security to death in a fireball of metal and exploding jet fuel, but yet there I was. There was obviously more than skill, cunning, and Martin Baker involved in getting me out of that jet alive. Now I needed to keep that "alive thing" going.

Seeing the ground rushing up I prepared for the parachute landing fall I had practiced in training. Unfortunately, I did not have time to release the survival pack that was my seat cushion. I was supposed to have released it, allowing it to fall away and hang on a lanyard about ten feet below me, which would have permitted an unimpeded parachute landing. But, with the ground being so close when the chute opened that did not happen and I smashed into the soft earth of the valley like a pile driver still sitting on my seat cushion. Stunned, I gathered my senses as quickly as I could to realize that only 100 or so yards away was a line of Vietnamese villagers intermixed with some Vietnamese military rushing toward me. The line reached almost across the entire small valley and left no escape in that direction. I could see that their intent was not cordial and it was time for me to depart their impending presence as quickly as possible. They were carrying every conceivable weapon, mostly tools for working the soil: crude pitchforks, shovels, hoes, hammers, spades, clubs, and then there were the ever-present AK-47s, M1 Garand rifles, carbines, and pistols including our Army 45s.

Chapter 10 | Lucky or Not?

Releasing my harness, I scrambled out of it leaving my survival kit behind. As I ran across the valley, I realized how I was both blessed and cursed. The soft soil probably saved me from breaking a leg as I landed ill-prepared to do so, and yet it had denied me the cover and evasion possibilities of the jungle, but it's necessary to utilize all the advantages one has and ignore those you don't. I was able to run and did so, with considerable haste. In the center of the valley was a ditch with trees and brush and it was all I had for cover nearby. When I arrived at the edge of the ditch, I felt fortunate that I had heard no shots nor seen any earth kicking up around me. The ditch looked as if it had a smooth bottom of ivy, much like English Ivy, so I jumped in only to discover it was a fake bottom. I fell through the ivy and landed face forward across a hidden log which the ivy had bridged and covered with its growth. Later I realized I had broken two or three ribs as I fell across the log. Not having time to concern myself with that issue, I ran up the ditch until I realized it ended before reaching the end of the valley and the covering brush and jungle. Assuming that if I made a run for it toward the jungle across the open valley, I would have no cover whatsoever and those with firearms could cut me down like a rabbit. So, I decided to hide in a thicket of bamboo and hope they would run by me leaving an opportunity to escape to their rear. With much yelling and commotion, they did just that, leaving me a clean exit to their rear, which I started to take only to notice two older men completely clad in black carrying very large rifles and walking slowly and deliberately up each edge of the ditch toward me. The boisterous group that preceded them had just run by, but these black clad men were methodical in scrutinizing every bit of that ditch. In a moment, they spotted me. One on each side of the ditch, they raised those huge rifles and took aim. It was at that moment I realized a bullet with the enormous velocity it would have being shot from one of those guns would be very hot as it blasted through me. I am not quite sure why that seemed to be important at the time, but again fate would have its way and no shots were fired. I remained frozen like so many rabbits I had hunted in my youth, but now I was the rabbit. A few loud and harsh commands by the older man in black to the right of the ditch and the charging mass of villagers reversed their course and returned while I remained at bay. As the now quiet group stood more curious than threatening at the edge of the ditch, I remained still and quiet. After all, it was their call.

I'm sure I looked somewhat threatening with a handlebar mustache, dark tan, my helmet still on, the loaded .38 Smith & Wesson in my pocket and standing 6'3" in my boots, all to their modest 5'2" – 5'8" height and slight stature. Realizing I was far outgunned, I chose to not draw my .38 and provoke a shootout, which I would have lost. About this time, I heard three or four smaller caliber shots, perhaps from a .38 pistol, which we carried. They came from the east where the plane had crashed and I had seen Ed's chute. Shortly following were two or three heavy caliber shots, more like a .30-06 caliber, like an M1 Garand, the same weapon being held on me, and the same caliber as my dad's rifle I had shot many times as a young man. I knew what they sounded like.

I did not surrender with raised arms; I did not remove and drop my weapon and I did not offer to leave the bamboo thicket. Why the useless taunting bellicosity in such dire circumstances I'm not sure and I am doubtful that it made me any more heroic. It became apparent that the group discussion now concerned who would be crawling into the thicket to disarm and drag me out. At this point, I felt somewhat more secure because I assumed if they wanted me dead, I would already be dead. I was, however, just as convinced that should their security or safety be threatened, I could be quickly made so. Somewhat to their alarm, I held my position in spite of their gestures and shouts which I assumed were commands to come out.

Subsequent to this standoff were murmurs, pointing and comments regarding what to do next, besides just shoot me. Obviously, as long as I was not a security threat to them, I had some hostage value and would be taken alive if possible. I glanced at my Seiko watch and the date number on the "day & date" readout was a red number 12; Sunday, March 12, 1967 around 10 o'clock became etched into my mind forever. Speculative bickering continued about who must enter the thicket after me. Finally, the older gentleman in black settled the issue and selected a couple of tall slender young fellows who demonstrated little hesitation but, nevertheless, exercised considerable

Chapter 10 | Lucky or Not?

caution in advancing through the thicket. I quietly waited with eyes constantly scanning my captors but concentrating mostly on the pair who were now my companions in the thicket. Just out of arm's reach, they gestured for me to raise my hands, and no longer feeling bellicose nor heroic I did so. Once they were in arms reach, they began to feel for my .38 and removed it. Then, one pocket at a time, they opened each of them and removed the contents: my survival radio, that I should have destroyed but had no time to do it, helmet, the orange survival switchblade knife, my .38 ammo, maps, and gloves. I was told to remove my G-suit, shoes and flight suit, leaving me barefoot and wearing only my shorts and t-shirt. During this process they led and pushed me from the thicket. By now any resistance was purely token and I was being treated humanely, although a bit rudely. Having examined my flight suit to their satisfaction, they returned it for me to put on but kept my shoes and socks, still leaving me barefoot. It was about that time I noticed two of the men in the gaggle who were wearing military uniforms had come to the front, now that the villagers led by their "seniors in black" had resolved the crisis. They looked like kids but the .45-pistol held in the hand of one of them certainly did not look like a toy. Pushing and poking me with their gun barrels and a wide array of tools and weapons, the victorious crowd took turns urging me down the valley toward the village. The kids in military uniform tried to be in charge but clearly, they were not. The two older men in black, who had lowered and put their huge rifles on safe, were issuing directions that were executed respectfully by the village members with little regard for the comments of the in-charge wannabes.

When the roar of jets overhead signaled the arrival of some search and rescue aircraft, I was pushed into the bottom of the ditch and one of the Army types put the .45 to my head and demonstrated by gesturing that I kneel in the ditch and put my head down. At this point, I again became defiant and refused. I replied in gestures that if they were going to execute me, it was going to be with me standing looking at them. I would not be executed by being shot in the back of my head kneeling at their feet in a ditch! It was at this moment, the barrel of the cocked quivering .45 came into perfect alignment with the sun shining behind me through a break in the canopy over the ditch, and I could actually see the bullet in the barrel pointed at my face. Our military and police members are taught to hold their weapon with the finger beside the trigger guard and off of the trigger until you want to actually fire the weapon. It is because of a stress characteristic called "adverse pressure," which is a tendency for the muscles of the body to contract under stress without the voluntary command from the brain to do so, like squeezing the trigger without knowing that you are, or intending to do so. This obviously stressed, shaking kid with his finger on the trigger of a loaded and cocked .45 pointed at my face about a foot or two away, all while rescue aircraft roared overhead was not a good situation. I was nervous and concerned but nevertheless remained defiant. The old man in black grasped the seriousness of the standoff and gently pushed the .45 aside and spoke with the young man in a calm but firm manner and stepped in front of me. He pointed to the sound of aircraft overhead, indicated bombs going off and told me to lay down in the ditch for my own safety, all by gestures. I nodded and laid down in the ditch on my side while looking up at the group of villagers crouched around me. The rescue aircraft overhead, having not seen us under the tree canopy in the ditch, eventually departed. My hands were bound and I was again poked and prodded toward the village where a crowd was gathered to view the captured "American air pirate." After passing the villagers, who kept their distance, I was marched towards a hump of karst nearby at the edge of the valley. Arriving at the small karst hill, I was shown an entry to a dugout cave no larger than a small bathroom and a ceiling too low in which to stand. Crawling would be necessary to even enter. The cave appeared to have been intended to store crop harvests off season, but it would be my temporary jail. It was empty except for a few bamboo sticks scattered on the dirt floor.

Shoved into the cave and followed by the two uniformed kids who had holstered the .45 and taken the AK-47 out of my back, I was unceremoniously set down. The bindings previously placed on my hands behind by back were harshly tightened and some commands were issued, which I accepted with very much the same attentiveness as would have one of dad's Herford cows. I assumed it was something

Chapter 10 | Lucky or Not?

like "stay in the cave or we will shoot you." Being left alone in the small confines of the cave with a guard posted outside, I began to feel the pains of stressed and injured parts of my body. However, upon a cursory body parts inventory, I decided that under the circumstances, I was doing pretty well. Little did I know....

I was to later learn many of my fellow "air pirates" were beaten and tortured by their captors who had a score to settle because of past bombing raids. This village had not suffered such a fate and found me more of a curiosity than the icon of a hated enemy. I have always thought that the army kids would like to have been tougher and exacted more revenge except they were badly outnumbered by the villagers who took their orders from the older man in black. Contemplation came easier now, and I realized how fortunate I had been, how hopeless the situation was and how much my destiny was in the hands of those who hated me.

It occurred to me that I did not know if I had been looking at North Vietnamese or Pathet Lao* uniforms on those ".45 totin'" kids. If I was considered in Laos, previous intelligence reports indicated I would most likely die in a cave of malaria and malnutrition. Was this my fate? Was this my cave, and were they Laotian? However, if I was captured by North Vietnamese, I would most likely be transported to Hanoi, tortured for intelligence, perhaps brainwashed as in Korea, but likely kept alive to be used as a future hostage. Neither option seemed particularly desirable. Nonetheless, I was opting for the latter, but only the future would reveal my fate.

An ominous shadow fell over the entrance to the cave. All was quiet. Then with a few small shuffles, in came a calm looking fellow dressed in black and as I write even now, I ask myself if he was the "man in black?" I cannot recall but he was in black, self-assured, and interested in how I was doing. Why was I not able to know whether he was the village elder that had been so in charge? I don't believe that the adrenaline allowed me to make that determination at the time and as many of us who are Anglo-Saxon know, all those who are not, look alike. He gathered up some of the small bamboo sticks scattered

---

* The Pathet Lao were the indigent Communist guerillas in Laos allied with the North Vietnamese and were equivalent to the Viet Cong in South Vietnam.

The Eagle Hunts

about the cave and systematically laid them on top of each other on the damp dirt floor as if he were making a small campfire. He explained, again in gestures, I should sit on them rather than the floor of the cave. Then he checked the security of the bindings on my arms behind my back, untied them and told me to keep my arms behind my back as if they were still tied should the guard posted outside look in. I nodded in acknowledgement and gratitude as he departed. I thought, that if I was in Laos and this was my cave maybe I had an advocate, or was it the old "good guy, bad guy" interrogation routine we had been taught about in survival school?

The day progressed into evening. A small group of men including the uniform clad youngsters and the man in black arrived at the cave and beckoned me out. I crawled out to see the sun low over the western ridge and a group of villagers gathered at some distance down the path leading to the village. The armed group at the cave and the elder who untied my bindings, seemed anxious to escort me somewhere. One of them gestured, suggesting I might straighten and give a bit of a twist to my mustache, which I did to his satisfaction. I supposed from this, that it was time for "show and tell." The crowd was congenial and curious as I walked down to the area where they were gathered. As I was encircled by them, those guarding me seemed more intent on the crowd than on me. Ironically, I assumed I was in relatively safe hands for the moment. There was lots of looking up, pointing and murmuring. If I turned, or took a step, the seemingly friendly crowd would stiffen and quickly pull back only to relax when I continued to be nonthreatening. Escape was never very far away in my thoughts but this did not seem to be the time nor place, perhaps later. Whatever I could do to present a "resigned to my fate" attitude would lighten the security consciousness of my captors. After a few minutes of getting acquainted a small bowl of dark liquid was thrust toward me from a small middle-aged Vietnamese lady, or perhaps Laotian lady, standing in the crowd. Thirsty, hungry and sore I was nevertheless, reluctant to do more than just observe it. It was a very dark almost black looking liquid, and seeing my reluctance to accept it, the man in black took it and sipped out of it and again offered it to me. This time I accepted it and drank. It was a strong tea and I

Chapter 10 | Lucky or Not?

welcomed it. Then someone offered a white root of some sort that was just out of a boiling pot and still hot. It was about the size of a large carrot and I accepted it with more enthusiasm. Later I was to discover the root, which had the texture of a boiled turnip and the taste similar to a potato was cassava. Some of us may know it as tapioca. It was a staple of the mountain farmers who grew it.

After "supper" with the villagers, I was left in the hands of the militia troops who walked me, still barefoot, down the winding trail to where I didn't know. We crossed a small footbridge of bamboo that took us over the dry stream that had been the focus of my earlier capture, then a short distance to a point where the trail met the end of a rocky dirt road. The road, which came down the edge of the ridge that enclosed the valley to the west appeared to be the only connection this small village had with the outside world. I was directed to a pile of old dirty straw and told by one of the two guards that I could sit on it, so I did. As the sun had now been down over the ridge for a while, the sky was darkening and the air was turning from balmy to cool. As I relaxed a bit, I felt something crawling on me, invading my flight suit. Closer investigation in the disappearing light revealed the straw was infested with leeches, and now so was I. Standing up quickly enough to alarm my guards, I picked the leeches off my flight suit and legs before they had time to attach. Both guards watched intently with drawn AK-47s pointed at me. It was interesting to realize the young guards, though seemingly at ease, were very vigilant. Since I was up and the guards were full of adrenaline, they decided to build a fire out of the straw. They motioned for me to join them by the fire. I think it was more about having me closer so they would be able to watch me better than any consideration for my comfort. As I had not relieved myself all day, I communicated the need to the guards in a most male and international manner and they gestured to a spot for me to perform the act. It was a rather impressive event. It was so long in duration that the guards begin to chuckle then commented "holy moly." Well, I don't really know what they said but it was inflected like that.

It wasn't long after dark that the clumsy rattle and rumble of a truck came into earshot as it approached on the dirt and rock road

The Eagle Hunts

coming down the ridge. Olive drab in the dark shadows and crude looking with the canvas cover over the back, it was the style of army trucks the world over; its headlights were a weak orange and hardly lit anything. It reached us and stopped. A couple more army guys exited the cab and exchanged salutations with my guards. Orders were given and I recognized they were for me to get in the back of the truck with a couple of guards. I sat on a bench along the edge of the truck bed and the guards sat across from me on the opposite bench and held their AK-47s between their knees. I noticed a pile of stuff in the middle of the truck bed but it being too dark to see, I just ignored it. With a lot of rumbling and jostling we moved slowly up the ridge to an open area where I was ordered to get out. Directed to the front of the truck, I was told to stand in the headlights. An officer stepped forward from a small group of uniformed men and delivered an oration, a political tirade that seem to generate some emotion among those to whom he was speaking. They responded pumping their fists in the air and exclaiming "whota whoa whota," or something like that. After the "whota" thing, photos followed and they were all taken with no flash. Knowing what I know now about the Vietnamese command of technical things, the night photos in front of a truck with a 6-volt electrical system and dim headlights, would suggest there was not even one chance in hell of any of them being usable. I did not consider they may have been the only proof, or even indication, that I escaped the fireball and explosion that morning. Indeed, it was to be three and a half years before my family had any indication I was alive. They were told Ed and I went down with the aircraft. Not surprisingly, because the crew in the other aircraft could have easily missed seeing us and our chutes during their breakaway from the same anti-aircraft artillery that got us, our chutes, the most visible of everything except the huge fireball, were open so briefly that when they recovered from their breakaway and reviewed the scene our jet would have been a burning smoking mass attracting most of their attention, with our chutes no longer open.

   After the photo op and commending speech to the gun crew, which I assumed was the crew of the guns that shot us down, I was ordered back into the truck and off to who knows where in the clear

Chapter 10 | Lucky or Not?

black night. The old truck which had run the Ho Chi Minh trail, no telling how many times, was carrying me either west to Laos and toward a certain slow and agonizing death, or east toward Hanoi for certain months as a tortured hostage. The direction of travel would tell me, but we were twisting and turning so much I had not a clue as to which direction we were going. Even now, as I sit and compose at the age of almost 71, enjoying my later life in the pleasant surroundings of Cabo San Lucas where we are vacationing, I wonder from the point in time of that dark trip forward to now, how my fate might have changed if I had attempted escape. Survival school taught us to attempt escape early, the earlier the better and they were correct. Perhaps my best opportunity had passed, but at that time, there, dark of night, jungle, guards hopefully somewhat relaxed by my passivity, to jump out of the truck and take off into the jungle might have been my best chance to escape. Then I took the opposing view—I had two

A 57mm anti-aircraft gun like the type that shot down Captain Clark over North Vietnam. The anti-aircraft site seemed to be composed of both 37mm and 57mm guns. The 37mm guns looked just like the 57mm except a bit smaller. This photo was taken by the author at the air museum at Nellis Air Force Base, Las Vegas, Nevada.

The Eagle Hunts

or three broken ribs, my left arm and shoulder were injured and painful due to flailing in the windblast, I had a spinal compression, my body was very sore, exhausted and dehydrated. I had bare feet, no survival gear, no radio, no map, no weapon, no light and nothing for infection control. The chance for a successful escape was very slim. It seemed the biggest problems I had were no shoes and no way to contact rescue, nor map to navigate. With no shoes, a cut or bite was certain within a few minutes of escape and infection in the jungle was fast and certain, much faster than we are accustomed to. The jungle survival school I attended in the Philippines taught me that. A cut on your foot one evening, if unattended, could develop overnight into a serious infection making walking very difficult. Without some sort of protection for my feet, survival for anything but a couple of days was unlikely and I was not going to get back to the Mekong River separating Laos and Thailand in a few days. So, I made the decision to stick it out until a better opportunity presented itself; perhaps a better opportunity that might include shoes. That was not to happen. Just guessing now, but I expect the gooks had already figured that out and that's why I had no shoes. To my recollection, there were extremely few, only one or two, who in the history of the American conflict ever made a successful escape from capture in North Vietnam. There are lots who claim it, but as former POWs know, there are three times the number of imposters as there are of actual former POWs. It is the imposters who brag about being the only one of a very secret group that was captured and able to escape and survive.

Being resigned to the road trip, I decided to grab some sleep. I laid down on the bottom of the truck on what felt like my parachute and went to sleep. I was jarred awake as we bounced over a large rock lying in the road that had not been seen by our half-awake driver and now realized my chance of survival had just increased to "possible." We were driving into the sun. Hanoi, here I come. That did not seem a reason to be particularly cheerful but compared to Laos and dying of malaria and starvation in a cave, it had more promise. As the sun rose, the more nervous the guards became, after all, "The Eagle Hunts" by day. Unfortunately, I was separated from the flock and I was riding with its prey. I guess I should have been nervous also.

Chapter 10 | Lucky or Not?

I immediately noticed on waking that the chute on which I had been sleeping had a large spot of fresh blood on it. That was not good. It was not my blood and that only left Ed. There were two sets of flying gear, mine and now obviously, Ed's. I was alone in the back of the truck except for the two stoic guards and I could only assume that Ed had been killed in the exchange of gunfire I had heard the morning before. As I was to learn years later, Ed's wife had received a letter where he had written that it was his intent not to be captured alive. Now the source of the shots I had heard the day before was confirmed. Ed had decided to shoot it out with his intended captors. It was made obvious by the way I was so out gunned during my capture that he had lost.

The Eagle Hunts

CHAPTER 11

ON TO HOA LO

The truck came to a halt and there was a big commotion, always a commotion. Exiting the truck on command, I saw a small river perhaps 150 feet across. Then for a reconnaissance pilot an interesting sight, a concrete river crossing built under the water so as to escape observation from the air but fully functional at a somewhat lower river level than now. Such a structure in Missouri is called a "low-water bridge," but here it was called a water crossing camouflaged by being under the water it crossed. Our infrared capability would have found it easily; too bad I was only able to collect intelligence from the ground and, at this point, had no way to transmit it. Oh well, I guess I fancied myself still fighting the war. There was a small flat bottomed Jon boat moving across the river with two more army guards in it and lots more chattering, talking and commotion.

I was transferred from the guards with the truck to the guards with the boat and we crossed back over the river. By my account this was the Black River, the southern tip of which we were going to use as our checkpoint for entry into the Red River Valley, wherein Hanoi was located. I was marched to a small village and into a bamboo hut about the size of a large dining room table. On one side of the hut was a small bench, which left only a couple of feet between the bench and the opposite wall. The door at the end of the hut was similarly of bamboo and hung loosely on makeshift hinges. After I was inside, the door was closed with a guard posted just outside. It was hard to see out of the hut but what I could see indicated just basic village comings and goings with some curiosity as to who was in the hut and why

The Eagle Hunts

army guards were posted. My limited survey indicated no damage from previous air attacks.

The sun was overhead when the woven bamboo door opened and more cassava and tea was thrust toward me to eat, or not to eat. These guards seemed to be older, more experienced, and I came to assume they were the prison guards that would take me on to the old French prison in Hanoi, the location where our intelligence had indicated American POWs were being kept and named Hoi Lo Prison or the infamous "Hanoi Hilton." The village chatter became quieter and had almost ceased; what was going on? Then I heard it, quiet at first but getting closer, a crunching of the dry grass as someone walked slowly but deliberately toward the hut. It attracted my attention because all else was very still. The slow deliberation of the pace caused me to be extra cautious, so I moved back from the front of the hut as someone approached and halted. In a flash a long sharp machete was thrust through the thin bamboo wall followed by an exclamation in a female voice which I did not understand, but assumed from its apparent anger that it was damning. This was followed by the machete being plunged through the wall in a different place again, and then again, as she worked her way around the hut while I jumped away from the

Old French Hoa Lo prison in Hanoi, North Vietnam circa 1965, dubbed the "Hanoi Hilton" by the American prisoners of war.

Chapter 11 | On to Hoa Lo

location of the next anticipated thrust. As the thrusts continued and I kept moving, I hoped she did not have an accomplice, for she was predictable and I felt confident in staying ahead of her but, another machete coming through from the other side could've made me uneasy. The guards started hollering and running to the hut. An argument ensued between the chastising guards and the vengeful woman who with exclamations of disdain was escorted away. A guard looked in on me and seeing I was unharmed closed the door. Sometime subsequent, maybe a few minutes, or maybe a few years, I learned she was an older woman who had lost a family member in a bombing raid and vengeance was her motive.

With the excitement over, what little liquid I had so far received was working its way through my system and now I needed to pee. Not wanting to mess my own nest, and as I had no idea how long this location of interment might last, I started to make some kind of racket which attracted the guards' attention. I was issued out of the hut to a small short screen which was obviously available to those of the village needing to relieve themselves. So, I did and gathered a crowd of curious villagers interested in what a pissing, big, mean looking, barefooted American air pirate looked like. The guards kept the crowd at a somewhat polite distance but by this time my attitude was very much "what the hell." Back into the hut I went until dark, then another truck ride down a bumpy dusty road for an hour or so then lights, paved roads, small roadside sheds with a single yellowish light bulb hanging by a wire from the top casting an exotic golden glow. Small Vietnamese people were going about their life cooking on broken and uneven walkways and eating out of bowls with chopsticks while squatted around a small fire. Up and down the street they were going about living. I felt like a traveler back in time in an exotic place. But the fantasy did not last long and it was the last truck ride I would take without a blindfold for six years.

The exoticness of the night became lost as the truck rattled to a halt. We had arrived in an area where the lights were placed on top of a long concrete wall and over a large arched double door creating light and dark spaces that were industrial looking and not the least pleasant. Closer observation revealed large shards of glass stuck into the concrete at the top of the wall and old rusty strands of barbed wire running above the glass with insulators installed between the wire and its supports, electrified wire. This place looked like a prison and indeed it was. I had arrived at the old French Prison of Hoa Lo. It was a large prison built in Hanoi during the era of French colonialism and was now used to house criminals, the politically incorrect, wives and children of the politically incorrect while they are taught the correctness of the communist doctrine and, of course, the American Air Pirates. The front entrance was ugly, algae stained concrete dimly lit and ominous looking. Climbing down from the truck I realized this was a survival situation.

This is the front gate of the Maison Centrale (Hanoi Hilton), which opens onto a street also named Hoa Lo in downtown Hanoi, circa 1960s.

CHAPTER 12

THE KNOBBY ROOM

I remember thinking the war, which could be ended in six months if we were only allowed to fight it the way we should, might last two more years and I cannot cope with the thought of being away from my family and home for two whole years. Therefore, I will do this new tour of duty six months at a time. I will assume release in six months and if that doesn't work out, I will reset the clock for another six months. Little did I imagine I would do that for the next six years. The son that was born to Bonnie and me on January 18, 1967 was still unknown to me except for the Western Union telegram saying he and mom were fine. He was six years old when I first saw him upon my return in February of 1973 in the military hospital at Scott AFB. The road to then would be one of torture, beatings, starvation, intimidation, threats of rape and death for my family, deprivation, political indoctrination, solitary confinement, fake executions, illness, malaria, a near death experience, bombings, drugging, hallucinations, and the worst of all, a fear not of death or disability but of losing one's mind and returning home scrambled; it was cause for suicide. There was a constant quest for survival, a renewing faith in God, all in an ever-present shadow of death.

My thought process was broken by a blindfold being tightly secured around my head and my arms pulled behind my back and tight steel handcuffs roughly applied around my wrists. Being prodded and pushed I was guided through doors and down hallways, up and down short steps and around numerous corners, mostly I assumed to disorient me. When the journey was over, I was halted and the blindfold removed. The two guards departed with some form of gesturing that

The Eagle Hunts

indicated I was to remain in the drab green room to which I had been taken. It was old and dingy looking with a steel hook that protruded from the center of the high ceiling. The rusty looking thing resembled a hay-hook I had used for many summers on the farm in north Missouri as a young lad to pitch hay bales. The walls were knobby and looked like they had been formed with egg cartons filled with plaster and smacked against the walls. It appeared to me as having a sound deadening function. Although it was perhaps fifteen feet square, the only furniture was a table, probably six feet long, of the type you might see at home sitting on the curb waiting for the trash truck. It had a plain worn wooden chair behind it; in front of it was a crude three-legged wooden stool reminiscent of the milking stool grandpa used, small, short and rickety. On the table was a bad garage sale type of lamp, and in the corner of the room another one of those tables perhaps four by four foot, worn, scarred, with remnants of paint that age and use had mostly worn off. It was ominously filled with rusty and bloodied torture devices: rolled and looped flat letdown tape from some pilot's parachute, forged iron wrist and ankle mandrels, clubs, rods, short sections of rubber garden hose, fan belts and some other devices with chains and screws I didn't take the time to identify.

The room was cold. It is cold in Hanoi in March. Having been stripped of my flight jacket and accustomed to the warm climate of Thailand I was chilly, but I knew soon it would likely be the least of my concerns. Having been left alone with a guard posted outside, I walked up to the table and placing my hand under the lamp I felt its warmth. Lying down on the table I put the lamp just above my neck and felt the warming blood start to move through my body.

The pleasantness did not last long as I heard approaching footsteps and hastily moved off of the table. I guessed I was not the first to come up with this idea as the first thing the officer did was to run his hand over the top of the table feeling the warmth where I had been laying. I was sternly informed that I was not to do that in the future. He was a slender man dressed in a North Vietnamese Army uniform and perhaps 5 feet 8 or 10 inches in height, tall compared to most of the Vietnamese.

Chapter 12 | The Knobby Room

He sat down in the chair and briskly issued the command "sit down." After I seated myself on the "milking stool," he proceeded to explain that I had been captured in the act of spying on the Vietnamese people and the punishment for that was death. However, if I were to "understand" the way of the Vietnamese people and ask their forgiveness I might be spared. I was to "demonstrate" a "good attitude" and obey the camp regulations then I would be sent home and I could tell the American people about the ways of the Vietnamese people and their fight for freedom against the American aggressors and their South Vietnamese "lackeys." He repeated the statement that should I repent and ask the Vietnamese people for their forgiveness perhaps I could go home before the end of the war which could last "10-20-30 years or more."

The interrogator then began to read the "camp regulations," which should they be followed to the letter, would require me to break every one of the items of the Code of Conduct of the American fighting man. I assumed that it was not coincidental because one of the first acts of the captors would be to start breaking down the military discipline and loyalty to our superiors which was part of our military lives. I have included below the Code of Conduct of the American soldier for your interest.

Article I
I am an American, fighting in the forces which guard my country and our way of life. I am prepared to give my life in their defense.

Article II
I will never surrender of my own free will. If in command, I will never surrender the members of my command while they still have the means to resist.

Article III
If I am captured, I will continue to resist by all means available. I will make every effort to escape and to aid

others to escape. I will accept neither parole nor special favors from the enemy.

Article IV
If I become a prisoner of war, I will keep faith with my fellow prisoners. I will give no information or take part in any action which might be harmful to my comrades. If I am senior, I will take command. If not, I will obey the lawful orders of those appointed over me and will back them up in every way.

Article V
When questioned, should I become a prisoner of war, I am required to give name, rank, service number, and date of birth. I will evade answering further questions to the utmost of my ability. I will make no oral or written statements disloyal to my country and its allies or harmful to their cause.

Article VI
I will never forget that I am an American, fighting for freedom, responsible for my actions, and dedicated to the principles which made my country free. I will trust in my God and in the United States of America.

Included in the camp regulations was answering all questions ask by the Vietnamese camp officer fully and completely and not communicating with any of the other "blackest criminals" (captured Americans or allies) in the camp. Upon hearing these "Camp Regulations" I wished to take several exceptions but not confident in the interrogator's receptivity I chose to just remind him that I was bound only by the terms of the Geneva Conventions. I was then reminded that North Vietnam was not a signatory to the Geneva conventions, and besides, as a "spy" I was not covered by the Geneva conventions. Well, being called a spy with a big star and U.S. Air Force written on a 58,000-pound aircraft that I left behind and my name,

Chapter 12 | The Knobby Room

rank, and "U.S. Air Force" written on my uniform made spying a bit of a stretch. Again, I opted to not remind him of that in as much as he didn't seem all that receptive. The first questions were easy, name, rank, service number, and date of birth.

"Clark, John W., Captain, 474790A, 1 January 1940." Just in accordance with the Geneva conventions.

"Very good" I was told, now what type of aircraft was I flying?

"Clark, John W., Captain, 474790A, 1 January 1940."

"No!! You break the camp regulations." You must answer all questions fully and completely was the interrogator's response. What base did I fly from?

The answer was now becoming somewhat repetitive,

"Clark, John W., Captain, 474790A, 1 January 1940."

The response I remember well, with several exclamation points the interrogator informed me that I was demonstrating a "bad attitude" and would be "sev'erly bunished"* if I did not answer the questions fully and completely. Okay, so the pace seems to be picking up and I don't appear to be convincing the interrogator of anything nor in his estimation do I appear to be cooperating. That's good, I think.

What was the name of the other man in your aircraft?

And you guessed it name, rank, etc.

The formally composed but brusque interrogator began to show irritation. Somehow, I felt like we were just getting started. He became more aggravated with each unanswered question and as he finally stormed out through the mottled and paint chipped, worn green louvered doors he declared I was a "blackest criminal" with a "bad attitude" and I was going to be "sev'erly bunished" and to remain seated on the stool and "think deeply and carefully about my crimes."

A guard was posted outside leaving me to contemplate the unpleasantness of the forthcoming promised severe punishment.

Not finding that pleasant, I availed myself of the opportunity to break the camp regulations right off and look through the louvers noting that the floor outside was red tile and I could see nothing else except the pants, feet, and black rubber sandals of the guard.

---

* "sev'erly bunished" is an intentional misspelling for severely punished, representing the interrogators inability to put the emphasis on the correct syllable and pronounce the letter "p."

The Eagle Hunts

I later learned the American Air Pirates called those black rubber sandals "go-aheads" because it was the only way you could go, "ahead." Looking something like shower clogs the soles were cut out of old tires and the straps out of inner tubes.

The slap-slap-slap of the rubber sandals worn by the North Vietnamese as they walked on the concrete and quarry tile floors of the prison was already becoming familiar and it seemed a good signal that someone was approaching. It had been a very long 36 hours since I left the security of my jet and saw it engulfed in a large fireball on the side of a jungle ridge. I was tired, cold, hungry, with two or three broken ribs, a compression fracture of the spine, flail injury of the left arm, shoulder, neck and very sore everywhere. I reasoned what could they do to me that wasn't already planned anyway. So, I squatted down with my back against the pimpled wall, assumed a fetal position, which exposed the least amount of me to the cold, put my head between my knees and informed my mind to awaken me whenever it heard the slap slap of those rubber sandals. If that sounds odd, then you have not discovered what the mind can do in extreme circumstances. I was to learn a great deal about that in the ensuing years.

I awoke with a start. That sound was approaching the room, and I sprang up and sat on the stool just a second before the doors swung open. There were two of them. The second gook looked like he was probably an enlisted man as his uniform, though neat, was not adorned with the same red epaulets and shiny stuff as the camp officer, but he was packing a pistol. I was asked again if I had decided to answer the questions. Oh yes, of course, name, rank, serial number, etc. The guard whipped out his pistol and cocking it, put it to my temple.

"You are a spy and will be executed unless you abide by the camp regulations and answer the camp commander's questions fully and completely," or something like that. Oh no, not this again, didn't we do this just a few hours ago? Anyway, as there were no black clad older gentlemen to settle the passion of the moment I was not as hopeful of the outcome. I thought of my family, and that a .45-bullet blowing my brains out of my head would probably not hurt, only just turn out the lights. But, the eventuality on which I had staked my

Chapter 12 | The Knobby Room

life played out and I was spared of execution in favor of remaining a prisoner of war and a political hostage, most likely with substantial payment from my country for my eventual repatriation.

It seemed our intelligence had been correct about the North Vietnamese preferring to keep American prisoners alive for intelligence, propaganda and hostage value, as opposed to summary execution. Torture, however, was never ruled out and so at this point I was not sure what should be my preferred course of action as things moved forward, death or torture. Ed had apparently already decided.

Nevertheless, as the gooks had not chosen the death route and there was still much information to be obtained, the interrogation turned ugly. The guard with the pistol left the room and that is when I noticed he walked with one foot somewhat towed in. Later I learned he had been named "Slewfoot" and was famous among other POWs as a brutal, sadistic torturer who enjoyed his trade a great deal. There was rumor, some years after our release, he was mysteriously and brutally executed somewhere in South America or Cuba. It was never verified by any authority, but was suggested that our friends at the Defense Intelligence Agency or CIA had caught up with him and paid our respects. Sorry I missed it!

Slewfoot returned shortly with a rather threatening collection of old, unpainted, rusty steel devices that were added to the collection already on the table in the corner, evil looking devices of torture: mandrels, pulleys, chains, clubs, switches, whips, straps, and whatever else I cannot remember.

Ironically the straps were loops of a long, flat, let-down strap taken from a pilot's jungle survival pack. It was in our survival pack so if our parachute was hung up in a tall tree canopy we could hook one end of the strap to our parachute harness and the other end to our body harness and after unlatching our body harness let ourselves down to the ground below. No one ever said my new captors were not creative and I was about to "learn the ropes" possibly with part of my own survival kit. Slewfoot then grasped my arms and twisted them behind me and clamped a set of iron mandrels around my wrists.

These solid steel cuffs were nearly two inches wide with a screw that tightened and pinched them into my twisted wrists. The skin was intentionally pinched between the two halves and was smashed and cut by the crushing tightening action, much as one might pinch and cut skin with a pair of pliers. This was not a quick numbing process like missing a nail with a hammer and hitting a thumb or finger; it was a deliberately slow process with long lasting, and ever-increasing pain. I discovered I don't scream with pain, but more grunt, pant, or maybe I just don't remember screaming.

I was to lay on the cold tile floor, actually a pleasant sensation by contrast to the other sensations, and think "deeply and carefully" about my "bad attitude." I did think about my bad attitude, for how long I don't know, but upon their return my attitude was unimproved. Slewfoot always seemed to hold back another trick in the art of causing pain, and so another trick it was. Each time the thinking deeply and carefully period became longer and the pain inflicted seemed to never end.

As we progressed to the next phase I assumed Slewfoot had tightened and twisted all he could on the mandrels and decided to add the "rope trick." The flat nylon straps, which comprised the "ropes" were interlaced and wrapped around my upper arms with the mandrels still in place allowing the straps to be tightened over my upper biceps. The abrasion of the straps literally tore the skin off as they were tightened. These masters of pain had developed the skill of using devices like flat straps and wide mandrels that, though not lacking in delivering pain, created more surface injury than cutting into the muscle below, as would have an actual rope, leaving big scars which would make the acts of torture obvious upon repatriation. It seemed when they went to that extent to inflict more pain, they tortured the American prisoner to death, hence less evidence among the returnees of injuries inflicted during torture. If internal injuries as a result of ejection and capture were experienced, then it was used against the prisoner. Any further scaring or disfigurement by abuse of the injured area during torture would be concealed by the results of the original injury suffered by being shot down, i.e. a broken leg or arm could be twisted and bent to produce tremendous additional pain.

I was grateful that I had not revealed the broken ribs, but unfortunately the flail injury to my left shoulder was being fully exploited by

Chapter 12 | The Knobby Room

the straps that pulled the arms backward behind my back; it seemed until they were almost touching. For some who had similar greetings and who were no more "understanding of the camp regulations," shoulder dislocations occurred. The straps which were wrapped around the arm were loosened and retighten even more to take full effect of the abrasion and to slightly relocate to areas where the nerves had not yet been numbed by the preceding trauma. With the wrists in mandrels it twisted them even further. Things seemed to become foggy as time passed, but I remember at some point a guard armed with an AK-47 entered the room, and I would discover why a bit later.

Slewfoot stood in the middle of my back as I lay face down on the floor and yanked up as hard as he could on the straps. The pain shot through me as never before and I leapt up to a crouching position throwing him off. Still crouched over I shot under the table in the corner and stood up flipping it upside down into the middle of the room while scattering everything on it. When I stopped to realize what I had done, I was looking down the barrel of a cocked AK-47, "oh crap not again," but this time, I'm not sure I cared whether he blew my brains out or not, at least it wouldn't hurt anymore. My attitude seemed to be more of, "either shoot me or get that thing out of my face." I, being much larger, though trussed up, was full of adrenalin and could have seriously injured at least Slewfoot by smashing him against the knobby wall and most likely killing him with a knee drop to the chest as he collapsed before being filled with a clip of 7.62mm ammo from the AK-47.

Not caring if I was shot indiscriminately seemed one issue, however, intentionally committing suicide by AK-47 was yet another. Under such intense pain one's logic takes on a character not understood by those not having had such an experience. It baffles me today how many experts exist on torture, or life threating experiences, or the fog of war that have only "studied" but never experienced it. Nevertheless, I opted to not commit suicide. Being satisfied that I had decided not to deliver the violence, my captors let me collapse onto the floor. Then they left me to again think deeply and carefully about my "obdurate" behavior.

The Eagle Hunts

This time my opportunity to reflect on my situation lasted substantially longer and to end it, I implied I would talk and then stalled by repeating name, rank, so forth and added some relatively meaningless bits of info like the type of aircraft I was flying which would have been obvious by looking at the wreckage, or who the other pilot was in the aircraft, when the dog tags around his neck would have clearly identified him.

I guess when all the skin was worn off my arms and my arms were twisted and pulled together about as far as they would go, the ever resourceful Slewfoot then put mandrels and straps on my ankles with the same inconsideration he had shown with my wrists and ran the straps behind my back and around my throat pulling my legs and head backward together while choking me at the same time. Each pull became tighter and tighter but there was a limit as to how much he could choke me because that just turned the lights out and what was the sport in that. For some reason, he decided to take the choke collar off and resorted to pulling my arms upward from behind my back to my head using the straps newly wrapped around my wrists up to and around my throat. I was left repeatedly to think deeply and carefully about my bad attitude. I am not sure how much time passed but it was many hours, maybe a day or two before my resolve began to weaken.

I was certain that if I resisted very much longer, I needed more strength than I had at that point and so I sought help from prayer and the Almighty. I prayed for the strength to endure and I felt nothing, my thoughts were empty, not even the satisfaction of faith and the comfort of forgiveness should I die from this torture. I had lost my faith, there was none. I had become agnostic in allowing my knowledge in science to question the teachings of the church and my Christian upbringing. My faith was an empty vessel. I then knew I was on my own. A very empty and lonely feeling settled over me as I again heard the slap-slap–slap of those sandals coming down the hall.

The instructors at survival school were correct, name, rank, serial number, and date of birth would only last so long. It was a fact we needed to face. The enemy tortured us to the point we finally failed in the ability to continue to resist and even if we could, we should not, for the injuries suffered in doing so would greatly weaken our resolve to continue future resistance and very likely compromise our ability to recover and survive. Being tortured to death was not part of the Code of Conduct as it was being taught, however, to what extent one was expected to resist became a much discussed and difficult aspect of the subject due to the widely varying strengths and capabilities of each individual. It turns out that both ends of the spectrum were displayed in the group of which I had just become an unwilling member. There were those who took it absolutely and had enough strength to resist until they died, and there were those who made no effort to resist, accepted special privileges, forsook the rest of us and returned home early. We call them traitors. Fortunately, there were only a few of each and I fell somewhere in the middle of that spectrum for I am not particularly proud of my effort, but I gave it all I had, and lived to spring back which always greatly aggravated my captors.

The captor's general assumption seemed to be once we had been broken their work was done, and now all they had to do was threaten their unique form of "sev'er bunishment" and we would be putty in their hands. Not so, and it really surprised and pissed them off. The more pissed off they were, the more successful we felt. It seemed they needed to be cleared from some higher authority to torture and sometimes, if it was not authorized, their bluff would have been called. They would have lost lots of face, what more could one expect? We reveled in our gamesmanship until the next time when torture was authorized and they settled old scores. No man was ever condemned by other POWs if he gave in after trying to resist and then sprang back to continue to resist, never forsaking his fellow Americans and allies.

The answer to the ability to continue resistance and maintain your mental and physical health to recover was called the "second line of defense." It was some kind of sham we made up and practiced in survival school that allowed us to stall the torture, to make it look to our interrogator like we were willing to talk while wasting their time and giving them false and useless information. This needed to be done with some forethought as just pure lies were easily forgotten, allowing the interrogator to entrap you with follow-up questions. Also, they used the same questions on other crewmembers or flight members and compared the answers. For me, this was not an issue because Ed was the only other crew member in the aircraft and he had been killed before any interrogation took place. However, any discovered lies would be cause for further "bunishment."

It was beginning to look like the time was coming. I would rather give in with some control about what I was saying, and what I was willing to do, rather than be broken completely and then be mentally and physically unable to further resist at all. Time was passing and when I began to gradually give a bit, I did not know. Sometimes I was released from my painful bonds and left alone to think again deeply and carefully which allowed some form of feeling to return. But it only allowed the slewfooted henchman to reintroduce the pain even more intensely. On one such instance I recall looking at my wrists and hands and realized they were bloody, badly swollen, raw and

Famous Knobby (torture) cell in the Hanoi Hilton (from "Home with Honor, Thirty Years of Freedom").

oozing with huge protruding veins, perhaps the size of a large ball point pen. It seemed I was looking at someone else's arms, not my own. I decided to see if I had any feeling in them and banged each on

Chapter 12 | The Knobby Room

the table harder and harder, with nothing, only a thud, but yet that slewfooted SOB could always find some way to extract more pain.

My second line of defense, to which I resorted, was being stupid. When I acted stupid, it furthered their confusion by putting the blame on them for not being able to understand the answers being given by the "idiot" they had broken, all the while the "idiot" could act sincere and earnest in my intention to give them the information they wanted. The fog and haze in which I existed seemed to make it more realistic and easier to pull off for they knew well in what mental state I existed.

They assumed the higher in rank of the prisoner, the smarter he was. I was a brand-new Captain which meant I was basically a First Lieutenant and not very smart so I played into it. I killed a lot of time not understanding what they were saying, explaining things so they only heard gibberish, having a problem forming words, being easily distracted, correcting their English to make it worse, all the while seeming to comply with their demands. Many of the questions were answered in some form except one, what was the next target to be bombed. That I did not know and it cost me a lot of pain until they decided I really did not know, however, I led them down a lot of blind alleys hoping for something they would accept.

The Eagle Hunts

CHAPTER 13

HEARTBREAK HOTEL

It was a bright sunny day, perfect for a bombing raid, and I was being issued down a wide outside walkway of broken and deteriorated concrete bordered on both sides by planter boxes full of some sort of greenery. Behind the boxes on each side was a two-story building of typical French design with covered walkways and small apartments on each of the two floors with open arched doorways. The covered porches for both floors, which were supported by tall columns and extended the length of the building, seemed to be community property and was shared by all. Most of the doors were open with families, including children hanging around outside. I was told by someone that these were political prisoners that not having yet seen the "truth" were being "allowed" to understand the Communist doctrine, much as I had been allowed to understand the way of the Vietnamese people. Of note, the whole family, even children, were being exposed to this political "reawaking." If any of the family was slow to accept the "doctrine" it would reflect negatively on each member of the family.

Everything I saw, the buildings, doors and windows, planter boxes, and walkways were in the same disrepair as what I had already seen and I suppose the white paint on the buildings at one time gave it a nice look for a prison, but the worn, tattered buildings I was seeing gave it a depressing look.

I walked as straight ahead as I could, standing tall, with my head up. I was determined to walk with pride, and not stare dejectedly at my feet. I might not have resisted as well as I hoped, but I was damn well not going to show it. It was probably a 150 to 200-foot walk to the end and a right turn into a dark, damp, slimy, and dingy narrow hall lined on both sides with heavy iron-wood doors. The hinges were crude, rusted steel straps riveted through the doors. At about five foot high and in the center of the door was a peep hole about six inches by six inches with iron bars and a swinging steel cover plate that could be locked from the outside. A single bare bulb hung from an electric wire that descended from the tall ceiling overhead. Halting me at the first or second cell on the left the guard unlatched the large dungeon-like padlock and swung the squeaky door open ushering me inside and slamming the door behind me. A quick survey of the cell showed a similar unpleasant environment as in the hallway except more light as the back wall had a large two or three foot high open barred and arched window, the bottom of which was perhaps eight foot above the floor. Even standing on either of the two foot wide concrete slabs on each side wall my view of the outside was limited to just the tops of the other buildings with their disheveled orange tile roofs and similarly large barred windows. The smooth knee-high concrete slabs jutting out from each side wall had a three foot aisle between them that ran the length of the cell which was approximately eight feet. The concrete slabs were just long enough for a six-foot man to lie down with his ankles in the leg stocks at the front end. The stocks were reminiscent of the same artist that had produced the torture devices and the large iron hinges and straps on the outside of the cell doors. They looked like they had been hammered by hand out of half inch by three inch iron stock in a mid-19th century blacksmith shop with a coal-fired forge in Milan, Missouri then thrown onto the dirt out back to rust for a couple of years. These jewels of crude antiquity were located in each of the small prison cells that I was to inhabit over the next six years at the "Hanoi Hilton." I don't recall ever seeing a piece of painted metal in the years I was there and the stocks were no exception. These things seemed to have lots of overkill as I found skin and bone didn't measure up well against iron, even if it was rusty.

   The walls of the cell into which I had been cast were covered with names, dates, and strikes used to keep track of time. There were words not in English, which I could not read, and names that

Chapter 13 | Heartbreak Hotel

were French. I was reminded that the French who preceded us were imprisoned here, and died here, captured at Dien Bien Phu, and abandoned by their country after having survived the death march to Hanoi.*

The French were Christian, and I'm certain prayed to the same God from which I had hoped to derive strength in the days just past. But now it became clear to me that prayer for deliverance from this predicament was not very realistic for there have been many in the history of wars and captivity that have not been saved, why should I now? Prayer, it seemed to me, should be directed to asking for strength to withstand my trials, and should it be my fate to die, salvation, and for the grace of God upon my family and my fellow prisoners. But before that, I knew I must develop some religious strength, born of true faith, and communication with God. I reasoned, in my youthful years I had faith, then I doubted. I was exposed to the conflicts of science, evolution, and creationism. Was I abandoned as I became the doubting Thomas? Perhaps, but I felt the God of which I was taught would not forsake me were I to begin a search to rediscover the faith I had lost. So, I decided to begin the quest in earnest.

It seemed that earnest prayer could even take the form of conversation, most likely one way, at least at first, mental, whispered, or even spoken. If I believed in God, and I had true faith, then could these conversations become two-way, even answered? No, I really didn't expect a big deep voice from the clouds to answer me, but maybe some guidance, some direction as to the way not yet clear to me. Maybe, maybe not, but how would I know if there was not an earnest faithful quest? My God would listen, guide me, and test me in the quest. I know now at age 71 God would do all that, and the story of my quest is one of which I have spoken very little but which I hope to be able to tell in the coming pages. Even by my recollection

---

* Authors note: the most accurate depiction of this prison cell environment I have seen was at the National Aerospace Museum at Wright Patterson Air Force Base in Dayton, Ohio. The biggest difference was the new, clean look of the museum display. I expect the actual prison may have appeared as the display when the prison was new but the display lacked the nastiness, it lacked the slime, algae, peeling whitewash, broken up and deteriorated floors and walls, frayed electrical wires, stench, rats, insects, vermin, and teak relics of the French occupation many years before.

years later, in some cases the casting aside of logic and science in favor of pure faith was the only answer to some of my most astounding experiences. Yes, God will answer, but only if you can listen, only if you can hear, only if your mind is awake to see. In my six years as a prisoner in a Godless Communist political system I learned that faith in our all-knowing, all-powerful God can answer many questions about the path on which we choose to walk our life. However, in 1967, I was very alone, and started to pray, talk, conduct a one-way conversation without expecting any response, just having hope and faith that my God for whom I was baptized at the youthful "age of reason" would listen and perhaps respond. Indeed, my God did respond in manners unknown to me then, but so dramatically revealed to me now.

The slap-slap-slap shook me from my meditation. More so soon? A new sound, which I was to learn and dread, came from the hall. The jingle of keys in the lock to my cell door, the loud metallic scrape and plunk of the iron bolt as it was slid to open my cell door. The guard standing full in the now open doorway exclaimed:

"BOW DOWN!!"

"What?"

"BOW DOWN!!"

Okay, I thought, I'll stand up.

"BOW DOWN!!"

He stated it firmly followed by a demonstration of a full 90° bow from position of attention. In hushed tones intended to be experienced by me only I uttered "dream on, you little prick!"

So, after being smacked around a bit I reminded myself of what I had just been through and that perhaps now was not the time to draw a line in the sand. After stepping back to the doorway and assuming he had made his point the guard again repeated,

"BOW DOWN!!"

With my best passive aggressive conduct, I assumed a slouching, insulting position of attention and nodded only modestly. Seemingly satisfied with his imposition of an act of subjugation he moved on to other camp regulation and housekeeping matters.

Chapter 13 | Heartbreak Hotel

The day passed into evening and there began a very primitive banging of a gong, slowly at first and quickly increasing in tempo. Gong---gong---gong---gong--gong-gong-gong gong gong gong gong. Shortly afterward I heard the small barred window in the door open. The round childish face of a different guard peered through the barred cubbyhole saying "bow down." Okay prick, and I nodded. Then in a somewhat more soothing voice he uttered "saa-leep."*

What?

"Saa-leep"** he answered again. Oh, sleep…It was going to be an uncomfortable night. I was still in my shorts and blooded T-shirt and trying to sleep would be challenging on a cold concrete slab in a damp open cell in the middle of March in North Vietnam. With injuries, open torture wounds, and accompanied only with what would become the ever-present single yellowish light bulb hanging from the ceiling at the end of a badly frayed wire I actually passed into sleep.

One of my cold catnaps during that night was interrupted by the gong I had heard the night before and from a speaker somewhere came music, perhaps the national anthem, and some stretching sounds like "oooo" "ahaaaaa" "oooo" "ahaaaaa" for a short period. This, I came to realize, was the national wake-up call for the entire country.

All of Ho Chi Minh's North Vietnam went to bed and woke up at the same time by the gong. I was becoming familiar with the finer aspects of communism. A few days later the slewfooted "slap-slap-slap" came down the hall, stopped at my cell and swung open the door, waiting for the "sort of bow," before escorting me out, down the hall and through the courtyard to the green knobby room. Not a good sign. The interrogator was already in the room seated behind the trashy curbside desk and commanded:

"Sit down!"

"Now," he said "we talk about your family." "Where does your family live?"

My response was a rather demented "whaaaaat?" I was now into my second line of defense to stall and waste time. He asked again and this time my response was:

---

* Authors note: Language is represented in its colloquial form to better create the setting.

"You-you-you already know," referring to the threats that had been made on my family in the days before.

"Do not show bad at-tee-tude" was his response in broken English.

Thereupon I was given a blank sheet of crude yellowish broad lined paper and a pencil, which reminded me more of a crayon, to write about my family. The interrogator cautioned me not to show a bad attitude or I would be severely "bunished." I had a pretty good idea where this was headed, nevertheless I did not pick up the pencil or paper but instead decided to talk silently to God in prayer. I used the words exactly that way because I knew it would be a one-way conversation. My gut was in a roil, my heart was in fear, I did not know how much strength I had to again endure what I had just been through. After some sitting time, measured in hours, but unsure of the exact number because my watch had become the property of one of my captors, the interrogator returned. Seeing the untouched paper and pencil exactly as it had been left, he spoke briefly to the sadistic slew footed torturer and abruptly left stating "you will be bunished!" Slewfoot ordered me out of the room and led me down the walkway through the courtyard with an armed guard following. I began to imagine what the real torture chamber must look like. In this prison in the Red River Delta it probably was not like a dungeon in an old French castle because of the high-water table, but another dark, dank and slimy room within an isolated part of the prison with hooks and old rusty torture devices hanging from the wall. To my premature relief, I was returned to my cell. The armed guard watched closely as Slewfoot locked me in the large iron leg stocks at the end of the concrete slab, slammed the cell door and laughed. I thought, this can't be all. I can deal with this. After all I can now lay on the bunk during the day. But it was not very long before I realized laying on a concrete slab and shifting around to move the pressure points is one thing but being required to sit or lie in the same position because your ankles are clasped together in a leg stock is yet another. There was no opportunity to relieve myself other than to do so in the same position and sit in it. Fortunately, I had a young bladder and not much opportunity to drink any liquid

Chapter 13 | Heartbreak Hotel

except the sorry pumpkin soup that was served in a chipped porcelain bowl with a weird aluminum spoon stamped out of a piece of one of our airplanes. The hours passed, spots got sore, the agony of wanting to move and not being able exacerbated it. Some mental games helped to pass the time and keep my mind off the misery. Day turned into night with the ringing of the gong, and an almost sleepless night, with that infernal bulb always lit just overhead. It seemed it would never end. Sunrise came with another gong. Cell doors in the hall opened and closed—pumpkin soup time. I suppose I was in the company of some other "blackest criminals" who had bad attitudes or perhaps some political prisoners, or maybe no other Americans at all, maybe I was alone after all.

My captors told me that I was the only one who had not seen the way of the Vietnamese people and was being punished. True, I did not like the way of the Vietnamese people and especially the slewfooted SOB. But I was starting to see that I could tire of these leg stocks sooner than I had previously thought. I cannot remember if it was this day or the next or the next when my cell door swung open and slew foot unlocked the leg stocks and beckoned me to follow him out of the dark hall and down the courtyard to the knobby room. The interrogator who I was to later learn was endearingly referred to as "the rabbit" by the other blackest criminals who preceded me through the "rope program" sat smirking behind the table awaiting my entrance. I noticed the blank paper and pencil on the table. "Sit down!" came the firm command, then in an almost kindly fashion, he explained that I must obey the regulations and write as I was told then perhaps the Vietnamese people would forgive me and I would be able to go home before the war was over. Blah blah blah and I was left alone to write about my family. Being able to get out of the stocks and move my body gave me some relief but the sore spots were getting really sore! Nevertheless I wasn't ready to make it that easy for them, so still no writing. Back to the stocks I went, but this time one arm was handcuffed into the stocks with my ankles causing my body to be held in a twisted, sitting, and slouching position. Now, added to the sore spots, were aching muscles and twisted body. As I slouched and pulled back against the handcuffs trying to relax the sore and cramping muscles the handcuffs dug into the swollen and sore wrists creating enough pain that there were to be no cat naps, no sleep at all. The broken ribs stabbed me like a knife and the compressive back injuries were equally painful from the twisted slouched position. The "rope tricks" were violent and painful but the pain fairly quickly eased if I acted as if I might be willing to share some information. The relaxation of pain was nice, but what was not so nice was the increased pain when the torture began again due to my unsatisfactory response. This agony and pain from the leg-stocks came on more slowly but became more and more intense and agonizing, passing to constant pain as time crawled by. The mind could not escape it. It grew and grew; there was no relief. Slewfoot never came by to ask if I was ready to write. I would have, a short bit of nonsense, just to get an hour or two of relief. But no opportunity was given. I expected on different occasions that I would be walked back to the knobby room to again discuss my attitude. Nope, it was not to happen. I prayed "Father give me strength. I hurt so much and my mind is playing tricks on me, I see and hear things. I try to divert my mind from the pain with any thought that seems to occupy it, strong emotions like hate, love, sex, nothing seems to work always the pain breaks through."

Time passed slowly, a few minutes, an hour, until the gong, but never any sleep. Eventually the door swung open; it was daylight. That's all I really remember. How many daylights passed, I don't know. The cuffs came off and the legs stocks were opened but I could not move, I could not even feel much of me. I was numb. How could numb hurt so much and so constantly? I could see my body was still all connected, but it didn't want to move, so I just sat there looking at my free legs and arm in a cloudy stupor. Slewfoot stood there and waited as I willed my body to get off the slab and it responded slowly and agonizingly to the point I was on my feet but I could not stand upright or untwist my back. So, with my shoulders twisted almost perpendicular to the ground and my back hunched over almost 90 degrees, I slowly drug my feet stumbling alongside the jerk that seemed to find it amusing. I imagined the movie portrait of the Hunchback of Notre Dame, except I was

Chapter 13 | Heartbreak Hotel

living it. Yes, I wrote on the paper, but with all the lies I thought I could pull off. But in my heart, I knew I had written too much. My mind told me it was time to recover some before the next episode. Guilt overwhelmed me. I had forsaken my country, I had forsaken my family, I had not lived up to the standards of the American fighting man…I was no longer worthy of my status as an officer in the United States Air Force. How could I return home?

The poorly written sheet of paper strangely seemed to satisfy the Rabbit. I think maybe that I had written something more meaningful than it actually was. Returned to my cell, I was given two red and purple vertically striped pajama type pieces of clothing. These I viewed with a considerable amount of consternation. The word "brainwashing" kept coming to my mind.

During the Korean War of the early 1950s, resulting in the American engagement with Chinese forces and inevitable capture of many Americans, the concept of "brainwashing" became part of the English vocabulary. It comprised the utilization of mental trauma on the captured, reportedly by such acts as placing a bucket over the head and beating on it causing constant loud and reverberating sound, pain, extended periods of no sleep, fear of one's life, confusing those less educated with distorted facts of their form and manner of society and government, and constant recitation of distortions and lies about the benefits of their captor's way of life. These tactics must have been effective evidenced by the larger than anticipated number of American defections and mental trauma evidenced in those POWs repatriated after the war. Movies such as the Manchurian Candidate became popular in American and the free world cultures of entertainment. The effective nature of brainwashing was attributed to the selection of candidates from the population of POWs by the Chinese interrogators. They were largely made up of poorly educated young men whose perceptions of the society from which they came could be challenged, distorted and reformed.

As a result of brainwashing by the Chinese, the curriculum and conduct of American Air Force and Naval aircrew survival schools were built around the resistance of such treatment by those who might be exposed to becoming prisoners of war in future conflicts.

The Eagle Hunts

The Air Force survival training school was conducted at Stead AFB, located north of Reno, Nevada. Earlier I described my attendance there after I graduated from pilot training. In that program, there was a "hot war" and a "cold war" phase. The hot war was a more brutal phase, and the cold war one of more isolation and longer duration. The hot war phase was intended to expose us to the torture and harshness utilized to quickly obtain information that could be of importance to the immediate conduct of the war. The cold war phase was more of a long-term imprisonment where one could expect to be locked away and forgotten, a Francis Gary Powers[*] situation.

    Had I been selected as one of these brainwashing candidates because of a weakness to the brutal treatment I was experiencing? In my sleep deprived and traumatized mental state I reasoned that the seemingly bold clothing must be to identify me as a candidate for Korean style "brainwashing." I had reconciled the fact that I could deal with returning home as a cripple, or an invalid, but I could not return having lost my mind. I could not return being someone about whom people would explain in hushed tones that I was much different after having returned from the war. I started thinking of ways to end my life should the "brainwashing" process began. The more time that passed in that cell the more possessed I became with the thought. Realizing how preoccupied I had become with the idea of committing suicide, the more it was predisposing me to assuming that future actions by my captors might be "brainwashing" when in fact they were not intended for that at all. I set out to force myself to think of other things. So strong was the specter of having my mind taken from me that I turned to the only thought stronger, prayer. It seemed to start working because I was being left alone. I decided the initial interrogation phase must be over. Four days passed without any further contact with the rabbit or the slewfooted sadist. I did not suppose, nor did I pray for them to stop the torture for that

---

[*] In May of 1960 Francis Gary Powers, flying a U-2, was shot down over the Soviet Union by a new SA-2 surface to air missile developed and deployed by the Soviet Union to shoot down American high altitude reconnaissance aircraft that were unchallenged by Russia's existing air defense fighters and missiles. As it was a "cold war," he was convicted as a spy and held alone in a Russian prison with little expectation of ever being released.

Chapter 13 | Heartbreak Hotel

This painting depicts the typical Vietnam prisoner of war garb worn by American aircrews captured and detained by the North Vietnamese. It is copied from a picture presented on the back inner cover of "Home With Honor, Operation Homecoming", July 1976 by Henington Publishing Co., Wolf, Texas, donated to each of the returning Air Force POWs.

seemed a hollow prayer but, instead, for the strength to withstand it and the clarity of heart and mind to not overreact to it; to not interpret the torturous actions, perhaps incorrectly, as brainwashing and prematurely end my life. I asked for hope and faith and the way back to God. I asked for a dawn to the darkness of the night that had befallen me.

As my prayers became more involved and more sophisticated, I began to feel more of a sense of comfort with the one-way conversation. Did I feel I was talking to someone? I don't know, but I talked as if I did. It was at about this time that I became bold enough to ask God for some kind of response, a simple sign that I was being heard. I clearly remember in the first days after being released from the legs stocks that I began to again search the walls, a search that had begun weeks before when I first arrived there. The search involved combing each square inch of the wall to that prison cell, to as high up as I could see by standing on the concrete slabs,

The Eagle Hunts

to below the concrete slabs and all around the walls. There were the names, the French names that I mentioned before, strikes and cross strikes, obviously an attempt by some previous occupant to keep track of the days. Some strikes and cross strikes were sickeningly numerous, there were dates, there were words I could not identify, probably Vietnamese but I was looking for a simple cross and there was none.

The day was cloudy and humid as it moved into afternoon and I lay prone on the concrete slab. It was a day of prayer and patience, for I did not, after all the years of selfish waywardness, expect a glorious sudden awakening of faith. But, the patience and praying were both soothing and I passed into sleep, blessed sleep. I awoke to find myself as if in a piece of artwork, with a ray of bright sunlight beaming through the window above my head, striking the whitewashed wall in front of me with such brilliance as to be almost iridescent. The beam was further highlighted by a hazy and foggy atmosphere in the cell that made it as a painter would display a beam of light streaming from the window and striking the wall. Surprised and taken aback, I leapt upon the concrete bunk, stood on my tip toes, and looked out the window to see from whence came such an uncommon beam of light. The cause was a commonly seen event. The sun had dropped down just below a cloud deck before it settled on the horizon. As it did so, it shone brightly into the window just a little bit above the roofs of the adjacent buildings of Hanoi and the prison wall, framing a perfect ray of light coming in the window and smashing onto the opposite wall. The outside air, having been cleansed of pollution due to the rainy day, made the sun shine brightly, and yet the air in the dank cell gave the ray of light a misty atmosphere into which to shine. Having satisfied myself that this sensational ray of light seemed to be a perfectly logical and understandable meteorological incident, I looked to the wall, for I could not help but be drawn to the high intensity of the light. And there I found it, a cross, a perfectly etched cross, about one foot high and about an inch thick. The fact that the cross was there did not surprise me; I had expected to find one before. But what did astound me was that I had been over that entire piece of

Chapter 13 | Heartbreak Hotel

This photograph is of a painting, which depicts with amazing accuracy, the moment Captain Clark awoke from a nap and was stunned by a bright ray of light entering his cell and illumining a Cross in front of him on his cell wall. It is a partial photograph of the original acrylic painted by Vevonna M. Kennedy who is Col. Clark's younger sister.

Original painting by Vevonna M. Kennedy. Not to be used without expressed written permission of Colonel John W. Clark, USAF (Ret).

wall little by little and never saw that cross. I could only take it as a sign from my Father. I chose to believe that the cross was an answer. He had been listening, and I had been heard.

The days passed agonizing slow but the swellings in my arms and legs had been going down, the injured places had scabbed over and were beginning to heal. Each day had started to take on a routine; the gong in the morning, and the guard coming around to insure I was not laying down. Occasionally a new piece of prison equipment would be handed out, like a small water pitcher, perhaps a pint or maybe a quart in size, which would be filled three times a day with hot water. At another time, I received a thin cotton blanket, crudely woven and held together by course cords of cotton twine, so crudely manufactured that one could pick out cottonseed hulls and pull the cotton twine out of it.

We were fed twice a day, the first time perhaps around 9:30 or 10:00 o'clock in the morning and the second time around 3:00 o'clock in the afternoon, with a siesta around noon. There would be the usual clanging of keys in the padlocks, creaking of the opening and closing doors, and clunking of the big locking bolts.

My primary interest had drifted to what was going on outside my walls and door, to expand my environment to include the other cells which shared my hallway. My ears were becoming more acute, if only gradually, but they were starting to become my eyes. As the time passed, having been greatly boosted in my long walk up the road to faith with the cross incident, I prayed for some way to know or believe that I was not alone, that I was not the only "blackest criminal" in the prison. In my heart, I couldn't believe I was. Not that I felt at all bad for being a "blackest criminal," just that I could not believe all the Americans that proceeded me had given in more easily than me. Me, the blackest of the black, hummmm?

The ever-present single, weak, seemingly "orange" tinted light bulb which hung from the ceiling on a long-frayed wire was always on, day and night, all night… forever. Maybe it would go out one of these nights and I would be able to discover a peephole or crack in the door from the hallway light shining through that would permit me to see out in the hallway. But it was not to happen. I could

Chapter 13 | Heartbreak Hotel

hear the guards yell, stomp, strike and generally express displeasure and frustration with whomever was across the hall from me. If the bow was not deep enough, you did not move quickly enough, or stand at attention then they would exclaim "eep" or "bow down" or "come back." I never was quite sure how "come back" translated. It seemed to mean "move back" but sometimes it would suggest "come on." Anyway, whoever was across the hall and not in good favor, had seemingly figured out the fine line between pissing off the guards and creating an incident that would cause him to be beaten or sent to visit with the camp officer who would seize upon the opportunity to use the straps and mandrels, or fan belt, or other very painful device to correct a "bad attitude." I was doing pretty well at pissing them off but I was still gun shy from my first encounter with their rude welcome. The days passed and yet I continued to include in my conversations with God the suggestions that it would give me great strength to know that I was not the only "American air pirate" in this slimy, cold, hell hole of a prison.

It began as a night like all the rest, cold and damp. There was the dimly lit single light bulb, the cold hardness of the concrete slab now somewhat softened and insulated by a thin bamboo mat that resembled a reed beach mat, which kept me from direct contact with it. And let's not forget the ever prominent rusty, crude leg irons at the bottom of my bunk which had so endeared me to my accommodations. The gong-gong-gong signaled it was time to sleep and sleep I relished for it was escape.

I awoke abruptly, what time I do not know, and the cell was black. The bulb was out. Quickly, for I was afraid the bulb might suddenly come back on, I looked at the door. There it was, a crack that I had not seen, even with close scrutiny. The weak light from the hall shining through beckoned me for a peek and sure enough the field of view was aimed right at the door across the hall. I studied other little slivers of light from the hall looking through each of the cracks they revealed. The rest were indirect, a crack that would let light through but was obstructed so as to not allow me to see through the door. Of course, nothing was happening in the hall for me to see, it was the middle of the night and even "goo-yen"* was snoring and slobbering when I'm sure he was supposed to be standing his post, alert and erect. It was as though I was afraid if I quit looking through the crack it might close up. Eventually I realized just because I wanted so much to see who was behind that door across the hall nothing was going to happen until the morning meal so I gave up and went back to the bamboo mat over the concrete slab to sleep. But I was very anxious for the morning and the door across the hall to open. Who would it reveal, another American, a Vietnamese political prisoner, an air pirate or spy like me? Perhaps it might be one of the guys from my squadron who had taken off on a mission and not returned. The Vietnamese were not releasing the names of those killed or captured so there was no way of knowing who had survived being shot down and who had not.

I awoke early as usual, and contemplated my predicament, my survival, and just how long this less than desirable turn of events would last. I laid on the hard mat and stared up at the "forever on" single bulb, wait, wasn't it off last night? It was on now! Was that just a dream? Oh, please no! I leaped up and sought out the crack in the door I thought I had discovered. It was not there, but it seemed so real. Calm down, regain my mental discipline and systematically look again at the area of the door where I thought I had seen the crack. With a more deliberate and systematic search I found it and sure enough I could see the door across the hall. I looked back and up at that bulb, that dim, ever on bulb. I looked over at the cross that was now mine, I reached out and touched it and whispered a soft "Thanks Father." There will be answers to prayers if you are aware. There are many ways in which they can be delivered, have true faith, and listen with your heart.

The crack in the door proved fruitful. With the clanging of the morning breakfast process or brunch or lunch, or whatever one calls basic yard cuttings boiled in water until the water turns green and then served as some sort of nourishment, I was able to peer through

---

* Author's note: This was a particularly insulting iteration of the word "gook" that added a context of child-like idiocy which also included a very demented facial expression. It was coined at a later time by a very creative Navy Lt. Jg. Paul Galanti who was a future cell mate of mine and a Navy A-4 pilot and whom we will hear a lot more about. Think prison humor here.

Chapter 13 | Heartbreak Hotel

A cell door in the Hanoi Hilton. (from "Home with Honor, Thirty Years of Freedom")

the crack and see the person across the hall. He was a tall wiry F-105 pilot from the Northeast, New York, I think. He looked a scoundrel for sure. His bow was barely a head nod and his contempt was obvious. He was Charlie Green. I know all that because Charlie and I were to live together in a four-man cell two or three months later. Euphemistically my shoulders went back, my head came up and I continued up the path of faith in God with new conviction and the comfort in knowing that there was at least one other "blackest criminal" who had not seen the way of the Vietnamese people. That

The Eagle Hunts

gave me hope and a strengthened belief in my quest for my God that continued to grow into a faith that later saved my life.

The marks on the wall were starting to add up to a larger and larger number when I discovered that I did not need that system to keep track of the passing days. The sounds from outside the window and over the wall helped also to track the days and weeks. With increasing frequency, I was marched into the green knobby interrogation room to rehear the stories of how we air pirates, having been duped by our leaders into killing innocent peace-loving Vietnamese women and children, were now being punished and would be tried as war criminals and would be executed or imprisoned for life, never to return to our families. But, should I understand my crimes and be forgiven by the Vietnamese people, I would be allowed to return home with the others who have realized the way of the Vietnamese people and tell the American people about how illegal and unjust the war was against the Vietnamese people.* It began to appear as if

Photo of one of the actual leg stocks in the cells of the Hanoi Hilton. This photo was taken after the Hilton became a museum and the rust and filth was removed and painted over. The manikin is of a Vietnamese prisoner showing the harsh treatment of the Vietnamese by the French.

---

* Authors note: The frequent use of the word "people" is intentional to highlight the emphasis on the word utilized for the connotation that they, the "people", had anything to say as to the conduct of their Communist government, which they did not, none whatsoever; they were only duped pawns.

Chapter 13 | Heartbreak Hotel

Charlie Green and I were the few who had not yet realized our crimes. Things were not looking good, but I had been schooled in propaganda and political indoctrination techniques and I wasn't buying any of it. Apparently neither was Charlie Green.

The Eagle Hunts

CHAPTER 14

LITTLE VEGAS AND THE TAP CODE

The jingle of keys, the opening of the lock, and harsh "thud" of the steel bolt being slid open when it was not mealtime was not a welcome sound. But this day, instead of being given the signal to put on my long-sleeved purple and red striped shirt and long pants and "come back," I was also told to roll up my bedroll. A move? Good sign, bad sign, war's over, going home, whatever, I didn't have much to say about it. Blindfolded I was led down halls, around corners, through little doors, up and down steps. In fact, I recalled its similarity with the disorienting route we took upon my arrival. I was halted, my blindfold removed, and I was standing in front of a wooden green and ivory louvered door, one of about five or six in a single-story building with a red tile roof situated on one side of a rather basic prison courtyard surrounded on two sides by high walled prison cell blocks. They were like the one I had just left, but on the other two sides was a less secure looking "L" shaped building with louvered doors, which more resembled modest living quarters than a prison cell. Was this a good sign? Doubtful. I had found nothing so far to be a good sign except my march to faith. I suspected only a change in my captors' tactics to adjust my attitude, which after not succeeding, degenerated into the usual intimidation, threats and if my attitude was particularly egregious, torture. Ushered into a room, I found it completely bare, about the size of a small bedroom with stucco walls painted a light yellow, no concrete slab bunk, no iron leg stocks, no

The Eagle Hunts

hooks hanging from the ceiling, but yes, there was that single dim light bulb hanging from the ceiling on the frayed wire. There was also a window on the back wall that was also louvered but boarded up. The room was light and roomy by comparison to the cell from where I had come. As I unrolled my mat and blanket onto the broken and crumbling concrete floor, I heard the lock on the cell next door open and I took advantage of the louvers to check out what was happening. I saw a very skinny American "G.I." walk across the courtyard with his bedroll under his arms; his legs were boney and his knees were large by comparison, his face was drawn but upright and proud. He looked like the pictures of starving prisoners I had seen from German prison camps. Dachau came to mind. How long had he been here? How long before I would look like that? He was to be my new neighbor; Navy Lt. Cmdr. Howie Rutledge, shot down almost two years earlier he was to tell me by tapping on the wall over the days that followed.

Howie was one of the many heroes that risked suffering the abuse and sure torture to make certain no "new shoot down" was left to confront the Communist indoctrinations alone. From the time I met Howie on the wall, I was never alone again. It started that same day with a "shave and a haircut" he tapped on the wall between us. Then he waited for me to respond with the "two bits" that seems to be known by every American of any generation. Of all the lectures and talks I have given about the tap code over the years since, the audience always responds immediately with the "two bits" when I tap a "shave and a haircut." Of all the differences in our communication between generations, the technologies of which we, as an older generation are inept, "shave and a haircut – two bits" is somehow like a bad joke that won't go away. It is the code that as a child let you in the tree house, and although not everyone in the world knows it, Americans do, all of us.

After Howie's greeting was tapped on the wall and my immediate "two-bits" response, there followed a storm of erythematic, meaningless taps and all I could do was listen. He paused and obviously waited for a response while I waited and wondered what to do. Again, "shave and a haircut," now I quickly responded to tap the customary

Chapter 14 | Little Vegas and the Tap Code

"two bits" and again off he went with the taps, the meaningless taps, and again I listened and did nothing. We did it again but this time the taps were much slower but still retained the erythematic nature still meaningless to me. The activity had increased outside and he gave me as single "thump" on the wall and went silent. While waiting for our next episode, my first thought was why we weren't using the Morris Code. Then I realized there was no way to tap a dash, only dots, and I was at a loss at to what might be next. I desperately wanted to talk to my new mystery friend and countryman. The next day about noon we started out again but this time the taps on the wall were just a number of single taps and grouped together but not forming the usual rhythm like before. This time they were like + + + + + + + + + + + +   +   + + + + + + + + + + + + +   + + + + +. Still they meant nothing to me, but his patience was endless. During the next couple of days for an hour or so in the middle of the day he tapped. When I didn't respond, we did the shave and a haircut again and started over. Eventually I noticed a repetitiveness in the length of the groups of taps he was sending so I decided to count the taps. First there was fourteen taps, then one tap, then thirteen taps, then five taps, then a long pause, over and over again he was tapping the same thing. Okay, now what did that tell me? Lying on my bamboo mat on the floor I wondered what could he be repeating so patiently, so diligently, so bravely? Then I decided to count each tap for a letter in the alphabet, 14 would be the letter "N," 1 the letter "A," 13 the letter "M," and 5 the letter "E." Putting it together--"NAME!!" My name, he wanted my name, how could it have taken me so long to figure that out, but thanks to his persistence we now had communication. With eager anticipation, I awaited the next day for the shave and a haircut, my response of the two bits and his 14-1-13-5 taps wherein I responded by tapping my name.

   Over the days that passed I learned from Howie much about camp life. The guard's names, "slew foot," "the rabbit," and others, about siestas, when everyone took a nap even the "ever alert" guards. That's when we tapped. Howie explained that if we were caught tapping there would be torture and we would be forced to write and sign papers explaining how "good" our food and treatment was as guests of

The Eagle Hunts

the North Vietnamese. These "voluntary" documents of appreciation would then be turned over to the antiwar groups to foster their movement at home. That's why we tapped during siestas. If one of our intrepid guards were to position themselves properly, tapping could be heard coming from all corners of the camp during these siestas.

Over the ensuing months and years, my tapping partner in the adjacent cell and me, with the indispensable assistance of our cell mates who acted as clearing partners, became more and more adept until we arrived at the capability of tapping and communicating very rapidly at almost any time, but this was just the beginning and not yet that time. I passed Howie the key information he requested, such as my name, rank, what I was flying, where I was shot down, the other crew members name and rank, what I thought happened to him, and where we were based. At the same time, he provided me the same information about himself. It was a lot of information and we tapped for several days, one siesta at a time. At some time in the process I learned how he had already been a captive of the North Vietnamese for two years. Two years I thought, that is what I will look like in two years. Little did I realize it would be six years! Howie was doing me a heroic favor. He was the answer to prayers; it was he and others like him that made sure we were all unified… that there were no "lost sheep."

Although I was not a fan of our president, Lyndon Baines Johnson (LBJ), nor the manner in which his administration was conducting this war, Howie made it clear that to remain unified and strong against our captors, it had to be "LBJ all the way." And so it was.

After this basic info was passed with the one two three, ABC manner of tapping Howie tapped "this code is too slow, we have a much faster code and I will teach it to you." "Are you kidding me!" "You are going to teach me how to tap a complex code by tapping through the wall with nothing on which to write?" Yep, that's exactly what he meant!

First, you draw a box and put the numbers 1, 2, 3, 4, 5 across the top of the box, then the same numbers 1, 2, 3, 4, 5 down the left side of the box. Okay I thought, I've got that. Now, draw lines between the numbers up and down and horizontally so that it divides the box

Chapter 14 | Little Vegas and the Tap Code

into 25 small boxes. Let's see, as I review my mental handiwork, 5 rows x 5 columns is indeed 25 little boxes and that seems to check out so far. I reminded myself that this mental exercise was good for my stagnant memory and so while waiting for the next siesta and continued education in the new Code, I repeatedly went over what I had learned. With nothing by which to write, all of my work was mental as we moved through the details, siesta by siesta. Howie

	1	2	3	4	5
1	A	B	C	D	E
2	F	G	H	I	J
3	L	M	N	O	P
4	Q	R	S	T	U
5	V	W	X	Y	Z

The Tap Code matrix, which Capt. Clark learned and memorized by tapping on the wall using the 'one number tapped is one letter of the alphabet' code.

explained that you fill the boxes with the letters of the alphabet starting in the upper left-hand corner with the letter "A" and go across the top filling each box with a B, C, D, & E, then go down to the next row starting on the left with the letter F and proceed across on that row to the letter J. About now I realized the 26 letters of the alphabet are not going to fit into 25 boxes so where does the Z letter go? Anticipating my approaching dilemma, he continued that since there were only 25 boxes and 26 letters the C also doubled as the K,

The Eagle Hunts

problem solved. "Now memorize that, you will use it a lot." "Okay, not too bad, I just hope I memorize the same box Howie has."

With this matrix well in mind, we continued the next siesta with Howie explaining that each letter has two numbers associated with it, the number of the row in which it is located, and the number of the column in which it is likewise located. For example, the letter A is in row 1 and column 1, whereas letter Z is located in row 5 and column 5, and then also the letters C and K together occupy the space at row 1 and column 3. Got it?

To send a letter you tap two groups of taps, the first group of taps is the number of taps of the row in which the letter is located and then second number of taps is the column in which the letter is located. For example, the letter A is one tap for the row 1, pause, and then one tap for column 1, and the letter Z is five taps, pause, and then five more taps, likewise the C and K will be one tap, pause, and then three taps. Howie told me to practice this in my mind because the hard part will be to decode each letter as it is tapped and remember them until they form a word. Howie tapped, "I will quit tapping at the end of each word until you have figured it out. When you do, you respond with two taps to tell me you have it, then I will continue to the next word. If you did not get it and want it tapped again send me a series of taps starting loudly and diminishing in volume like this. We will work out some abbreviations as we go along."

It didn't seem as hard as it turned out to be, partly because my spelling had always been horrible. I was an engineer by degree you know, so why would I need to know how to spell? Now that chicken had come back to roost. Howie had the patience of a saint, over and over he would tap a word, sometimes substituting another word that seemed easier until I finally figured it out. I improved with time to the point Howie said, "When you think you have figured out the word before I have finished it give me a rapid two taps and I will go on to the next word."

We used two coughs for a call up (invitation to tap), then two coughs from the cell invited to tap for clear, or one cough or thump on the wall for not clear, or danger. If we were tapping one cough or thump meant danger, knock it off immediately. I often wondered

Chapter 14 | Little Vegas and the Tap Code

what the guards must have thought upon entering a cellblock with all the resounding coughs and thumps, not much I assume, for they never seemed to be the wiser.

There would be many applications for "the tap code," as it was to become known. Any way to make noise in short pulses would serve the purpose of communication. Coughing, sweeping, chopping, and then there were tactile and visual applications. We were limited only by our imagination. A future cellmate of mine was given the task of chopping up a large limb that had fallen from a tree in the courtyard during a storm. Paul was not given to cooperating in any manner with our captors, but in this situation, he was quick to see the opportunity it provided. He appeared to grudgingly accept the task and for the ensuing day this young hero utilized the machete provided to transmit to the entire camp all of the POW names he had memorized. It was a substantial list. Two chops then three chops, "H," two chops then four chops, "I," "HI PAUL GALANTI" and he continued to chop the names one after another all while the guard watched and the camp officers could not help but hear the crisp and intriguingly rhythmical sound of Paul dedicating himself to the "peoples" task of cleaning the courtyard. How pleased they must have been with themselves assuming their indoctrinations of this "hardened criminal" was showing results by his willingness to help the "people" clean the court. Then how confused and disappointed they must have been when this converted hardened criminal suddenly reverted to his former "obdurate and bellicose" ways. We did occasionally win a conflict in our six and some cases eight years within the barb wire. And to give due credit, Paul was the origin of the particularly degrading term of "goo-yen" previously described. Oh, yes it was sweet!

From time to time we cleaned the badly deteriorated concrete floors of our cells with a bamboo brush that resembled a two foot long handful of bamboo sticks tied tightly at one end and flared out at the other forming a crude but effective short handled broom. That, and the bucket of water thrown on the floor, made for great swishing as in "swish swish swish – swish swish," so by now I'm sure you get the idea. One of my favorite applications of the code was using a cotton cord from the Vietnamese blanket we were provided.

As previously described, the manufacturing process must have been a masterpiece of crude ingenuity because we could easily pull one out. A removed cord could be knotted in a carefully spaced series of knots so when the seemingly discarded length of string found in the "bath" was pulled between a finger and the thumbnail at a constant rate it would clearly snap, unheard, but felt as each small knot slid by, snap-snap, snap-snap-snap, snap-snap, snap-snap-snap-snap ("hi"). It was a great way for a new arrival from another camp to let those from whom he was isolated know he had joined them. As more and more of the bellicose and resistive Americans arrived in their camps, it became obvious to the prison officers the strict code of conduct, which required each American prisoner to follow the commands of their senior officers, was being strictly adhered to. This created a closely united and cohesive group of criminals, when it was hoped by our Vietnamese captors that converts to the cause of the "peace loving Vietnamese people" could be made. Sensing any communication between these "criminal air pirates" was not conducive to that goal, the POWs were separated into cells of "solos," pairs, and cells of four which were strictly forbidden to talk between each other. The Vietnamese reasoned that to further confuse and inhibit communication the criminals should be kept moving from camp to camp. As you must surmise for a proficient tapper, which everyone became, moving from camp to camp was a perfect opportunity to pass news of other camp activities, names, orders, and inspiration from senior leadership. Particularly cherished were words from our senior officers who were held in solitary confinement in the most harsh and miserable conditions for years at a time. Their encouragement kept us united and helped us adjust to the changing tactics of the North Vietnamese. When the gooks finally realized that continually moving us around from camp to camp was only enhancing our communication, they stopped the practice and began to keep us within our own camps.

One can easily see that communication and the tap code played a key role in the unity and strength of the American prisoners of war interred in North Vietnam. Howie had, in an act of selflessness and at considerable peril to his own well-being, brought me into the fold. He continued to issue guidance and insight as to what had been

Chapter 14 | Little Vegas and the Tap Code

suffered by others. What I had suffered and the remorse I felt was very normal and experienced by almost everyone. He made sure I knew I was still an American warrior and together we would survive this ordeal. When I became "conversational" in this new and much faster tap code, Howie continued, "Were you tortured?"

"I don't know, they haven't been very hospitable. I didn't get my nuts cut off or any splinters driven under my nails but whatever they did…hurt like hell and made me say things I shouldn't have. I feel very bad about that."

"Did they wrap you up with your parachute letdown straps and peel the skin off your arms and legs?"

"Yes!"

"Use your injuries against you like straining your shoulder injuries or tying your arms behind you and pulling them up over your head?"

"Yes!"

"Did they hit you in the face and beat you?"

"Yes!"

"Did they threaten you with execution by putting a cocked gun to your head?"

"Yes!"

"Were you locked in leg irons with your hands until you couldn't walk?"

"Yes!"

"Did you ever feel like you were a traitor to your country because you gave in against your will and wrote down things that you did not want to?"

"Yes!"

"You were tortured!"

And, Howie continued, "My countryman, have you considered suicide because you have forsaken your family, your country, and your fellow airmen?"

"Yes, I have, but I am ashamed to admit it and it makes me feel very weak, I haven't measured up, I'm sorry, I tried."

"Have heart Captain, you have shared the same experiences and feelings as most of us. Suicide has been a common feeling. That is why it is so important for us to talk to the new guys and let them know they are not alone and their feelings of despair and hopelessness are our common bond. The thing that sets us apart from any who would actually abandon their country or fellow countrymen is the fact that we will make the gooks torture us all over again for anything they continue to get out of us, but only to the ability each of us has to resist. Our combat continues, our resistance goes on with all we have but we must maintain our ability to continue to resist both mentally and physically. You are learning fast and you have a heart full of resistance. Remember the byword is 'LBJ all the way,' regardless of your political persuasion. Never give in easily, make them pay the price and they will look elsewhere. You are now one of us and always will be regardless of where this experience takes us. We have faith in God, country, our fellow POWs, and ourselves; believe this and you will be strengthened more than you can know."

The day was bright and the sound of keys in the lock came from next door. I was quick to look out the louvers to see Howie walking away with his bed role wrapped up. There was a sudden feeling in my gut of loneliness, of abandonment. When would I see Howie again? With perfect composure, there was no glance back, no gesture, nothing to indicate any association with me in the next room at all. Howie realized had there been, it might have caused a suspicion that could have had dire consequences for us both. I would hear of him on occasion and then six years hence after our release be very pleased to meet in person, this man to whom I owed so much.

My earlier fears of being selected as a candidate for brainwashing were put to rest by my communication with Howie. He had made it clear my treatment was not due to any special selection. From those shot down as much as two years earlier no such treatment seemed to have been meted out by our captors, not that it wasn't brutal, but not specifically aimed at mental discombobulation. Political indoctrination took the form of a generally low key discussion where the interrogator asked political questions and explained how we had been deceived into killing innocent children and pregnant women by a bellicose government who wanted to oppress and enslave the Vietnamese people and on and on for an hour or two. We called them "quizzes."

Chapter 14 | Little Vegas and the Tap Code

It was interesting to note in the earlier days of these "quizzes" our minds would wander aimlessly, taking some humor after frequent syntactical faux pas of the English language but never really listening to the content of the lecture. However, as the months and years passed our minds, lacking even the most basic stimulation of everyday life became void of experiences, except maybe those brutal ones the mind naturally tried to forget. Simple experiences like what you had to eat for breakfast, the news on TV, the weather, all which comprise the experiences and memories of a day of being free were not there. Ours was day after day of staring at a blank dirty concrete wall and the ever dim light bulb. Our minds became vacuums, stimulated only with our own mental activity and memories, which made us even more and more susceptible to the political jabber that we received during quizzes. It was not beyond our realization that this was occurring, and we allowed it to occur so as to receive some mental stimulation, but we placed it in the context of communist political indoctrination.

I likened my recollection of memories as a free man to a scrapbook, one that I looked at hoping to keep my memories fresh. However, the pictures began to fade as if being bleached out by the sun, the pages became tattered and frayed, and I recall even now how the specific details of my wife's face began to gradually disappear. As you can well imagine, almost any mental stimulation was welcomed. Your mind sucked it in like a vacuum would suck in air. Our job was to try to qualify the information we absorbed, to place it in some context. I divided their claim of the numbers of American troops killed by ten. I found that my approximations were generally verified from time to time by information from recent "shoot downs" or contained in the articles of American publications they might show us as proof of their other victories.

Because the extended time away from contact with the outside world made us eager to absorb all of the distortions and propaganda, banging on a bucket over one's heads was not necessary. There was time to wait and wait, and that they did. Fortunately, our education, training, unity, and communication allowed us to absorb it, qualify it, and use it to fill the void without it affecting our allegiance.

The Eagle Hunts

The days passed and I received a new neighbor. Oddly enough, I do not remember who, but he was one of us. It was during that time I noticed floating around in my mid-day bowl of watery soup were crumbs of bread, or perhaps "dregs," stuff from the bottom of the pot out of which it had been dipped. My new neighbor at one tapping session told me to watch out for the dregs in the soup. It didn't make much sense to me but since the soup was "dreggy" I supposed there must be something to watch out for. Nevertheless, it was a survival situation and after inspection and finding nothing that I thought was not consumable, I ate. Shortly afterwards, that afternoon or the next day, I vaguely remember I found myself in a fetal position huddling and shivering in the back corner of my cell, not even remembering how I got there. The cell had taken on an iridescent hue of yellow. Had I flipped out? Was I beginning to lose my mind? Was this what it would be like to be in a mental institution when, or if, I made it home?

I had already reckoned with the thought of returning home with all kinds of physical problems and disabilities, but mental problems? No! As you recall in my previous comments, I did not want to go home that way, but I had dealt with the suicide issue. Perhaps I would retire to the solitude of the mountains somewhere. God's creatures would accept me as I would be.

Somewhere in the yellow haze came the usual rattling of keys in the lock, the swinging open of my louvered door, the especially booming bright light of the outside and the guards order to put on my long-sleeved shirt and follow him. We marched down the front of the five rooms to the end, which I had learned was the interrogation and political indoctrination room, or "quiz" room. There it was, the wooden table but with a blue cloth and a fan which was pointed somewhat in the direction of the stool on which I was told to sit. The fan was a new twist, and like most things Vietnamese, would have been found on the curb at home. I noticed it had a kinked-up wire running to the wall with no plug on the end. Apparently, the plug was only an unnecessary detail because the two wires had been stripped bare and were shoved straight into the old French outlet. From my days in Europe I remembered that the old French electrical

Chapter 14 | Little Vegas and the Tap Code

system was a direct current 220-volt system that had never been changed over to the 110-volt alternating current system to which we were accustomed in the United States. We made the conversion because it was a much safer system as one could take a shock with it and generally survive, the old European system, not so; it was lethal. Therefore, the bare wires casually poked into the 220-volt wall outlet could be deadly with a slight mishap while plugging in the fan or unplugging it. Really, I guess I didn't care one way or the other. It was not my job to be in charge of the fan.

The interrogator made a brisk entrance which seemed out of character for his diminutive size, seated himself, and ushered the command to "SIT DOWN!" He began his well-rehearsed lecture on how the Vietnamese people would be lenient if the "blackest criminals" would confess their crimes and ask the Vietnamese people for forgiveness. That which I describe in one sentence would drone on for minute after minute and while doing so the interrogator kept moving the fan more and more toward himself and with each movement the wire would wiggle and with that the wall plugin would spark and emit a bit of smoke. Of course, the fan would spastically turn off and on, thus creating a distraction from his well-rehearsed presentation. Having reached the limit of his patience because of my amusement of this spectacle, which I tried to hide, but I guess not very well, he exclaimed, "I know to fix" and yanked the wire out of the wall with even more spark and smoke and commenced to straightening out the kinks and curls, explaining that to do so would allow the electricity to flow more easily. He then grabbed the end of the wire and shoved it back into the wall socket with great authority. The fan worked flawlessly. If he had been touching the bare wires when he shoved them into the socket it would have lit him up like a light bulb and most likely killed him. But for the benefit of both of us it did not, and now fresh off of this proof of his knowledge of all things electric, I was asked to write a statement, which the interrogator would dictate to me, describing the good food, treatment, tolerance and humane treatment by the Vietnamese people.

Suddenly it became clear that I had been fed hallucinogenic drugs and called in to write this statement supposedly under the spell of

The Eagle Hunts

these drugs. The "dregs" that my neighbor warned me about were in fact drugs, and I either by virtue of stupidity or the drugs influence already, had not correctly decoded the message. However, it seems, the hallucinogenic aspect of the drugs and my cognitive thinking were not well coordinated with the interrogation intended to coerce me into writing down lies which they would dictate, but I was not completely free of the influence either. So, I asked him to begin his dictation and I waited to see what they wanted me to write before I committed myself to writing it. His English syntax and grammar were so bad it was laughable, so my first impulse was to correct it, however I quickly came to my senses and realized that if I let him babble on, I couldn't possibly screw up a statement as badly as he and any other cohorts in the composition had already done. So, having no intention to write the lies and nonsense they wanted me to, I refused to write and was sent back to my cell, perched on a wooden stool, and kept awake for some days. I eventually told them I would write so I could take advantage of the opportunity to get off the stool, to walk and stretch before again refusing to write. After a certain amount of pounding on the table and shouting by my interrogator I was sent back to the stool. It occurred to me during this process that I might again be meeting the slewfooted sadist. That was unnerving but an unescapable possibility. After this on the stool, off the stool, then back on routine became tiresome, the sores on my butt painful, I began hallucinating from lack of sleep. I decided to try and maintain some reserve of mental comprehension and write their dictation before I truly became a drugged idiot doing what I might never know. So I wrote, but only with all of their grammatical flaws, plus a few extra of my own. I came to the phrase "to la rate," I had no idea what "to la rate" was supposed to mean, except after a bit of contextual examination I realized I was asking the Vietnamese people to "tolerate" my crimes and impertinence. With the English being that botched up there was some relief from the stress of writing this letter knowing that doing so would send the message that not only I was alive but that we were being tortured and coerced into making statements that were lies and untruths. I wrote what they dictated knowing no American would ever read this and not know that it was coerced.

Chapter 14 | Little Vegas and the Tap Code

There was never any further mention of my so-called expression of the "kindness" of the Vietnamese people. I often wondered why not.

As a group, we continually misused the English language in order to send a message to those who might be reading it, a message that the text they were reading was forced, thus creating an embarrassment and serious loss of face for our captors. Even though I enjoyed the gooks own gross misuse of the English language, I assumed I would eventually pay the price. Upon being discovered, too often those screwed up texts would return causing the composer to be "sev'erly bunished." Punished meant a great deal more than merely being scolded and perhaps put in solitary confinement for a period, it meant torture, repeated beatings and extended confinement in shackles and other medieval treatment. But it didn't happen to me, and I can only assume that the composers of the dictated text were so embarrassed, they would not show it to anyone and reveal their incompetence. To the best of my knowledge, this encounter with hallucinogenic drugs was my only one, but it was disturbing, unpleasant, and an awakening that my captors would use drugs to their benefit.

One of the hygienic issues we were afforded was to shave, not very regularly but once every week or so. While I resided in the cell behind the green and beige door, for some reason my shaving privileges were suspended. It certainly was not for humanitarian reasons which may sound odd but it hurt a lot to shave with those dull razor blades and the only shaving cream or lubricant being lye soap, which we were issued on occasion. One did not "shave" anything but simply hooked each whisker and pulled it out. My unshaven look turned to shaggy and then to "werewolf." I had never tried to grow a beard but now I was solid hair from my head to my shoulders. My ears protruded, as did my cheeks and nose and a bit of my forehead, and the almost hairless Vietnamese found it quite amusing. There was no trimming at all so I looked as though I had been stranded on a jungle island for months, all scraggy, dirty, and tangled.

One day when the green and beige louvered door was thrown open, a miniature guard with an AK-47, the butt of which was almost dragging the ground, showed the familiar aggravation at my lack of an acceptable bow, but nevertheless responded with the order to wrap

The Eagle Hunts

up my bed roll signaling a move, but to where? "Away from here." And I was just getting used to the routine.

My anxiousness of another move proved to be unfounded as I ended up just a couple of doors down, and my cellmate was Fred Crowe, a middle-aged lieutenant colonel who was the operations officer of an F-4C squadron based out of Ubon, Thailand who was shot down about the same time I was. It was good to see him and we quickly set about getting to know each other. At one point in our brief stay together I made the comment that our guard looked like a child and Fred responded by saying "yes but he has a 21-year-old AK-47." How astute I thought. We compared war stories of course, and one he related was of an air raid over North Vietnam where one of the F-4Cs in his flight of four disappeared into a cloud along with a surface to air missile (SAM), and neither came out of the cloud. He used it as an example of how aircrews that were killed in action must be called "missing in action" unless a corpse is seen, and how difficult it is to actually see a body or remains while involved in air combat.

I thought it illogical that I as a junior captain would be paired with another officer as senior as a lieutenant colonel and a squadron operations officer. I suspected one of us might be expected to exert some specific influence on the other. Or maybe due to his senior rank he would tire of this "idiot" of a junior officer creating friction and animosity among us that would lead to hatred, fulfilling their purposes of conversion of one or the other of us. I was a fair amount larger and much younger than Fred and in a physical confrontation would have prevailed. If that was the hope of our captors, our like for each other certainly dashed that.

The time Fred and I stayed together was short, but quite long enough for me to experience separation anxiety when the guards signaled for me to roll up my gear. Was I to return to solitary? Did this mean my relief from political indoctrination and the threat of torture was premature? My walk was short, but took me into one of the foreboding large cell block buildings from which I had heard the clunk of heavy cell doors, like the last cell block I was in before the interment behind louvered doors. It was a most unpleasant recollection, and just as I hoped I had graduated from the likes of it, I was ushered up

Chapter 14 | Little Vegas and the Tap Code

to a door very similar to the one of my first experience in Heartbreak Hotel. When the door swung open the eyes of three Americans met mine, one of them I recognized. How could that be? Fred and Howie were the only Americans I had seen since I had been captured. But now it came to me, the light, the crack in the door, Charlie Green an F-105 pilot from the Northeast United States and an answer to my prayers. Charlie was joined by two others, Paul Galanti a Naval Academy graduate who was an A-4 pilot with whom I would spend a great deal of my time "up north" and Dave Gray who was a 1st lieutenant and flew back seat in F4-Cs. Dave used to pat his plump stomach and say "this is all beer and steak why should I eat the swill they give us?" "We will be home soon anyway and I need to lose a few pounds!" Oh, if only. Dave learned to eat the swill but he was always the eternal optimist. Much of the time our mental stability depended on the hope these optimists provided. It was the hope we dared not have.

To balance the eternal flames of hope, those hopes of living, those hopes of going home, which were fanned by the Daves in our group, the realists, like me, never allowed ourselves to give very much credence to the optimism. Nor would we have the emotional courage to confront the pessimists and atheists. They were among us, and yes, their beliefs were respected, mostly because we felt sorry for them, but likely no more so than they did us. They thought we deceived ourselves into believing that should our God not see it in his Almighty way to save our lives, there was the hope of a place to go afterwards. The views of the pessimists were too depressing so we would generally seek the views of an optimist. It was amazing how they could find the good in a bad turn of events. But I get ahead of myself for most of the ability to seek the comforting counsel of others came in the later years after the raid at Son Tay when we lived together in larger cells of 30 or so.

Dave's recounts of his shoot down were very interesting as he told of the final maneuver taken by them to avoid a pursuing surface to air missile, a maneuver that took them into the clouds where they were no longer able to see the missile tracking them. To be most effective in escaping a pursuing missile one needed to be able to see it, and as they could not, it found them. Dave ejected and his chute opened as he fell earthward a few thousand feet. At about that time I realized his story was the same one I had heard from Fred. Here was one of the guys Fred had talked about dying, but whose corpse could not be verified so he could not be reported as "killed in action" (KIA). There was a reason for that, he was not dead! From Fred's explanation, those who fell into that category were reported as "missing in action, presumed killed" to their families.

Remembering the useless photos taken in front of the old truck after my shootdown I begin to wonder how I was reported. After my release six years later, I was told what I suspected. The other jet in the formation broke away from the anti-aircraft fire and in doing so turned its belly up to our direction and by the time they turned back to look no chutes were seen, either in the air or on the ground, only the huge fireball, and so we were officially reported as "missing in action presumed killed." Later, it was privately presented to the family by the guys in the other jet upon their return to the states as almost impossible either of us would have "gotten out." It would be three and a half years before my family was to receive word that I had survived, was alive ,and a Prisoner of War in North Vietnam. The official word came by a seven line postcard that we were allowed to write. Although the North Vietnamese refused to accept it, the card was in compliance with the provisions of the Geneva Conventions. It took about six months for it to be delivered home. The Vietnamese studied it for covert content and by holding it so long, outdated any intelligence info that might have been contained within. Of course, various U.S. agencies also studied it, the Department of Defense, the Defense Intelligence Agency, the Central Intelligence Agency, and who knew what others, to discern if any cleverly concealed messages were contained within the tiny writing. The evaluation by the government's agencies delivered finally with the card was the handwriting appeared, by their analysis, to be that of Capt. Clark and that he "appeared to be somewhat stressed." STRESSED? What the hell! Do you really think so? Very well, I think we can reasonably say that torture and fear of torture and death causes some stress. One, however, must keep in mind that I had been reported as "missing in action *presumed*

Chapter 14 | Little Vegas and the Tap Code

killed" due to the fact that no parachute was seen when our aircraft was hit and crashed into the side of a mountainous ridge. It had been over three years with nothing to indicate that there had been any survivors. This was my first contact with the outside world and a certain suspicion was understandable. I learned the aircrew in the other jet upon returning home a few months after I was shot down, visited my family and as they told the story Vevonna (Vee or V), my younger sister with whom I had always had a close, even somewhat spiritual connection, said "He is alive, I feel it, and besides he has the fastest reactions of any man I have ever seen. He got out!" I do not know if I rate that much praise but I can recall that my ejection from that hurling jet only four seconds before it became a fireball in the side of the jungle ridge was not the only time in my yet young life that my quick thinking and reactions accounted for my being able to relate this story now at age 75. Of course, Vee was correct and she, the romantic optimist, kept hope alive for those who wanted to believe so. God Bless Her.

The realization that I was still alive wasn't the only one. Dave Gray's family and other "presumed killed" aircrew members were similarly surprised. The receipt of postcards for some families was celebrated in the realization their loved one was alive and yet for those who did not receive postcards, it was disheartening and discouraging.

The Eagle Hunts

CHAPTER 15

UNCLE TOM AND FAITH

Tom Storey, whom I have written about previously, was sent with us to join the air war over Vietnam and was shot down flying a mission on the only target I can remember ever missing. Tom was to become known among us as "Uncle Tom" while we endured the hells of North Vietnamese imprisonment due to his moral, spiritual advice and counsel over those years. Tom and I lived together alone for two and a half years, mostly in a single cell with two bunks made up of heavy wooden planks against one wall, with about a foot distance between those bunks, and the crude "once upon a time" whitewashed concrete wall opposite them.

Tom and I endured a great deal over the next few years. You will come to know Tom and his great influence on my life, on my quest for faith, and on my compassion and consideration for others. Tom was a man with a deep faith and love of his family and country.

A discussion I well recall, which Tom and I had as I confided in him my quest for faith, was an earnest thoughtful one. It was

Captain Tom Storey (Uncle Tom) with camouflaged RF-4C Phantom II at Udorn Royal Airbase, Thailand, circa 1966-67. Source is Lt. Col. Tom Storey, USAF (Ret).

not merely carried on by the need to fill time and occupy our minds, but to delve into the thoughts and feelings that made our faith. Tom was the strong faithful one who put the Christian lessons into the reality of his own life, the one who was a devoted, loyal and loving husband and father, a friend of great character, yet also the warrior who could justify and place into Christian context the need to defend our rights to faith and love of God. I was the lost one, yet who searched in earnest, and yet who had realized some of God's great power, the power of prayer against all odds. The peace that came, not by physical reward but, by faith and the promise of salvation.

One of our discussions took us to the realm of free will, the question of whether God has pre-ordained our lives or has given us the power of free will. We seem to assume we are given free will, but are we? Think about it. You are born who you are and no other. You have no need to exercise the free will extended to those whom you are not. Or perhaps said another way, if you do not possess the stature, talent, agility, strength and other physical attributes of a good basketball player, then why exercise any free will to play college or professional basketball? You don't have it. So, it would seem, we have the free will to do only that by virtue of what or who we are. Over a century ago, Charles Darwin theorized about evolution with little probability of God's direct hand in our lives. More recently, however, computers have allowed scientists to produce previously unimagined findings and potential for human growth and societal change. Thus, it seems that creationism and God's presence, in whatever form, cannot be put aside in favor of pure evolution

So, it was at some depth we discussed faith. The teacher, the wise one, and the student, the believer on the quest for the capstone to be placed on the arch between faith and what was not faith, the world of the doubter. Find the capstone and forever have the arched passage of faith open unto you. Tom, understanding this complex and thoughtful search laced with shards of fear and doubt, fell back upon a solution as logical as Rene' Descartes's philosophic theory of the cave, flawlessly logical and absolutely mechanical in its explanation, "The Matrix."

Chapter 15 | Uncle Tom and Faith

Slowly and deliberately "Uncle" Tom began to explain the question for me to ponder. Consider a matrix with two items on each axis. On one part of the axis consider there is God, a recipient of blind faith, on the other part of the axis there is no God, we simply evolved by probability and evolution alone, there is no divine guidance, no salvation. For the other axis of our matrix one part of it will be we believe in God and are rewarded and buoyed up by the hope and guidance of the Christian teachings. But for the other part of that axis, we don't believe in God, disregard Christian teachings and have no hope for forgiveness and salvation. We accept as moral guidance only what seems to be the current sociological and environmental rules of acceptable social behavior.

A Matrix for Belief in God and Non-Belief in God

	God Exists (Win)	God Does Not Exist (Lose)	
I Believe in God (Win)	Win Win	Lose Win	I Win three times and Lose once
I Do Not Believe in God (Lose)	Win Lose	Lose Lose	I Lose three times and Win once

If you believe and there is no God you give up the teachings and morals of faith and leading a good Christian life and the hope of salvation. However, if there is a God and you don't believe, you are but a lost soul wandering through the jungle of life influenced mostly by the changing societal norms of others who may themselves see the teaching of Christianity, like the ten commandments, as beliefs of fools who worship a nonexistent idol, and whose actions suit their own selfish purposes.

Consider please the four options this matrix affords: (1) there is a God and you believe ("win" & "win"), (2) there is no God but you believe ("lose" & "win"), (3) there is a God and you don't believe ("win" &"lose"), and (4) there is no God and you don't believe ("lose" & "lose").

Tom then so clearly and logically posed the question before me: "How do you pick John, believe or not, faith or not?" He silently watched as the question sank in. The matrix says three "wins" to one "loss" in favor of having faith and only one "win" to three "losses" in favor of no faith. If I needed a logical, mathematical, physical, or a probability crutch I would have to pick for faith in God, for the matrix gives me a three to one chance of winning. I picked to believe in God's matrix as Uncle Tom knew I would.

The capstone? Maybe!

Uncle Tom had apparently paid attention in school, church, and done his homework, or maybe he was just smarter than I was. Nevertheless, he was a deep reservoir of things to memorize, many of them religious and spiritual. He was a great boost to my search for faith. He may literally have been God sent. He taught me much about the Bible, the Old Testament, and the New Testament. I memorized all of the books of the Bible and who wrote them. He taught me many of the scriptures and the prayers that I continue to recite today, The Lord's Prayer and 21st Psalm. I recited them a lot and they comforted me. He taught me the words to many of the songs I used to hear in church but of which I never learned the words. Due to his suggestion, we started our own church service on Sunday and quietly sang the songs to which he had taught me the words. "Wherever two or more of you are gathered in my name, I am there also," he used to say, and we were gathered. I hope I was a good student because I am forever indebted to his contribution to the faith that I will always have with me.

During one of our discussions Tom posed this question, "Why is it that when we are looking for a spouse, a mate, we clean up, dress

Chapter 15 | Uncle Tom and Faith

up, wash and polish the car, pick her up on time, hold the doors open for her and compliment her on how nice she looks. Then after marriage we hardly ever go out, "have a date" with all the attention to being considerate and attractive to her as we did before marriage and still expect to be as alluring to her as we were then. You shouldn't, so have an old-fashioned date once in a while; show her you think she is still the center of all your love and attention."

Tom not only spoke from the heart, but he practiced the life of which he spoke. He and his wife, who I knew then as Sally and whose name is really Sylvia, continued their marriage after the six years of being a prisoner of war, and raised a family of which anyone would be very proud. Most of us returned to broken homes and started over. Thanks to Tom, I allowed a great lady to find me and after 35 years we are more in love than ever, and we even go on dates.

The Eagle Hunts

CHAPTER 16

BABY RUTH AND BERKSHIRES

 With so many different types of people in this world the selection process to find those who will make good pilots, and more specifically fighter pilots, is a very exacting process. For me, it began in my second year of ROTC in college which progressed through expansive officer qualifying and aptitude tests, physicals and three more years of ROTC and summer camp. The process for me was no different than any of my compatriots and, therefore, it was not surprising to find we were all very similar in intelligence, education, aptitude, attitude, physical abilities, training and demographics. As one might say it was the "nature of the beast." I was, however, to discover that there were some who needed lots of contact with others. They needed others to communicate with frequently. Then there were those, like me, who seemed to be perfectly comfortable within their own mind. Tom was one of the previous types, whereas I was one of the latter, and it played a major role in the months and years to come.

 Keeping track of time was never an issue. I, as with the others, was always aware of what day it was, and what month it was. They came and went, each day seemingly taking an eternity, but when one looked back over a collection of days they seemed to have passed rapidly. However, keeping track of them was just a normal occupation of one's mind. As the days passed, I tried to keep my mind busy, but there wasn't much real achievement or experience gained during that time, and consequently as I looked back there was little to relate to the past. It was mostly blank and empty, and seemed to have passed quickly. I did, however, have a couple of pet projects that I worked on, often with Tom, who questioned the nature of my sanity.

During the first part of pilot training, as well as survival school, I had been exposed to different ways POW's occupied their minds and how important it was, especially for those in solitary confinement. Keeping one's mind occupied helped ward off an affliction known as "barbed wire psychosis" wherein captives became resigned to their fate, gave up their desire to survive, just allowing themselves to die. It was an affliction which seemed relatively common, not only in Korea, but in all preceding wars where individuals who were not among the sickest and weakest seemed to just die when others survived.

Another such affliction was "The Stockholm Syndrome," where having no contact with other captives, prisoners gradually started identifying with their captors who, in their harsh circumstances, seemed to befriend them and become compassionate. It seemed to be a common tactic among our captors, except when it did not provide immediate results they lost their cool, blowing the whole compassion thing.

One of my first efforts to keep my mind from falling into the preceding pitfalls was to recite all things I memorized in my school years. That did not work very well because I had not done a very good job of memorizing anything and so my recitations were incomplete and fractured. It became frustrating for me to keep my mind sharp, especially during the cold, freezing winters in North Vietnam. The thick stone and concrete walls of our cells cooled during the cold periods and continued to refrigerate the cells even when the weather warmed. The cells were open to the outside air with large barred windows high up on the narrow back wall. There was no way to close off the windows and, therefore, cold damp air freely flowed into the cell from the outside, settled to the floor and presented a constant refrigerator-like environment. In any short span of time, it would not have been that bad, but 24 hours a day, day after day, it cold soaked us to the bone. Our feet were bare and sometimes wet for much of the early years. Later, after a "treat the prisoners better" and "stop the

Chapter 16 | Baby Ruth and Berkshires

A typical two man cell looking through the bars in the cell door. Captains Clark and Storey's cell, which they shared for approximately two and a half years, was less than one half that size with a wooden bunk above the bunk below.

torture" movement in the United States, the Vietnamese allowed what we termed as "care packages" to be sent to us by our families. One of the items not removed from the care packages by the gooks were socks and they were a blessing.

With little food to act as fuel, and no opportunity to exercise except within the close confines of our cells, we were constantly cold and hungry. We lost weight rapidly and got our exercise from walking three paces twisting sideways one way in the cell then turning and returning the three paces the other direction. We harbored thoughts of that special food we would first select when we were released in the spring at war's end. Recall that I was doing this prisoner tour six months at a time. My special food was a Baby Ruth candy bar, with its chocolate, caramel, and salty peanuts, the embodiment of all things sweet and good. Oddly enough, I had never been a big fan of Baby Ruth candy bars. I was mostly a Butterfinger fan, nor did I become a Baby Ruth fan after we were released six years later. Suffice it to say, however, I did enjoy a few.

During my summers on dad's farm in north Missouri where I lived with my grandparents in a white two-story turn of the century farmhouse, I personally experienced the lack of simple pleasures that

The Eagle Hunts

we took so much for granted in the city. So, I decided to mentally take on the project of modernizing the old farmhouse. Heat for the old farmhouse was provided by a potbellied stove in the living room and leaving the doors open into the other rooms that needed to be warmed. One improvement, specifically, was to install a fireplace that opened into both the living room and the bedroom which were adjacent on the ground floor. By some manner of my thinking, fireplaces back-to-back using the same flue and chimney were not unusual, but because the fireplaces themselves were not common and were separated by a wall, they required building another fire at bedtime in the bedroom fireplace. Why not utilize the same soft burned down fire with glowing coals that was in the living room as one retired into the bedroom for the evening? However, the same fireplace opening to both rooms concept seemed impractical when retiring with people still in the living room. Engaging my gadget mentality, I decided to design steel and asbestos (asbestos was the way to deal with heat problems at that time) doors covered with tooled copper that would automatically sequence to close off the fire to the bedroom. Thus, it would display the fire when we were in the living room, and then when we moved to the bedroom, close off the living room and open the fire to the bedroom. I must say it was a masterpiece with specifications for electric motors, wiring actuators, switches and everything else to make it work, all in my mind, sitting in a cold, damp cell.

Next came my most creative work. Dad had always raised purebred Berkshire hogs and I always thought they were the most handsome of pigs, long bodied, low to the ground, black with a white blaze on their forehead and a short snout that looked like it had been smashed running full-bore into a brick wall. When time came to castrate the males, they could weigh anywhere between 100 and 150 pounds. Guess whose job it was to wrestle the stocky, quick, squealing, kicking juggernauts to the ground? Yep, me. I'm sure this was an experience with which most people cannot relate. One must appreciate the relatively small pen, in a muddy barnyard, where it took place. I'm not entirely sure I know why it was always muddy, except that hogs cannot sweat and hanging around mud

Chapter 16 | Baby Ruth and Berkshires

holes allowed them to stay cool. Not that dad would set his pen over a mud hole for this operation, but somehow or another it turned into a muddy operation, perhaps because if the fields were dry then we would be in the fields, so castrating hogs would happen at a time when recent rains kept us out of the fields. That's important. Because hogs have sharp hooves that dig through the mud into the solid earth below, they have full time four-wheel drive and mud cleats giving them very solid footing, whereas tall gawky kids wearing rubber boots slip around on top, with only two wheel drive, unless on their hands and knees, then they still slip around except on all fours. Purebred Berkshire hogs that are of castrating age are compacted within a relatively small package no more than 18 inches above the ground. That's about knee-high on that tall gawky kid. The speed, strength, and agility of a young Berkshire bore about to be relieved of his vital male-hood is indeed something to behold.

The technique is to back this young hog into one corner of the small pen and as he charges forward to run past you, snatch a leg, flip him over on his back, and as I recall tie three legs together and, with assistance from the surgeon (dad), lift it into a V trough where the operation is performed. When dad did it, it looked easy enough. When my turn came and the speeding "Berk" flashed by I countered with a firm grip on a rear leg, having missed the front, and immediately was yanked facedown into the mud and manure and dragged on my belly while hanging on to the hind leg of this kicking Berk. It seems now that letting go should have been as intuitive as letting go of the water ski rope when one falls, but somehow it wasn't. Dad found it much too amusing and could barely maintain his "serious" composure as he reminded me to cross one front leg as I grabbed for the other, tripping and flipping this hundred and fifty-pound rocket with its center of gravity sixteen inches off the mud.

So, with the motivation that should I find myself helping my father castrate hogs again and hoping to avoid the humiliation of being thrown into the mud and manure and trampled by a creature that was supposed to be my victim, I set to the design my "automatic hog castrator" with great enthusiasm. The design was a marvel, made of steel tubing, and painted John Deere green. The hog would be driven out of a pen into a small but sturdy fenced corridor that led to a device, which would put it in a headlock, close tightly from each side, lift the hog up, flip it over, present it for the operation, after which it would be returned to its original position, headlock and side rails released allowing the now neutered Berk to explode from the device with acceleration that would make any rail dragster jealous. If you can imagine the hinges, joints, bearings, gussets added for strength and adjustments available for varying sizes and weights, let there be no doubt it was a masterpiece, and still all in my mind, while sitting in a cold, damp cell.

I have never found anyone who ever took me seriously when I attempted to explain the intricacies of this cleverly designed mechanism. When I returned home, I should have drawn it up and patented it. But as I'm sure any farm co-op would confirm, there are none in service today so, I wouldn't have made much money on the patent infringements, but I could have framed it and hung it on the wall for all those who had never castrated a Berkshire hog to look at and wonder "what the hell?"

CHAPTER 17

THE POWER PLANT

The Shrike missile "wooshed" in overhead and impacted the radar aiming van located next to the prison walls in what the Vietnamese hoped would be the "no shoot" shadow of the prison. An afternoon fighter strike on a strategic target in the Hanoi area was on. Tom and I listened with interest to see if the strike would be close. The guns around the prison began hammering away while we heard the roar of afterburners and the scream of F-105s followed by explosions, which were not close enough for us to dive under our bunks but close enough to unnerve our guards, which we enjoyed. The eagle hunts today!

I wasn't fearful of the bombing attacks around us. Any time the Navy or Air Force guys attacked Hanoi there were lots of those shrike missiles, bomblets, and bombs going off around us. The Vietnamese stationed their anti-aircraft guns around the prison and around other POW camps because they assumed our aircraft would be reluctant to bomb those locations for fear of hitting the POWs, and they were correct. The big guns just over the wall behind us hammered away with certain impunity. However, Shrike missiles were ones that followed the radar aiming beams from the guns and were indiscriminate, striking anything that emitted a radar signal, next to a prison camp with American POWs or not. Generally low yield, they did not blow up very much around the radar site but gave anyone on it, or in it, or close by, a very bad day. They were launched from F-105 "Wild Weasels," which was the term for the fighter aircraft whose mission it was to blow up the radar guided gun positions. They launched from several miles away so as to take the anti-aircraft guns down before the

The Eagle Hunts

bombers struck. The Shrike missiles came blowing in from nowhere and blast the hell out of the radar aiming site with the guns just outside the back wall. They made an unmistakable "whoosh" overhead just before they hit the radar van. Often you would hear the shrike inbound and explosion even before the air raid sirens sounded. That was exciting but disturbingly predictable because the attacks always seemed to occur about 10:30 in the morning and 3:00 in the afternoon. Nothing like establishing a regular schedule so the gooks could clean up after the morning raid, eat lunch, take their siesta, load their guns and get ready for the afternoon strike.

An F-105 Thunderchief flying with a full load of sixteen 750 lb bombs on its five hardpoints. It usually flew in groups of four and was a supersonic fighter-bomber flown by the U.S. Air Force. Capable of Mach 2, it conducted the majority of strike bombing missions during the early years of the Vietnam War; a two-seat "Wild Weasel" version was later developed for the role against surface-to-air missile sites.*

One evening while Tom and I still lived together alone in the Hilton, probably about the fall of 1967, the guards began to rattle keys. We heard the large iron bolts clunking back as the doors were unbolted and the heavy squeaky Ironwood doors opened. The guards began issuing instructions to roll up bedrolls and we knew a move was on. Cell by cell we were blindfolded and led, carrying our bed rolls, along a crooked and wandering route to the main entrance where we were loaded onto canvas covered army trucks and driven

---

* From Wikipedia

Chapter 17 | The Power Plant

off. The tap code was rampant, everyone was bumping each other in an odd rhythmic way. The guards never noticed but we quickly established that our group in the truck were the same guys who had been in our cellblock. Such was not a big surprise except one of us was missing, Jerry Coffee. We arrived at our destination and were led to our cell, which turned out to be a sizable room with a louvered door on one wall and along the opposite wall a barred normal sized double window with louvered shutters covered with boards and nailed shut. On the floor were two single size mat frames made out of split bamboo sticks stuck between 2 inch x 2 inch wood frame pieces. Oh, and let's not forget the forever single light bulb and, umm toilet can! These were luxurious conditions compared to where we had just been. The single louvered door on the front was secured only by a simple hasp and padlock. Within the next couple of days, we were allowed into an open-air hallway off of which were numerous cooking sites. There appeared to be one cooking site per room and the cooking site itself was little more than a barbecue pit in the patio attached to the room. All of this was connected with the long narrow open-air but covered hallway.

Sometime during the next few days Tom and I were ushered out of our room and handcuffed together in the cooking area. We were handcuffed around a steel water pipe which ran through each cooking unit and although we could not see them, there were others of us who were likewise enjoying the fresh outside air. Hummm, steel pipe running between us, steel handcuffs, what better to tap with, and so we did. These cooking units had been well used and it became clear that we were being housed in quarters once occupied by workers in an adjacent industrial complex. We had been hearing about it from others before we saw it ourselves. It was described by those who had seen it as heavy industrial with considerable bomb damage. There was much speculation as to what had brought us to this place and it was surmised that we were there as hostages to keep American aircraft from continuing to bomb it.

The complex loomed above us as we stepped outside, tangled steel girders with welders and acetylene torches cutting them free and welding in new ones, chunks of scattered concrete with steel reinforcing rods protruding out, and large steel boxes and cylinders interconnected with pipes of various sizes. We were literally in its shadow. I knew immediately what it was, for old Professor Scorah, my engineering thermodynamics instructor, had those of us in his mechanical engineering class design one. It was the Hanoi Thermo-electric power plant. The word was passed. President Johnson had said no American POWs would be used as hostages on targets but there we were.

In a few days, several of us were paraded under heavy guard unbound and unblindfolded around the plant. If we were to be useful as deterrents to future bombing attacks, we would need to be seen at the power plant. I suppose our status should have been of some concern to me but it did not seem to be as I was enjoying the tour and the opportunity to see something other than the inside of a concrete cell. Several things came to my attention. One was a huge brick wall being built around the plant. It was probably 30 to 40 feet high and 15 feet thick. The labor was being done by peasants whose activity reminded me of the ants we often observed swarming a task in our Hilton cell. Peasants carried bamboo poles over their shoulders from which were hanging a basket at each end containing mortar and brick. Wearing tattered black pajamas and coolie hats, they were climbing up the brick stairways constructed for access on the outside of the huge wall. Like the lines of ants, they shuffled to the layer of brick on top and delivered their load to the busy bricklayers. I wondered if the designers of this monstrosity knew they were only making a massive chimney for the bombs that could be dropped within it. The shock waves from the exploding bombs would ricochet off the inside walls making several passes through the power plant before it would be blasted out the top in even smaller pieces than it was now. Should I warn them? Let's see -- no, I don't think so.

Most depressingly, I saw several young girls being forced into labor carrying bricks and mortar just like the much larger and older men. These young girls should have been in school with their long black hair in ponytails, giggling and whispering, as young girls of this age are want to do the whole world over. I watched as one of those small young ladies trembled to take the last steps to the top with her load of

Chapter 17 | The Power Plant

bricks while several men stood around laughing at her misery unwilling to assist in any way. I wished they were manning a radar site with a couple of shrikes inbound. The North Vietnamese did imprison and torture their youth so that they could know the way of their great leader, Ho Chi Minh, if they were initially disinclined to do so.

As parts of the large boilers had been blown away, very large sheets of steel were being bent into curved pieces to replace them. At home, we would have utilized massive steel presses that slam down on red-hot steel plates bending them into the precise shape before being shipped off to the construction site via heavy rail. Here, however, this heavy thick steel plate measuring a minimum of 10 feet by 15 feet was laying on the concrete floor with each end supported on a section of railroad rail. In the middle was another rail sitting on the top with a couple of "steel workers" banging on it with heavy iron malls. Blow by continuous blow bending it ever so little, but nevertheless bending it. Somewhere back in my college years in a metallurgy class, I had heard that this could be done but I would never have imagined it being done by two small men standing in the middle of a huge sheet of steel with a couple of iron malls, blow by blow --- brick by brick. Amazing!

We had been shown off to the population, and most importantly to those who might notify our intelligence that POWs were being held at the power plant. If you bomb the plant, you bomb us. Oh well, such is the fate of a prisoner of war at war.

One fine day, a couple of weeks after we had arrived at the power plant, Tom and I were having a contest about who could catch the most mosquitoes out of midair, the count being verified by the size of the small stack as we piled up our unfortunate prey. I recall it was a close contest. Tom was as good at snagging mosquitoes as he was flying F-4's. Suddenly we were jolted out of our competitive aerial combat exercise by the familiar whoosh of a Shrike missile and a very close strike. The walls pulsed in and out with the concussion, the guns started going off, bombs started exploding, not at the plant I don't think, but somewhere nearby and the unmistakable ear-splitting scream and roar of a diving F-105, lots of F-105s. Damn we were glad we were on their side. Again, the familiar scene was playing out just outside our walls; indiscriminate shrike missiles hunting their targets, and explosions with unnerving closeness. Although things shook quite a bit, everything seemed to be secure, so after wiping the mess out of their pants, the gooks gave us a post-strike inspection and all seemed to be okay. Tom and I decided, however, to prepare for the next strike by raising our bamboo bed panels up against the wall like a lean-to, then hunch down behind them at the first indication of the next bombing attack.

We didn't have to wait long and our planning paid off. The sirens, the guns, big guns probably 85 mm, blasted away, each detonation moving the walls and in and out like a drum head. Then, a heavy concussion. Instantly everything turned white as the pressure caused moisture in the damp air to condense; this was a bomb and a close bomb at that. Things went flying around the room, pieces of wall, pieces of door, and pieces of things from whence they came I did not know. The attack didn't last long, they never did, but we kept our heads down for every bit of it, and then some, in case of a delayed detonation. From behind our flimsy bomb shelter we could see our door had been blown off its hinges and into the room with quite a bit of plaster and pieces of wall littered about the floor. The dust had not yet settled when the gooks appeared in the blasted open doorway with handcuffs and ordered us out to the open kitchen to the iron pipe, a distance of maybe six to eight feet. We were again handcuffed with our hands around the iron pipes to alleviate any escape attempts.

I don't remember trying to sleep that way so I guess by night Tom and I had been moved into a concrete closet sized cell that was perhaps a four or five foot square and so dark you could not see your hand in front of your face. There were no windows and only a very small air vent at the top. The floor was wet gravel and the mosquitoes were so thick you could not breathe without getting them in your nose, and if your mouth was open you had to keep your teeth closed to filter them out. We had no mosquito nets or blankets to cover ourselves as they had been left behind in the bomb damage, so by morning we were raw with mosquito bites over any uncovered skin. The box was a sauna in the sun with no ventilation at all. I don't know how many days we were there but fortunately not very long. Later we

Chapter 17 | The Power Plant

were moved to a hastily converted former living compound with old French colonial architecture. I'm sure at one time it must have been lovely but then it was in the same state of filthy rundown disrepair as the prison and the rest of Hanoi. A large broken up concrete courtyard formed the center of a square of rather large rooms with barred and boarded-up louvered windows, both front and back, and a louvered door at the front with barbed wire and various other medieval security devices. Carrying our reclaimed bed rolls, Tom and I stepped up the crumbling concrete steps into the large room and made ourselves at home. It was evident by our short walk from the power plant that they wanted to keep us close enough to still serve as a deterrent to the bombing but not living in the complex itself, which was okay by us. It was then that I was able to see via a sizable crack in the front door the arrival of our week-old French bread which was serving as the cornerstone of our current diet. The street, which I could see through an open gate, was covered with dirt, straw, and manure from the many buffalo, chickens, pigs and other animals that passed along it, as was our courtyard, which by the way, also contained one of those steel plate bending operations. Bounding through the gate came a Vietnamese soldier riding a derelict bicycle with bent wheel spokes, a wobbly wheel, cockeyed set of handlebars with a wicker basket on the front and a platform on the back. Except for the basket, all was painted olive drab, slightly reminiscent of the condition of the bike after I T-boned the massive steel Oldsmobile in downtown Columbia many years before. The basket was loaded, but not with bread and neither was the platform on the back. The bread was in a gunnysack tied at the top and attached to the rear of the bike so that it was being dragged along the street behind the bike. And so, arrived the staple of our diet, a gunnysack of stale, rat and roach eaten bread swinging wildly behind a bike creating a cloud of manure flavored dust. Oh well, it was food and this was a survival situation. It wasn't as if I hadn't peeled off rat poop that had been smeared between loaves and dugout roaches that had buried themselves in the loaves before. I will say, however, that on a few occasions we had fresh (sometimes even warm) French bread. This, however, was not one of those occasions.

The Eagle Hunts

With communications restored, everyone was accounted for except Jerry. No one had been seriously injured in the airstrike and that was good news and very fortunate. Within a few days we had another airstrike. I believe it was one we later learned was targeting the famous Doumer Bridge, which was one of the few, if not the only, road and rail bridge over the Red River which connected Hanoi and Vietnam to China, and it was, perhaps, the most heavily defended target in the world. The F-105s that screamed in sounded like they were going to fly through our window. It is a scream that you could never forget, one that cuts deep into your gut, one that ignores the hands cupped over your ears, and one that causes the flesh on your body to scream with it. The only thing worse is waiting for the bombs it dropped to explode, hopefully not near you. Not being able to see made it impossible to do anything but wait and hope. We had no foxholes, no tunnels, no sandbags, no bunkers, no protection of any kind, save a flimsy unreinforced brick wall.

After the raid the guard came around to tell us to stay down on the floor because the bombs which were dropped were made up of many bomblets, like hand grenades, and were timed to go off for quite a while after they were dropped. Several had landed on the street behind us and we could hear them exploding for the next hour or so, but none of the shrapnel ever punched through our wall or shutters.

Shortly after arriving at this courtyard camp a small lump developed on my back, just above the top of my shoulder blades. It was growing and aching. I could move it around under my skin and I thought it was another boil it first, but it was never sore like a boil, and did not come to a head. I couldn't keep my mind off of it. It possessed me. I knew deep down it was cancer. I came to realize that there was absolutely nothing I could do about it. I could not even imagine what death from cancer would be like there and any treatment would likely be worse. I finally realized I was possessed with this "cancer" and that I could go nuts or have a nervous breakdown because of this fear. So again, I turned to God in prayer, and the answer was not so dramatic as at times in the past, but an answer nevertheless. "God works in strange and mysterious ways" Tom said. Be open to his answers and you will hear them. They may come as a

Chapter 17 | The Power Plant

quiet thought, one that has a certain clearness to it, an easy seemingly obvious thought among the confusion of despair. Listen to it, there most certainly will be an element of faith involved which skews the perceived probability of disaster in your favor. There were times when those who lead us to faith, those like Uncle Tom, have said:

"What harm this faith, if there is no God and it frees your mind from its possessor then it is still good, have faith."

As I found my way along the trail of faith in our Father, the wonders of it unfolded before me, it gave me strength and heart… I found I had begun to find the real faith. When others said that there is no God, I could keep the faith, and it grew stronger. I know it is why I compose this book now. Did my cancer become benign, was it never a cancer after all? Who knows, who cares, but the answer was, as always, a simple one.

"Keep faith my son for you have passed through great trials and you shall pass through more, but pass through you shall, for if I had wanted you by my side you would be here" and again I heard the bombs and screams of the diving F-105s.

… The Eagle Hunts

CHAPTER 18

RETURN TO HOA LO

It was in the court yard camp near the power plant that darkness was coming earlier and earlier due to the waning summer. Through the crack in our door I could see the activity on the street had slowed down considerably, the low wattage single light bulbs cast a soft but exotic glow over the courtyard and street outside, and the constant banging of the malls curling the huge steel plate had ceased. I waited for the gong to unroll our blankets, hang our mosquito nets and crawl in to sleep, sleep that would bring an escape. If it was cold, I pulled the blanket over my head and warmed the air underneath with my own breath. If it was hot, I would sleep in sweat on my side with one arm propped up on my fist so that my arm would not touch my torso. If arm and torso came together during the night a heat rash soon developed from the two pieces of perspiring skin touching for long periods in the filth which was our existence. There was no way to treat a rash, no powders, no soaps, no medications at all, only a malnourished body. Rashes led to bacterial infections which could become serious.

The gong did not come but the guards did with the now familiar keys jingling, locks banging and put on the long clothes and roll up the stuff gestures. We were on the move, to where would it be this time? After being blindfolded, jostled, and a short ride we arrived back at our old cell in the Hilton. Diagonally across the hall from us we quickly discovered Jerry Coffee whom we had left behind when we moved out to the power plant. He was in solitary confinement ("solo" in our vernacular) and very happy to no longer be alone in that small cell among many empty ones that comprised the cellblock.

The Eagle Hunts

We were unsure at that time who was in the cells around us so we opted to not tap on the walls. Instead we signalled to Jerry by flashing our hands up and down under the door, which being lit by the light in the hallway shining under the door, was easy to see. At the same time I was flashing, I could also clear the hall of any guards, that is, if I was looking down the hallway toward the entry, otherwise, I needed a good excuse for being on my hands and knees at the bottom of the door should the guard look in. Because Jerry was solo, he had no one to clear for him as he flashed and as I have mentioned the repercussions of being caught trying to communicate were so severe that one could not risk it casually. The next day after we had adequately established who was in the cell block, who our neighbors were, and set up full cell block clearing, either Tom or I continued our flashing under the door to Jerry while the other tapped to the rest of the cellblock on the back wall.

Jerry was anxious to relate his activities while being left behind and alone. He said the gooks had known we were communicating via the tap code, but could not catch anyone in the act. In order to listen in on our tapping, the gooks decided to keep Jerry back and interrogate him. Jerry had a wonderful command of the English language with a lovely way of putting words together which caused him to become known as a "silver tongued devil." Therefore, I'm quite sure Jerry most eloquently told the gooks to "kiss his ass," whereupon they responded in an altogether too familiar manner, torture. He had no choice but to give up the information or die a horrible and useless death that would deprive us all of his future silver tonguedness*.

Having done so, he informed us as quickly as possible that the gooks knew everything about our tap code. Being forewarned, we proceeded with caution, but were surprised at first, then later took for granted, that they could not interpret our messages even knowing the system.

We realized our tapping system was almost impossible to decode due to the many personalized abbreviations between individuals who were regular tappers, the speed at which we tapped, and the common

---

* Words are misspelled and even created to give some contextual color to the situation and connote attitude.

Chapter 18 | Return to Hoa Lo

practice of the receiver tapping-on the sender when a word which was anticipated and confirmed with the first letters. On occasion whole sentences would be communicated by sending only the first letter of each word.

We even found it humorous when an English-speaking gook interrogator tried to set up a "sting" operation and go into an empty cell sounding like a new guy moving into the cellblock. They tried it while the normal occupant(s) were out, perhaps to a quiz. We heard a couple of coughs out the back window as per our usual call-up, go to the back wall and listen while the "plant" would hopelessly butcher the sign-on "shave and a haircut." Oddly, there was never a response. On occasion, there would be a guard planted outside the door who would quickly whip open the peephole to find himself looking at the back of a darkest American criminal, in our case usually Tom, doing something completely inane but blocking off all sight into the cell. Of course, the guard was expecting to see one of us with our ear to the back wall and hence caught in the act of breaking the camp regulations, which would cause both of us to be severely punished. "Eeeeping" and hollering, the guard required Tom to move, which of course, first he would fake misunderstanding and look at the guard straight in the face through the barred peephole, then gradually comply which revealed me with my pants down sitting on the potty-bucket, ostensibly enjoying one of the fine points of the day. After a couple of times, the guard with the quickest key was assigned to unlock the door and whip it open, thus being able to see around Tom and catch the me with my ear to the wall. Fortunately, I was quicker at getting my pants down and plopping onto the already strategically placed potty-bucket than goo-yen was in getting the door open. All this eventually disgusted the guards, the door was slammed shut, and they retreated in a pout at not having caught the "blackest of criminals" in the act of tapping on the wall. I know of no one who was ever gullible enough to fall for their ruse which was, of course, a great relief to Jerry, and frankly, an added source of one-upmanship and entertainment for us.

Jerry also revealed to us he had been pressed into acting the part in a movie of an American Army interrogator attached to a South

The Eagle Hunts

Vietnamese unit. The scene was one where a captured member of the Viet Cong (Vietnamese Communist guerrilla forces in South Vietnam) was being beaten by the South Vietnamese for information while Jerry was enjoying taking an active role. Of course, the whole scene was staged and Jerry was the only unwilling actor. The scene was filmed by an East German camera crew to be a part of an antiwar documentary which found itself in an American documentary film, award-winning at that, being played in the theaters at home.

As fate would have it, I verified this because I saw the film after I returned home and there was Jerry actively involved in the torture of a Viet Cong captive. So much for the reliability of documentaries, especially those awarded for their authenticity by the motion picture industry.

Jerry was one of those individuals who needed someone to whom he could talk. The long stressful weeks which he had endured alone was taking its toll. He told us he thought he was losing his mind, and we had returned just in time. It was clear to us, whatever the risk, we must talk to Jerry each and every day, as much as possible. So, we continued our flashing under the door while also tapping to the rest of the cellblock on the back wall. By now the risk of being caught was almost eliminated by coordinating with a clearing cellmate at the entry to the cellblock who would warn of impending danger. To begin the communications session, each cell in the block looked under the door to clear their segment of the cellblock ensuring no guard was standing quietly against the wall thinking he was out of sight. After doing so, there were two coughs from each cell indicating an all clear in their segment. Once complete, the clearing cell watched for anyone approaching via the only entrance and if a guard approached, they thumped the wall loudly. Why the guards never seemed to notice a huge thump on the cellblock wall just as they entered was always a mystery to me, but they never did.

It was on one of those eternal days that just kept coming and going that found me on the floor eye to eye flashing to Jerry, while Tom took the info and passed it on to the others via the back wall. I detected some small movement in the hallway out of the corner of my eye. Yet I had not heard a wall thump, or the single cough, that would

Chapter 18 | Return to Hoa Lo

signal danger from the clearing room at the front entrance of the cellblock. Quickly changing the direction I was looking, I noticed a small mouse just bounding along the hallway toward me. It was common to see large rats, sometimes ten pounds I would guess, lumbering in and out of the various holes intended for the drainage of the cells. I actually saw the guards hunting a rat with a dog one time. But a regular mouse was unusual, nevertheless, there was Mickey, just "be-bopping" my way. About six inches or a foot away, he spotted me, one big eye peering under the door. Mickey stopped and looked at my eye intently. I was a bit taken at having the opportunity to share a moment with this cute gray furry creature with long whiskers and dark eyes. I could see it pondering the unanticipated encounter and quickly making the decision to abort the intent to slip under my door. In doing so, Mickey made for what it expected to be a clear escape from my ominous, huge bloodshot eye, Jerry's door. It shot under his door apparently not noticing another big eye peering out. Jerry, however, did not share my same sense of communion with the little creature and sprang up from the door hitting his head on the bunk above and disregarding all abeyance of the camp regulations swore aloud for all of us to hear, guards included. Such a tirade of foul words only a sailor might have known. Oh yes, and by the way, he was a sailor, a naval aviator in more formal terms. Of course, guards rushed to see who and why the camp regulations had been so flagrantly disregarded. I assumed the knot and blood on Jerry's head must have been excuse enough for there were no repercussions.

The days and weeks came and went, the optimists found salvation and impending freedom in the slightest change of the food, a small sliver of pork in the pumpkin soup, maybe half a can of tuna with fresh bread, or sugar and a banana, whereas the pessimists pointed out the fate of the French before us and that we were just not worth the cost in lives, airplanes, and military equipment it would take to convince the North Vietnamese leadership to release us. Nor would our government be willing to pay the ransom that the North Vietnamese might demand. That less passionate but much more logical approach was disturbingly reasonable to me, and so I preferred to go with faith and the little sliver of pork.

The Eagle Hunts

Ants are a fascinating social collection of God's critters. My experience with ants was mostly spraying the unwelcome kitchen visitors with some sort of insecticide, or stepping on them as a line crossed the sidewalk. Now, I know they just wanted to survive like the rest of us, regardless of our position on the food chain. These ants of ours provided long periods of entertainment, and it became obvious to us that even creatures as small and insignificant as ants had a social order and organization.

Tom and I awoke from a siesta one day to observe a rather large spider making its way into the cell through the rat hole. The spider spread out to the size of a dinner platter with its body half the size of a computer mouse. Nasty looking! Tom threw his "go ahead" at it and missed which caused it to go from a casual visitor to one with a heightened sense of fight or flight. I was more interested in a passive approach and cautiously encouraging it to leave, whereas Tom was fully in favor of killing it. Realizing his "go-ahead" aim was not as good as his bombing aim, Tom decided to smash it with his remaining "go ahead" which he had in hand. Just one attack allowed the spider to demonstrate its considerable jumping ability, from a wall on one end of the cell to the wall on the other end of the cell without touching anything in between, a good eight feet.

It then pressed itself into the corner between two of the walls with half its legs toward the ceiling and the other half toward the floor resulting in a much smaller target. Nevertheless, it could still jump from that position and despite looking smaller, it was just as intimidating. Now my fight and flight sense had been aroused, and as there was nowhere to make flight and Tom had already selected the fight mode, fight it was. Holding both of my go-aheads, one in each hand, and Tom with his one remaining, we pursued our adversary feverishly, flailing and smacking in all directions while the spider leapt from one wall to another, flying over our heads or between us. But the ground fire was just too intense and on one such leap Tom calculated just the proper lead and nailed it in mid-flight smashing it against the wall opposite the bunks. After an appropriate victorious celebration, we observed it closely, ensuring it was dead. Satisfied with our victory,

Chapter 18 | Return to Hoa Lo

our attention turned elsewhere leaving it plastered on the wall like some hunting trophy.

We observed that our ants had scouts, and they were busy scouting all the time. Their task was security or finding food. If they found food, or they felt their security was at risk, a message went out on their tiny radios to the anthill requesting help to collect the food or fight the security threat. Or at least it seemed that way because a healthy sized group appeared shortly from nowhere. Quickly after the downing of our huge airborne spider, a couple of scouts found the smashed trophy. There was quite a bit of crawling over, under and around various parts of the spider. Shortly a crew arrived and began to bite chunks off the spider, carrying it away. The gong rang and we went to bed wishing our ants "good luck." When morning arrived, the entire spider was gone except one leg about six inches long that had been hammered tight against the wall. As we had the whole day to observe this masterpiece of organization and determination by our ants to also haul off the remaining leg, we set about doing so. It seemed a relatively small number of the original swarm were left behind to work. They got on one side of the leg and pushed it around as far as they could and then collected on the other side and swung it back the other direction hopefully breaking it loose. They were tireless and most of them worked together. From time to time there was an ant or two that did not get the word to switch sides, and was pushing against the others. But that was no problem because on the next swing they would be on the correct side. There were either some loafers that chose to ride on top of the leg or supervisors who were in charge of the operation, and being so, had to maintain a position to observe the progress. Back and forth, back and forth, they went. At some point several others arrived and when the reinforced party got ahold of the leg, it finally broke loose. They packed it off with some individuals in the party trying to carry it in the opposite, presumably wrong, direction. A few were simply riding, but for the rest of the mass all were working together to carry it off to somewhere to be devoured. Not a bad night's work I'd say.

A second impressive ant event occurred on another hot summer evening when we noticed a few small winged green bugs flying about,

The Eagle Hunts

then more, then a lot more! They were crawling on us, getting into our bed roll, and all over our bamboo mats onto which we would soon be sleeping. "Screw the camp regulations." We shook them off our mats, rolled out our bed roll, hung our mosquito nets over us and our bunks, and watched the small green non-biting or non-stinging bugs swarm over the walls and mosquito nets. Soon they started to fall off the wall and our mosquito nets to the floor, dead, piling up on the floor surprisingly deep, a quarter of an inch or so, completely covering it. The gong sounded and we were off to sleep leaving this mysterious etymological event to its participants. Obviously, the lifespan of these bugs was very short and their nuisance would have to wait until morning as the mosquito nets were working well. Morning came and there were none, the floor was clean! What the hell had we missed? Then we noticed a few ant scouts. Closer scrutiny revealed some few ants hauling off the last remnants of the green bugs. Each of the enormously strong ants was carrying a whole bug by itself while the scouts continued to maintain security. As always, we let them finish their task unencumbered and retreat, save the always present scouts. Considering the number of cells in our cellblock and density of bugs in our cell alone, it must've been quite a haul for some very large ant colonies.

CHAPTER 19

SICKNESS

Coming up on the late fall of 1967 or 1968, I began to sneeze, a few times at first, then more and more as the days passed. As I sneezed my nose would start to run. Eventually I sneezed 30 or more times in one session of sneezing. It was disturbing and concerning to Tom. What had I contracted? I decided to try to hold in the sneezes, but that did not seem to affect things much at all, until one day I decided to try in earnest. When I felt the sneezes coming, I pinched my nose shut and tightly held my breath, an act that would nearly cost me my life. The sneeze came and I held it back but almost passed out. I instantly felt weak and had difficulty breathing. In fact, I discovered I was so weak that I could not breathe and talk at the same time. It was against the camp regulations to lay down on the wooden bunk during the day, but it was that or pass out, so I laid down.

Tom called for the guard by yelling "bao cao!"* I expect I looked rather pale, gasping for air, and could barely talk. A guard eventually opened the door, looked at me, closed the door and walked away. Evening, then night came, and I slept very fitfully while gasping for air. It seemed worse. How could a sneeze held back have done this?

By morning my lungs were gurgling. I was coughing up lots of phlegm which seemed to help some, nevertheless I continued to worsen. From somewhere the thought came to me that my lungs were filling up with mucus and I was destined to drown in it. It seemed reasonable to me that if I could hang upside down maybe the mucus

---

* Bao cao (pronounced "bow cow") was an acceptable manner in which to beckon the guard if attention was needed. Otherwise speaking loudly was prohibited by the generally disregarded camp regulations.

The Eagle Hunts

would drain out through my nose and mouth, keeping my lungs clear enough to at least breathe.

There was no place to hang upside down so I kneeled on the bunk, laid my head down on the bunk so my chest was sloped downward and waited. I started coughing, then mucus started running out my nose, then the side of my mouth, small streams of thick mucus. Tom put the bucket/toilet under the edge of the bunk where I had my head and the mucus ran in a solid tiny thick stream, like honey, out of my mouth and nose, across the edge of the bunk and down into the bucket. It ran continuously; all day and all night, and so I slept in that position, when sleep came. Breathing was very shallow, difficult, and labored. I felt like I was always suffocating, but I was remaining conscious. I knew at least I was getting enough oxygen to maintain consciousness, so all I had to do was keep on breathing. It was the only task immediately before me. If I could just make it until night, then make it until morning, then make it to night again. The guards kept looking in and waiting for me to die, but I didn't. After several days some older guy in a white lab coat came to see me and did doctor things like listening to my chest and back with a stethoscope. He then departed to return with a huge syringe which resembled something with which my dad used to vaccinate cattle. He filled it with some outdated French sulfa drug. I knew this because I availed myself of the opportunity to look at the label on the small bottle which was written in French and dated a long time before. This "doctor," lacking any finesse whatsoever, shoved the needle the size of a wooden #2 pencil lead into my arm. On his first attempt the long needle went all the way through my arm, so he pulled it out and stabbed me again with a bit less vigor. Over the next few days, I was to get several of those shots, so much so, that Tom said my eyes turned yellow. I'm not surprised because everything I saw looked like I was viewing it through a yellow filter. A big yellow spot appeared on my arm, and my skin had a definite jaundiced cast to it. I could only assume that I was being massively overdosed with sulfa drugs. Over the next few days, the stream of mucus became even thicker and yellow and started to be intermittent. I still could barely breathe. I felt a constant sensation of suffocation. I tried to talk, but could not push the air out of

Chapter 19 | Sickness

my windpipe with enough force to actuate my vocal cords. The best I could do was to take a breath, whisper one word, then take another gasping breath for another word. I continued to make it to the night, then to the next morning, and the night again. The days were turning cold, and that seemed to further inhibit my breathing.

Eventually, I improved to where I was able to sit up during some of the day and lay down at night, but I was still very weak and could only sleep in cat naps, just trying make it to morning. Further reasoning told me that, although suffocating constantly, I really didn't need full lungs of air to just sit, or lay still, and so the short shallow breathing would be fine if no exertion was undertaken. It seemed to work, though I was always only one breath away from panic, and self-induced waterboarding.

The cold air was causing an increase in the congestion and coughing which further weakened me, something which put me back on my head and knees if it continued. I deduced that if the cold air was making it more difficult to breathe then I needed to warm the air up; it seemed obvious enough. That would be a good trick as there was absolutely nothing in the cell which was warm except Tom and I. Okay, that was it, I needed to come up with a way for us to warm up the air I was breathing without making it any more difficult to breathe, perhaps a rebreather. A rebreather works on the principal that even air which is exhaled contains enough oxygen to provide for effective rebreathing, hence pulmonary resuscitation. I thought, if I could mix a little bit of the oxygen-rich cold air with my somewhat oxygen depleted exhaled warm air, the result would be much warmer breathable air. Good idea, but how do I accomplish it? The toilet/bucket didn't hold much promise. We had all our clothing on to stay somewhat close to warm. Our blankets had to stay rolled up during the day and our bamboo mats were the only thing that even mildly insulated us from the cold wooden slabs. Then it hit me! Screw the gooks, and I threw my blanket over my head while I sat up on the bunk. I covered all of me and I could even tuck it under me. I was enclosed in a blanket envelope. There was plenty of air that leaked through that crude course cotton blanket and it worked like a charm. My whole body warmed the air under the blanket. The gooks seem to understand and

The Eagle Hunts

figured "oh what the hell, if the American Air Pirate is not going to die; why not."

It was difficult for Tom, who was a very gregarious person, that I had become a blanket blob, an absolutely inanimate object. I was unable to tap or clear to help Tom.

One of those nights in there somewhere when I had begun to lay down to sleep, and was able to sleep for longer periods, I had a dream I was being pulled upwards into a black vacuum. I began to move faster and faster, gaining speed away from somewhere. Where was somewhere? To my curious realization, somewhere was me, I was departing my body. Who was me now and where was I going? "Great Scott," I realized that my soul was leaving my body and I was speeding up. Where was I going? I did not know, but it was black, everything was black. Then it came to me. I was dying and my soul was headed home, wherever that was. **BUT I did not want to die!** So, I had no choice but to pull back, back toward my soulless body, and I did. I slowly stopped speeding up but still I sped somewhere, somewhere black. I could not see my body, but I knew where it was, so I pulled back harder, much harder! Although slowing down a bit, the harder I pulled the stronger was the pull away until I was pulling as hard as I could, but still I was slipping further away. Summoning from my own soul all its strengths and exclaiming into the black that I had a wife with my beautiful four-year-old daughter and a one-year-old son whom I had never seen, there was no force that could keep me from returning to them, there was no way I was leaving them to navigate the hills and valleys of life by themselves. I pulled with a strength from somewhere I shall never know. I pulled with a growing determination to return from where I had left. I did not know a spiritual soul had muscles that could strain and ache. Movement slowed ever so little at first, but increasingly more and more until we, the force pulling me away and me pulling back, had come to a standstill.

But I had to return over all that distance I had traveled so the pulling could not ease up, and so I pulled hard, very hard, knowing to give in only slightly I would die. Gradually I was moving back. My endurance during this effort was, for lack of a better description, super spiritual. The pull away seem to start to relinquish and then

Chapter 19 | Sickness

suddenly the opposing force broke! Instantly I awoke, gasping and choking, realizing I was not breathing. Through a badly inflamed and constricted windpipe and bronchial tubes I gently took shallow breaths, much as a thirst ravage person would be required to sip water so as not to choke. But I was breathing again. I then realized the involuntary function of breathing was no longer working. To breathe I had to constantly think about it. As long as I thought about it, I could breathe, never with a full breath and feeling in a constant state of suffocation, but nevertheless, maintaining a state of consciousness. It meant to me my sick lungs were still processing some oxygen. I had become my own iron lung. As my bloke friends would have said, this was a real "sticky wicket" because if I continually had to consciously breathe, I would not even be able to catnap.

I had never anticipated a development like this. I laid there my eyes open, flat on my back thinking about each breath, measuring my rate and depth of breathing to forestall panic. Was this the end? Was I to die in my sleep because my body would not keep breathing for me? How many times could I pull myself back? I knew I would eventually succumb, so I turned to where I had been searching and from where I had received encouragement and peace; The Father, The Son, and The Holy Spirit.

I prayed long and soulfully knowing that praying to live was an empty prayer. Many before me had prayed to live and many before me had died. So, I prayed to care for my family to forgive me my sins and wrong doing, help those with me to endure, to bless Tom and those who prayed and suffered with me and in the end should it be His will that should I pass, care for those who love me, and to shine thy blessing upon me. I closed my eyes and continued conscious breathing. I shall never ever forget what happened next, and 50 years later my eyes still tear as I write this. I have told only a very few, for it is almost impossible of which to speak. At first there was a soft warming relaxation that started at my feet and moved slowly, very slowly up my legs, then into my lower body. I had not realized I was so rigid and tense, but as the feeling moved up from my feet, I seem to almost melt, as if I were a puddle with no substance. The soft warmth reached my chest, heart and went out into my arms, out into

The Eagle Hunts

my fingers and up my neck into my head. It was a warmth like being cuddled in a fluffy electric blanket. I felt very at ease, very sleepy, and all seemed okay, all seemed at peace. With pure faith, I gave into sleep accepting whatever the good Lord had chosen for me.

Sometime later I awoke, wondering if I was home, or still imprisoned but alive. Through the fog and wonder of all this I could hear from over the prison walls, sounds of Hanoi beginning to awaken. I had made it to yet another sunrise.

The morning was dark and yet the gong sounded for the whole country to awaken, and I just laid there looking up at the bottom of Tom's bunk realizing he had not the slightest clue as to how close I had come to dying. Tom, who had been so important in helping me along the road to rediscovery of faith would not know because I just simply could not talk about it. He had given me faith; he had saved my life. I was not well but I had apparently recovered the ability to breathe while asleep. When I returned home, I learned I had advanced malaria which can affect the nervous system, including the involuntary nervous system which affected my ability to breathe without thinking about it. But if I had been infected by the mortal parasites why would it return to function. I cannot explain this, nor can the doctors whom I have asked. But the answer is simply faith.

To those who may read this, let it be known that there is a God, there is faith, and there is a plan. If you will work to help yourself, he will work to help you succeed with the plan. Don't pray selfishly, don't pray for riches, and to win games, pray for a fair game conducted in the attitude of good sportsmanship, pray to help others, and to enrich their lives.

CHAPTER 20

THE WITCH DOCTOR

Sometime during my early recovery my chest became very sore. Several spots on it hurt and were very sensitive to touch. Of course, I bitched about it, maybe because I knew I could get away with it. One very average day I was pulled out of the cell to go to the "clinic," a small unheated room probably 10 feet x 10 feet containing an odd assortment of old and antiquated medical gear, needles soaking in cold water, outdated drugs, and the old gentleman who wore a white smock. If the doctor, or whatever he was, had been made of wax it would have looked more like a museum display than the real thing. The doctor punched around on me and after I said ouch ever so often, whether it hurt or not, I was dismissed back to my cell. Some days later I was again summoned by the guard and delivered to the clinic where I was commanded to remove my shirt and lay down on the large stainless steel veterinarian's table. While I did so the doctor collected half pint fruit jars, alcohol, quarter size tokens, perhaps Vietnamese coins, cotton balls and a cigarette lighter. There was no explanation given and "Doc" proceeded with confident determination; me not so much. I didn't like the look of the cotton balls, alcohol, or cigarette lighter. Was he going to hack on me with those Civil War era instruments, then cauterize the wound with fire? Not being tied down to the table I surmised I had some recourse just before being shot by the AK-47 armed guard. Satisfied that he was now prepared for the forthcoming holistic treatment, the doctor started placing the tokens on my chest where I had exclaimed the pain. It was at this time I wished I hadn't been so flippant about saying "ouch" as he had poked around earlier. I recall he selected six or eight different sites.

He then soaked the cotton ball in alcohol and one at a time laid them on the tokens. After setting them afire and once burning nicely, like a fondue burner, he took one of the jars and gingerly placed it upside down against my skin over the token and burning cotton ball. Just as I was about to relieve myself of these odd bonfires all over my chest due to the rapidly increasing temperature of the tokens, the fires, having consumed the oxygen in the overturned jar, went out. The remaining alcohol proceeded to evaporate cooling the coin. So much for my concerns, but shortly the air in the jars began to cool and in doing so created a vacuum in the jar because it was sealed against my skin. As the vacuum increased my skin was sucked up into the jar. What an odd sight I must have been laying on that stainless steel veterinarians table with no shirt and old jelly jars plastered all over my chest with a token, cotton ball, and skin all sucked up into them. Where's a Polaroid camera when you need it? Gradually the jars began to fall off and I was returned to my cell with these perfectly round red circles all over my chest. Tom, when told of the incident, maintained his typical stoic decorum but clearly had a smile in his eyes, perhaps because it was outwardly amusing, or perhaps after all these weeks and months of fighting for life, day by day, I had found something amusing enough to relate. Oddly enough it did temporarily release some of the discomfort by relieving some pressure on the lymph nodes under the skin. I've always enjoyed that story because I can tell it without getting choked up, and those listening obviously get a chuckle.

I continued to improve slowly but never recovered to full health. Five years later on the flight home from Clark Airbase in the Philippines to Hickam AFB at Honolulu, Hawaii, I became ill and developed sweats and chills. The lovely flowered leis that had been placed around our necks started to make me choke. The malaria had become active again. Fortunately, it was the treatable type and was cured after a couple of weeks at the Scott AFB Hospital located close to home at Belleville, Illinois. But the parasite had done a lot of damage and it would take a year or two to recover fully.

However, during the ensuing years between my out of body experience and my release, my breathing went from times of seemingly normal to labored with a runny nose, some sneezing, and coughing, but

Chapter 20 | The Witch Doctor

nothing like that first winter. Sometimes my heart rate became irregular and in the last years of confinement I noticed at times I became extremely sensitive to only slight temperature changes. At the end of the war, we were given opportunities to bathe in a courtyard a couple of times a week. We dipped the bath water out of an open concrete tank about six feet by six feet by two feet deep. In the warm and hot parts of the year it was not bad. The water was always at ground temperature of about 55 degrees and we dipped it out with our drinking cups and splashed it over ourselves. But in cold weather it was brutal, and many of us did not partake in the interest of protecting our health.

It was on a mild sunny bathing day that I noticed while standing in the sun I began to perspire quite profusely. Others didn't seem to be perspiring nearly so much, if at all. I stepped perhaps four feet into some shade provided by the cellblock roof and immediately begin to chill, to shiver. This was a new and worrisome development. I did, however, learn to find an environment with a relatively constant temperature and adjust to it. It seems I had become unable to adjust to changes in ambient temperature. What system was breaking down now? Would we ever get out of there I wondered? What of these quirks of my health would become the ailment that would kill me? But again, if the good Lord had wanted me dead the opportunity had certainly been there. So, whatever ailment I was dealt, I kept the faith, did the best I could to minimize it, kept eating, sleeping, thinking, and being physically active when my state of health allowed.

Upon returning home I was told that the malaria parasites had found their way into the nervous system that helped control my internal thermostat and my heart rhythm. I'm not sure having known that at the time would have made me feel any better, but it did explain some things.

The Eagle Hunts

CHAPTER 21

SON TAY

The individual sessions of political indoctrination and physical abuse began to increase. One of the guys returned from a "quiz" and tapped that the interrogator had stated a campaign would be starting soon to convince us of our criminal ways. It would gain confessions of our crimes whereupon we would be tried and sentenced. Some would even be executed. This sounded a bit dire, but we had heard it before and there was nothing we could do but stand by and see how it played out. Actions up to then were beginning to indicate there was some truth in it. Apparently, our captors had decided we had been given sufficient time to voluntarily "see the way of the Vietnamese people" but had not done so. Then, suddenly it all stopped, and conditions seem to improve, more soap for bathing, and a few scant packages from home.

My first six-pound package from home, in compliance with the Geneva Conventions of which I will remind you the North Vietnamese disclaimed any association, arrived in a box about one cubic foot in size with one small package of Lifesavers rolling about, yes that was it, one small roll of Lifesavers. The gooks had extracted a heavy tax, most likely looking for suspicious items like crowbars, M-16s, shives, long-range shortwave radios, or whatever, and then maybe they just liked what they saw and decided to keep it. It was a start. The optimists went nuts, conversions were made, and the pessimists begin to pout.

Ho Chi Minh died in September, 1969, and being the author of the forthcoming torture campaign for confessions, it also died. Who among the Vietnamese leadership realized the importance of the

The Eagle Hunts

opinion of the American public I do not know. Vo Nguyen Giap, the North Vietnamese commanding general who had defeated the French at Dien Bien Phu perhaps, or the Prime Minister Pham Van Dong perhaps. The war was going well for the Americans, South Vietnamese and allies in the jungles and on the battlefields, although the American public did not know that.

About the time of the death of Ho Chi Minh, the news of the torture and mistreatment of American POWs by the North Vietnamese created a movement in the United States. It was a campaign to treat the POWs better, to treat them humanely, stop the torture, and to permit them to write and receive mail and packages according to the terms of the Geneva Conventions. Even though North Vietnam claimed not to be a signatory to the conventions they could, nevertheless, see the damage that a campaign against the brutal treatment of the POWs could do to the perception on the streets of America of the "innocent, peace-loving Vietnamese people."

We started to receive an occasional package from home, perhaps with a pair of warm socks or a bottle of vitamins. There was an occasional postcard and some reading material provided by our captors about how the "aggressive American forces that kill mostly old people, pregnant women, and children" were being defeated in the South. My heavens, the optimists were on a rampage.

On an evening in November or December of 1969 and not being entertained by the ants, geckoes, or terrorized by spiders we prepared to sleep, ahhh sleep, the great escape, awaiting only the gong. The gong did not come; what we heard was the jingling of keys, bolts banging, doors swinging open, and "eep eep," orders being given by the guards. And then our lock, our door and our very own "eep" -- roll up your bed rolls, put on long clothing, another move. As always, the question, to where? Of course, the optimists thought we were being released and the pessimists countered, we were going to a work camp. We were later sorry to realize the optimists were wrong, but not surprised, and the pessimists were wrong also, for they always were. But in their view of things, they were always mentally prepared for the very worst, and I might add, endured the mental depression that went with it.

Chapter 21 | Son Tay

> NGÀY VIẾT (Dated) 23 Feb 1972
>
> Dear Bonnie, Renée & Keith: Happy birthday Keith, the years keep passing bad and growth makes you now into a big boy. Help where home chores dictate & can't help but each day son follow mothers wishes, the Golden Rule and learn to be honest & truthful regardless of pride, temptation and what dishonesties may come of others. Bonnie my pet doll like T-shirts & shorts. Try & put some into packages. Also how about taking quite a few nice normal size pictures. I am interested, sweetheart, in you, the kids, folks & family, house, pets, lake, new cars etc. Please send the pictures only in letters. I was pleased to get your letter & pictures, also mom's letter. Love hope & faith
>
> John

GHI CHÚ (N.B.):
1. Phải viết rõ và chỉ được viết trên những dòng kẻ sẵn (Write legibly and only on the lines).
2. Gia đình gửi đến cũng phải theo đúng mẫu, khuôn khổ và quy định này (Notes from families should also conform to this proforma).

NGƯỜI GỬI (Addresser)
HỌ TÊN (Name in full): John W Clark
SỐ LÍNH (Service number): FR70477

TRẠI GIAM PHI CÔNG MỸ BỊ BẮT TẠI
NƯỚC VIỆT-NAM DÂN CHỦ CỘNG HÒA
(Camp of detention for U.S. pilots captured in the DEMOCRATIC REPUBLIC of VIETNAM)

NGƯỜI NHẬN (Addressee)
HỌ TÊN (Name in full): Mrs Bonnie Clark
ĐỊA CHỈ (Address): 1930 Doris Drive
Columbia, Missouri
United States of America 65201

This a typical 7 line form for a letter home, generally in compliance with the Geneva Conventions form even though the North Vietnamese disclaimed any requirement to comply with them. Captain Clark's family did not receive a letter for 3 ½ years after he was declared 'missing in action – presumed killed.' It was only after Ho Chi Minh died and the mistreatment of American prisoners of war became known to the American public that some letters began to be written.

The Eagle Hunts

The move was longer than normal, but otherwise uneventful. Morning revealed that we had arrived at something of a country camp in sight of the mountains at the eastern end of "Thud Ridge," so named for all of the F-105 fighter-bombers, of which I have previously written, that had been lost either over, or in it.

There before us were the mountains that most had seen so many times from above. Tapping to some of the other cells, which also contained American POWs whom had proceeded us by more than a year, and who had information gleaned from quizzes with interrogators, we learned we were at a country camp in the foot hills of the mountains near a small-town west of Hanoi called Son Tay. The camp was named "Camp Hope" by some of the POWs who preceded us, but it generally came to be known among most of us as Son Tay. A small camp, it was surrounded by a tall flimsy brick wall with guard towers at each corner and small number of buildings, three of which were divided into two, four, and six-man cells and named Opium Den, Beer House, and Cat House. In addition, there was a very small stand alone unventilated punishment cell that had a corrugated metal top and was extremely hot or cold as the weather varied.

We also learned the first arrivals had been told by the gooks that the camp was a work camp, and over the next several months some ditches in the complex had been filled in and a well dug. The well ended up being dry which would have seemed unlikely as the camp was positioned on the banks of a small delta as it flowed to the Red River and thru Hanoi from the northwest.

The open camp was, for the most part, a welcome surprise. All rooms were at ground level with one or two shuttered and barred windows. At certain times the guards opened the shutters and we could see outside into the camp grounds which were small and somewhat grassy. The gooks were constructing another small building between the wall and our cellblock and all of it was being done by hand. It was a source of entertainment for certain.

With the completion of the lighting, the lure and wonder of this advanced technology was just too strong, and at one point a guard walked up to the door, stepped partially inside, looked furtively about, and flicked the switch turning the lights on. Looking about

Chapter 21 | Son Tay

once more he flicked them off, then back on. Full of amazement he continued to do so, while all the time glancing about to see if anyone was watching. We were, of course, but from behind the shuttered windows which had ample cracks to make observation easy, but not obvious to him. Finally, he tired of his amusement and wandered off to resume his duties, or better yet, to discover another marvel of modern science.

It was about this time we learned, quite by accident, that Neil Armstrong had walked on the moon some six months or so before. It was within this heightened sense of light and moon walking technology which gave some of us the idea to inform the guards that if they did not treat us well, we would turn off the moon and leave them in the very darkest of night until our treatment improved. I can't say that our treatment improved much, but the guards demonstrated some concern.

The mountains to the west grew ever more fascinating, with jungle and streams of water and sparse roads. We could not help but wonder if those mountains provided an opportunity. Escape had to be carefully considered, for our tall Caucasian stature was not concealable among the native Vietnamese and there were no friendly Vietnamese in the general population of the North.

The repercussions of a failed escape were severe, both for the individuals attempting it and those in the cell that remained behind. In one such incident, one of the two men attempting the escape was beaten and tortured to death, and the other terribly tortured, beaten senseless, and after being revived and restored to consciousness so that more pain could be inflicted, was beaten again. The entire rest of the cell was beaten and tortured to varying degrees. It was generally considered by the gooks that a prerequisite to an escape attempt would be support and encouragement from the rest of those left behind and they assumed guilt by association.

Although the mountains had an allure to them it was a significant walking distance away and across a very densely populated Red River Valley, an adjacent Army base and the village of Son Tay. As matters were discussed among us in the cell of four, it occurred to me that those same mountains could screen a rescue force if they were to fly in low to the ground, and although the valley was heavily defended, ground clutter would confuse the radar and make it difficult to use radar guided missiles, guns, and aircraft. Effective defense would depend on optically sighted guns and barrage fire. Flying through a wall of barrage fire was pure probability. So, low at night gave the best probability, except for the potential of running into another aircraft in the task force, or the ever present very close ground. It so happened that the high technology RF-4C that I had been flying had just installed a very state-of-the-art ground radar which allowed us to fly up and down the hills and mountains along our route of flight, reasonably enough, it was called terrain following radar. One could get low enough to make oneself rather nervous, especially on a very dark night. Another mode on the radar would show a blip on the screen for any ground that was closer to our flight level than we had selected, which the crew could then fly around. This capability was tied into the inertial navigation and autopilot so that the aircraft could automatically fly around, or up and over the hills and mountains on the autopilot in the very darkest of night, or in the weather, or in clouds, if anyone trusted it. Since it was so new, and we had been the first to fly with it, we were still in the process of trying to be trusting, so most of the autopilot functions were not used and the aircraft was hand flown and closely monitored by both pilots.

Knowing of this new radar and flight technology, it became a reasonable assumption that helicopters and C-130 blackbirds could be equipped with it, and flown in low under the radar to the edge of the Red River Delta where we were located. Discussing this with my cellmates a plan was born to collect as much info about our camp and guards as possible and send it home via covert means. Knowing how to do this made it seem worthwhile to try, and we assumed that if the recipients of our intelligence were to receive information on location, size, composition and security of the camp the same thing might also occur to them. So, the thought was spread among others in the camp via tapping on the wall and soon took on a life of its own with each covert operative. A few weeks into our effort the high-pitched whine of an aircraft of some sort was heard over the camp at a very

Chapter 21 | Son Tay

low altitude amid a great deal of small arms fire both from within and outside the walls of the camp.

Some years earlier during my senior year at the University of Missouri, I was involved in a graduate course where we were experimenting with ground effect machines (hovercraft). To power our experimental craft, we decided upon a surplus four-cylinder two cycle drone aircraft engine, and I became quite familiar with its high RPM two cycle whine. Yes, your assumption is correct, we suspected the obviously unpopular aircraft that overflew the camp was one of our own reconnaissance drones. The thought occurred to me that we should've had more sophisticated drones than the ones they were selling the engines out of ten years earlier. Indeed, I learned later upon returning home, the drones that gathered most of the intelligence over North Vietnam were called Buffalo Hunters and were much more sophisticated. What had we heard that was so disliked by the North Vietnamese? It may have been a drone from one of our many intelligence sources that was doing their own collection of data off of the so called "grid." Or maybe not, but it gave us quite a boost.*

Clad in olive green uniforms and wearing rubber sandals cut out of old tire treads on their feet, our guards carried various weapons, among them were the AK-47 and a weapon that was a crude looking submachine gun stamped out of metal and resembling our old WWII .45 caliber "grease gun." It was so crude looking that it reminded the farm lads of the grease guns with which they lubricated their tractors and farm equipment back home. For a few hours each day, the tattered green shutters on the barred windows were opened, and we availed ourselves of the opportunity to interact with the guards as they strolled about looking into each open window. Not that there was much intellectual stimulation to be gained from such intercourse but it was part of a "Psy-ops" (psychological operations) plan to gain information while gaining a more human appearance with our captives. We were applying the opposite of what we were taught in survival courses. The thinking was should there be a rescue the guards would be less inclined to kill us to prevent our escape, or less inclined to resist our rescuers, or neither, but maybe just create a hesitation on

---

* Benjamin F. Schemmer covers this subject in detail in his book "The Raid."

their part that our 'maybe' rescuers could exploit to more quickly kill them. Conversation between us first concentrated on families. They were very receptive, showing us pictures of their wives, sweethearts, and children, as we did of ours. "Do you have a wife?" It was a fun question because we were able to gesture about long hair and breasts, short, tall, thin, and fat, big boobs, little boobs. Their wives all had little boobs, but some of our wives had much larger breasts and we would so gesture to their embarrassment. Some of the guards could hardly wait to come on shift, open our shutters, and show us new pictures of their homes, wives and kids; and yes, we found ourselves starting to kind of like some of the little pricks.

It didn't take very long for the camp supervisors to realize that their guards were being much too friendly with the prisoners. So, a new program sent the guards off to what we called "hate school." Every few months when they were observed being overly responsive to our questions, they disappeared for a week or two only to return with the demanding "bow down" and a hateful attitude. Clearly, they had been taken away to the hate school where they were again told about how the perfidious criminal air pirates bombed and strafed children and pregnant women. It was a bit humorous and gratifying to see how fast that attitude melted away when asked about their new baby or wife we had talked about before his temporary duty at hate school. Some liked to talk about going to America after the war, and some wanted to go to school there. Maybe they wanted to learn how to turn off the moon. Keep in mind we spoke no Vietnamese and they spoke no English, consequently, gestures, smiles, frowns, points, and pictures comprised the conversation. After the ice was broken all seemed to communicate well. Gradually the conversations became interspersed with questions whose answers might indicate the number of personnel stationed at the camp, nearby antiaircraft sites, and other meaningful information.

One such incident turned very humorous. It seems one of the guards was packing what had been named by us as a "tin-can machine gun" and we excitedly inquired about it. Of course, the excitement was infectious, and the guard set about showing it off with great enthusiasm. All was going well in this brief course on how to operate

Chapter 21 | Son Tay

a tin-can machine gun (should one fall into our hands), until it came time to shuck a shell into the chamber cocking the gun. The less than precision bolt would not cooperate. No amount of tugging, pulling, and yanking seem to have any effect on loading a cartridge into the chamber. In a state of embarrassment, the guard held up one finger, indicating for us to wait a moment while he disappeared around the corner of the building. A loud "smash" was heard, then a resounding "thud," much as we might suspect a tin can machine gun might sound if being slammed into the hard stucco wall of the cell block building. Momentarily, the excited young guard returned with a full demonstration of how the aforementioned stubborn bolt functioned. We, of course, demonstrated proper enthusiasm, not only at the demonstration, but also how adroitly this resourceful young guard had repaired the bolt malfunction.

Now, in a manner of which I am not able to explain to you the info we obtained was sent in the "blind" to our intelligence people at home whose job it was to monitor such activity. Sending a message in the blind meant it was simply sent info but we did not know if it was ever received. It was then that I realized why advanced survival skills were taught, and why I and some others possessed these capabilities. We were hoping to pique the thoughts of those who received our blind communications into considering that the nature and type of info which we were sending would be helpful for a rescue, and the collective effort being placed on it might suggest that those interred at Son Tay felt a rescue might be worthy of serious consideration. It was a correct assumption, for as we were to later learn, enormous effort was devoted to a rescue raid upon the POW camp. It is a story told in books and manuscripts and written by participants and historians alike. Those who have studied it in the military academies find it as an operation as classic as the Israeli raid at Entebbe. Though much more expansive, it was lesser-known as it involved a military POW rescue, not civilian hostages. A book I have already footnoted and would recommend reading if one is interested titled "The Raid - The Son Tay Rescue Mission" by Benjamin F. Schemmer can be found in my collection of books, or on Amazon.

The Eagle Hunts

In his book, Schemmer describes how due to a top-secret operation by the Americans to seed the rain clouds during the monsoon season in North Vietnam an abnormally high amount of rain fell in the water shed to the west of Son Tay raising the water level in the small river just outside the camp fence. When it looked as if the camp would flood, the order was given to pack up the camp and move it.

This photo is a simulated aerial photo of a mock-up of the POW camp at Son Tay which was used in the planning of the raid on the camp, circa 1970.

So, on the night of the 14th of June 1970 the camp at Son Tay was moved to another camp located at Dan Hoi about 13 miles to the east. I am not so certain that flooding was exactly the reason because the camp into which we moved appeared to have been newly completed, and it would have been pure coincidence that the completion of the new camp and the flooding occurred at the same time. Regardless, the impact of the move was to become historic.

The new camp was a dramatic change from what we had become used to. It was newly constructed, with fresh concrete and

Chapter 21 | Son Tay

white-washed walls. It was not necessarily plusher, for we had the same elevated concrete slabs for beds, bamboo beach mats for mattresses, open to the outside cold and heat, open to mosquitos, flies and other critters. However, the enhancements included ample space between bunks, which were all on one level rather than bunked and eight to a cell. Different cells from Son Tay were joined together to form larger cells, and in my case two four-man cells were joined together, which pleased us a great deal. It was great to be moved together with some of the guys with whom we had been tapping for so long, and whom we felt we knew very well but had only met through the wall. As I recall, the cell which could almost be called a room, opened onto a patio-like walkway on the other side of which was our latrine. It was not a bunch of buckets in a filthy, slimy, smelly, disgusting room that were emptied by us daily in an even more disgusting latrine used by the Vietnamese. It was rather crude by our standards but it was first class by theirs. Most of all, it was new and clean and lacked the slime and mold with which we were accustomed. Such a pleasant surprise was this new camp that the optimists tagged it with the name "Camp Faith." The name was fitting, as now the improvements were more than we had come to normally hope for. Moreover, I liked their thinking and was inclined to join their optimistic ranks.

However, we were also aware this new camp had a dark side. Because of the "treat the POWs better" movement taking place back home, and the impact it was having on the Vietnamese leadership, the need for the Vietnamese to make all appearances of treating us well was increasingly important. This was one of those moves. A new camp with bright airy cells, several men to a room, and more "leisure" time outside; it was a propaganda camp, and soon we expected to see the camera crews and questions from the communist eastern European and American traitors like Jane Fonda. She had already made her traitorous entry onto the political stage by being filmed setting on an anti-aircraft gun in Hanoi surrounded by very pleased and smug gooks watching as she ostensibly prepared to shoot down any intruding American aircraft looking for "innocent Vietnamese children and pregnant women" to kill. Jane Fonda, who had caused some of those among us to be brutally beaten to meet with her and describe the lie about how well we were being treated, so that she might return home to further inflame the anti-war movement, which she did with great pride.

While we enjoyed our new surroundings, we also prepared to meet the expected oncoming propaganda moves with firm resistance by implying that this improvement was nothing but a farce. However, we were also well aware of the brutal consequences of such resistance so we just decided to enjoy it while we could.

CHAPTER 22

HOT OR COLD WAR

Moving to this fresh new camp in the countryside where we could actually see the sky was encouraging in one respect, but likewise confounding in another. Better treatment was clearly foremost in the minds of our captors, but to what end? Was release at hand? Certainly, our optimists thought so. Was this camp built for another purpose, but only temporarily occupied by us just to provide an opportunity for the cameras to record our excellent living quarters, all for its impact on the war being waged in the streets and on university campuses back home? Our Vietnamese hosts had lost patience with our lack of any "identification with the oppression and plight of the Vietnamese people by the obdurate Johnson administration." Could this be an effort to demonstrate the pleasant confinement we could have for the duration of the "10-20-30 years or more" war? Or would we choose the hell of an existence from which we had just come? It would, of course, depend on if we chose to repent our crimes upon the Vietnamese people and beg their forgiveness, or a response to which most all of us seemed to be inclined, "kiss our ass." In that regard, this did not foretell a very desirable future.

I was enjoying the pleasant mental occupation of having listened to the lectures of the last few evenings given by Jim Warner, who was our "Mensa Marine." Jim was so smart he had no idea that he was supposed to seek shelter when it was raining. I'm not sure I ever knew, but perhaps it was not so much his IQ as it was his "Marineness" but he was an absolute contradiction in humanity. Jim had asked a few evenings before if the cell would be interested in bedtime stories in the form of lectures on the history of western philosophy and its impact on our constitution and republican political form of government. WHAT? And from a Marine! If not informative, this should be entertaining, a rather arrogant thought coming from an engineer that avoided spelling, got a D minus in his last course required for graduation, and who had just recently learned how to conjugate a verb from a Naval Academy fighter pilot.

Jim is a book yet to be written all by itself, and since I am not the author to do it, I can only touch on this fascinating individual. He had a confounding past with his education and ladies. His past with the ladies is for the other book to add spice. His past with education was one where he studied not what any institution of higher education wanted, but what was to his liking at any particular time. Consequently, Jim had a few hundred hours of education and no degree. I had never known what a person with a photographic memory was like, but Jim apparently had one.

All wholeheartedly accepted his offer and we started with Socrates, Plato and Aristotle and were proceeding through centuries of the West's great philosophers. It was absolutely fascinating how he could quote whole passages from their writings and teachings.

It was within this context that my hot war, cold war thoughts developed. It was a hot war in that guns were being fired, bombs being dropped, and armies in the field killing each other! But it was taking on a cold war aspect in that the population from which our military gained its support was tiring of the war and showing some impatience with continuing to support it. The Vietnamese people, living under the Communist totalitarian regime and having no say in their opinion, seemed to be resolute in their intent to continue their insurgence as far into the future as necessary. If they wore us and our allies down, as they did historical invaders, and more recently the Japanese and French, we might well find ourselves abandoned and living permanently in a North Vietnamese prison. This could, indeed, turn into what we had been taught as "cold war" imprisonment, which was a lonely isolated confinement, whereas ours was becoming one with several cellmates in communication with other cells. This afforded us an opportunity to confront one of the most insidious aspects of cold war confinement, that of mental atrophy. We would be able to gain

Chapter 22 | Hot or Cold War

from each other's knowledge and experiences, and as with Jim, often in considerable depth.

I reflected on the phases of mental activity I had passed through. During the initial period of interrogations, torture, and being kept alone and isolated from the rest of the American POW's, several things occupied my time. Daydreaming, of course, was a very popular way to pass the time. Planning my future, planning what I would do with my accumulated pay when I was released in "a few months" after the war (recall, I am doing this stint only six months at a time). Planning trips to exotic places was also a popular subject. As those "few months" became a lot more than a few, my mental plans became "tattered" and I went on to other more challenging endeavors.

In the second phase, when I moved in with cellmates and began communicating regularly with other cells, I decided to revisit and remodel the farm and old farm house. I still had nothing on which to write or draw, and nothing by which to do it, so I did all of the remodeling in my head. I started out by laying out various fields on the farm, reworking the barns and, of course, remodeling the house. Once an idea was conceived, I went into as much detail as possible to pass as much time as I could. So, each nail was hammered in with care and each board was fitted and joined in my head. Each facet of an idea was investigated very carefully. After the structure had been built it was necessary to compute how much it would cost to construct, the board feet, the cubic yards of concrete, etc. How much did ready mix concrete for that foundation I planned to pour cost? To find out might require tapping someone up on the wall of the cell next door, asking if anyone knew the price of ready-mix concrete. Within an hour or even minutes, an answer would return, perhaps even from several cells away, that the price of ready-mix concrete in California in 1963 was $22 a cubic yard delivered. There you have it, we had our own "Google." It was a great mental exercise and certainly did a lot to lift my spirit. It was hard to dedicate all that time to a project without some glimmer of hope that someday you might actually have an opportunity to build it. Understandably, this type of mental exercise was also very popular among many of us.

The Eagle Hunts

My thoughts and projects often followed my interest in things mechanical. I proceeded to develop a one-of-a-kind mechanical hay loader, the previously mentioned mechanical hog castrator, the fireplace and numerous other mechanical marvels which probably would have never worked if they had actually been fabricated. In the fireplace project my mental picture of it, including the electrical wiring, the tooled copper and the brick were all very vivid to me, even years after my release. It was as though I had seen it in a *Better Homes & Gardens* magazine.

Some of the men, who were more poetically inclined, memorized verses passed on by other prisoners while others collected various lists of things. We collected a list of the names of our fellow prisoners. As soon as an individual came into the prison system, his name and any information that could be gathered about him was committed to memory. An hour or so each day was spent going over those hundreds of names just to be sure that no one would be forgotten when there was a release.

Of course, most of us, except maybe the youngest and most junior, were well traveled and had eaten in restaurants and bars in different countries, and remembered the best of them. Through our communication system of tapping we compiled a list those places. The list comprised several hundred restaurants, eating places, coffeehouses, and bars all over the world. If another one of us had visited one of these places also, they added their own bits of information about what helped to make it great, novel or unique. "Voila," our own Wikipedia!

I could have traveled almost anywhere in the world and knew of a place to eat, which had made our "best" list. It was especially reassuring to know that these recommendations were made by individuals with interests similar to my own on the basis of a personal dining or drinking experience. It was a list I looked forward to using with great hope and enthusiasm one day.

During the period of time when I was very ill I felt I should try to take my mind off of that particular problem. It seemed when one has nothing to occupy their mind it gravitates to worrisome issues, and worrisome issues seemed to be plentiful. Dying was right up at the top, perhaps exceeded only by losing one's mind. Today the psychiatric

Chapter 22 | Hot or Cold War

world has a word for it, they call it "catastrophizing," assuming that an incident, regardless of how inconsequential will degenerate to a worst-case scenario, a catastrophe. This, it seems, was a demon that would again rear its ugly head years after my release from captivity. But, in order to settle my mind and relieve it of ever present thoughts of illness, torture and death, I decided on meditation. Never having been exposed to meditation, as my mind had always been a whirl of ideas and thoughts that were constantly in the act of being evaluated or activated, I was unsure of where to go, so I started with thinking about "nothing." Very well, what is nothing? The closest concept to nothing that I could imagine was the dark void of space, just black space. Try thinking of nothing but black space, a totally black vacuum. You can't do it, there are just too many other things going on in your mind. In the Zen aspects of Tai Chi, one is instructed to allow these meddling thoughts to pass through your mind. You can't keep them out so let them pass through without further consideration, like flipping pages of a book. This approach had not occurred to me, therefore, my solution was to think of the black vacuum of space, nothing but black. It was my goal. I quickly realized that just blacking out your mind did not work, so a strict mental discipline was going to be required. I started with a small black dot. I just thought of a small black dot. Then I concentrated on the small black dot to make it larger and larger. At first, I could not expand the dot very much before some wild thought came blowing in, but I persisted, and eventually the dot became larger before some spurious thought popped it like a black balloon. Eventually, I could gradually expand the black dot to encompass almost the entirety of my conscience mind and conscious thought process. I do not know what caused the black balloon to burst except that maybe I momentarily went to sleep or lost consciousness and it was burst by a subconscious thought. The thought control and mental discipline required to continually think the black dot larger, only to have it burst, and then start over, left little else to think about. It was mentally exhausting, emotionally relaxing, and did a great deal to achieve the desired goal. The very aspect of this mental mechanism was interesting to think about in its own right.

The Eagle Hunts

I'm sure I'm not the only one who had similar unique ways to rid their minds of stressful and mentally destabilizing thoughts. I built, created, designed, compiled information from others and concentrated on "nothing." Every day was indeed, a busy day.

It was these thoughts that brought me to realize that we POWs, collectively, were proceeding down a very healthy mental path and we should continue to expand on what had started out for me at Son Tay as learning some French from Paul Galanti. I was not the only one who was thinking this because, as you will see, it all started coming together when we returned to the Hilton much sooner than anticipated.

But before returning to learn French, because I had spent more time falling in love than studying in Mr. Stankowski's senior English class at Hickman High School, Paul sent me back to remedial English to learn the basic rudimentary aspects of my own language. Some of these aspects were parts of speech and conjugating a verb. Paul felt it was necessary to correct my lack of accomplishment in learning the English language so that he could then start teaching French again. I was beginning to see his logic. Okay, let's review; I started French, then oops English again, then back to French, and now not to forget our Mensa Marine, philosophy. Who had time to worry about being a prisoner of war?

CHAPTER 23

BIG CELLS

Our time in the new camp and the pleasure of such accommodations was experienced for only a few months. It was on the night of the 21st of November, 1970 at what I would guess to have been just a bit past midnight when all hell broke loose. There had been a bombing pause called by President Johnson in 1968 to hopefully entice the North Vietnamese back to the negotiation table in Paris. The incentive was that the pause could be ended at any time and the bombing resumed if the North Vietnamese would not cooperate, which they were not inclined to do.

The impact of surface to air missiles lighting up the night sky with bright flashes as they exploded, the firing of anti-aircraft guns, and sounds of attacking jets jolted us awake and made it clear that "Rolling Thunder" (the code name given to the previous bombing campaign of NVN) was back. It was a total surprise to the gooks; sirens went off, they shot their guns just willy-nilly, pure bedlam, and all we could do was look at each other in our large newly whitewashed rooms of eight prisoners and wonder what the hell was going on? A raid at Son Tay never really occurred to us as we had not been at Son Tay for several months and had tried to communicate that to our intelligence services.

The next day we were told to roll up our stuff and prepare to be moved. Really, again, where? It was the usual question, with the always unknown answer. There were the blindfolds, guard's eeping, exotic odors of water buffalo dung and food being prepared in large woks along the road. Arrival was a bit more involved; we walked around corners, through large doorways and gates arriving at a huge steel double door. It was dark green with peeling paint, rust, and a crude iron frame, perhaps 4 feet wide and 8 feet tall for each side of the door. Our blindfolds were removed and we were ushered in with 30 or 40 others.

The cell was large, perhaps 20 feet wide and 40 feet long with a solid concrete pedestal in the center about two feet high sloping from the center down slightly to the outside. The pedestal was wide enough for two "blackest criminals" to lay head-to-head in the center with feet pointed to the outside wall leaving ample room to walk between the pedestal and the outside walls of the cell. In each cell was an elevated Asian style "shitter," or bathroom, in a more polite vernacular. Polite as one might want to be, it was nevertheless a very nasty spot. It stood on an elevated platform perhaps two steps up from the slick and slimy concrete floor, a platform molded out of concrete and on the top of this platform were two or three bowl shaped depressions approximately two feet in diameter and six inches deep with a four inch hole or drain in the back of the bowl. At this point in my description one would be expected to stand in the bowl, squat, and dump down into the hole. One could, however, just stand on the edge of the rim and pee into the bowl. That was no problem. The problem was where do you put your feet if you have to squat. In their wisdom, the designers of this system realized one would find their feet in the middle of all the action and so they designed a couple of foot pads that rose out of the bowl so one could stand on the foot pads while squatting, take care of their business with any urine just running around the foot pads in the bowl arriving at the drain in the back. If one were squatting and aimed well the excrement would fall straight through the hole. As good aim was required and in the hard-to-find entertainment aspect of our confinement, a "bomb release" that hit the bullseye and passed straight through the hole presented a bit of a personal challenge to some excruciatingly bored fighter pilots.

One added aspect of interest were the ladies (not held in the same esteem in that society as we do ours) who changed the five-gallon pots that were under the drain hole. There seemed to be no regular time in which the pot changing occurred and as one might expect it was something of a startling event to be relieving oneself only to see the

Chapter 23 | Big Cells

ladies changing the buckets looking up at you through the drain hole. Well, if you find this disgusting then I can confess that we did too, even in our austere surroundings. How did one flush? A large drum of water in the room with a cup that's how. Dip some water out and toss it into the bowl and flee. Now place this operation in the prison setting, add lots of humidity, mold, fungus, slime, and no fresh air and how could you call it anything but a "Shitter?"

Shortly after arriving, we were able to communicate with some South Vietnamese pilots who had been interred in a cell next to us. As they could understand the Vietnamese on the public loud speakers on the street and the camp radio, they informed us that the Americans had attacked the compound at Son Tay in a failed attempt to rescue some American "blackest criminals" who were imprisoned there, but who were moved before the attack. During the next couple of years, we were able to gather more details of the raid from later shoot downs. After our release in February of 1973, however, actual details of the raid became known to us. American Air Commandos and Army Special Forces along with numerous other supporting Navy and Air Force operations executed a highly classified and dangerous mission within the very shadow of Hanoi. They snaked an attack force made up of helicopters and A1-E prop driven fighters all led by secret specially modified C-130 aircraft through the mountains and valleys of Laos and North Vietnam during the inky darkness of night arriving at Son Tay, where they crashed a specially modified HH-53 helicopter inside the walls of the small compound only to discover Son Tay was empty. The nearby buildings which were expected to only be a secondary school were instead a barracks for a large contingent of well armed troops, the nationality of which are not even yet confirmed. They did not appear to be Vietnamese due to stature and skin color. A shootout ensued as our would be rescuers secured and eliminated this threat, then moved their positions to secure the camp, while others performed a thorough search of the empty cells to make sure no POWs were accidentally overlooked. They departed on the other helicopters standing by to make the extraction. Numerous corpses littered the site but a head count upon extraction of our guys revealed no fatalities and only one injury, a broken ankle from the crashed helicopter due to an errant fire extinguisher.

Often, and to this day, I can only fantasize what it would have been like to have been there, in the dead of night, to see our guys smash in our cell doors, tell us they were Americans to take us home. And then to be ushered through the covering smoke with orange flashes of gunfire lighting up the areas around us and the smoke and smell of gunfire. I imagine being shoved or hauled aboard a huge ominous looking black rescue helicopter, the subdued red instrument lights from the cockpit, the helmeted pilot and copilot awaiting us as though this was what their life achievement was to be, the tethered and helmeted loadmaster's getting us strapped into the web seats along the edges of the seemingly monstrous helicopter with dim red and yellow lights scattered throughout its cargo hold. There would be the smell so well known to all of us, a smell of business, our business, to which we longed to return, canvas, jet exhaust, oils and lubricants, so familiar to the military and aviation. We would have heard the Loadmasters yell "they're all aboard sir," then the secure retreat of our troops as they jumped aboard and the windup sound of the twin jet engines and increasing rotor speed, the light bounces as we lift off and us craning our heads to look out of the portals along the side of the big blackbird as we leave the smoke, fire, death and destruction that had been our prison. As we watched it disappear and the lights of nearby Hanoi fade our escort A-1E fighters would join us and we and the other extraction HH-53's would disappear over the hills and mountains from where they had so silently come only moments before, to freedom - to home.[*]

We were ecstatic that our country had heard us and had tried to rescue us, what a lift. Nevertheless, we realized that a similar try would be impossible in the center of Hanoi. Years later during a joint reunion with the Son Tay Raiders we learned they thought we held a grudge and blamed them for not arriving before we were moved. They were heartbroken at what they perceived as a failure. But it was heartwarming to see their smiles, and even some tears, to learn that indeed we did not, even in the slightest degree blame them, that we

---

* Parts taken from "The Raid, the Son Tay Prison Rescue Mission" by Ben Schemmer.

Chapter 23 | Big Cells

held them in the very highest esteem, and in fact our morale was given a tremendous boost by knowing someone could "hear" us, and that our country in the form of our toughest, brightest, and best would take such a risk, on even a chance that we might be rescued. It gave us hope that our nation and its people had not forgotten us. That, my reader, is what being American is all about. It is in that belief we had faith, and which kept us alive. We will always stand taller, salute, and have moist eyes when the flag passes. We have always had the greatest regard, even love for those guys, and I am very proud to be an honorary Son Tay Raider.

In our communication with our South Vietnamese allies in the adjoining cell we used the wall at the back of our cell and it needed to be secured from the eyes of our watchful guards, especially after the raid at Son Tay. They were petrified that another raid might be in the making. After all it was apparent our country wanted us back in spite of the rhetoric from their leadership that we would be abandoned in their prisons. There was this two inch iron pipe stuck through the front wall of our cell about two feet in front of our side wall and about four feet above the floor. It was in an absolutely perfect position to see anyone tapping or otherwise communicating to the adjacent cell via that wall. Also, we had been provided with a reed short handled broom. It was bushy but the handle would fit into the pipe snugly and so there we chose to store it. However, our guards reported this surveillance inconvenience (plugged up spy pipe) to the camp authorities and our senior ranking officer was called out for interrogation to explain how we had made a radio by sticking their reed broom into their iron pipe. After pondering how to answer this impossibly difficult radio technology issue, even though we had landed a man on the moon, he gave up and came clean. He explained that since we had been given such a "nice" broom for which to keep our cell "neat and clean" we sought a way to keep it from being stepped on and abused. Hence, the perfect storage place was the pipe, off the floor but handy. The explanation had some merit and after a review of the broom we were able to keep it to block the pipe. Go figure. Maybe it's logical that those who thought we might turn the moon off if they didn't

The Eagle Hunts

treat us better could make a long range low frequency radio out of an iron pipe and grass reeds. Maybe?

The gooks lived in constant fear that our guys might try a Son Tay type raid again, which became acutely evident when in May of 1972 we mined the harbor at Haiphong located just east of Hanoi; it was North Vietnam's largest and busiest port. Such an operation required diversionary air raids, ground fire, and surface to air missile suppression, as well as a defense for our fighter bombers against those annoying MIGS, which in some cases were flown by even more annoying Russians. It was an attack that lacked nothing. Aircraft were roaring overhead, surface to air missiles exploding, bombs going off with reverberating detonations and the huge anti-aircraft guns firing in an almost continuous boom. From overhead came the unmistakably terrifying scream of the F-105 Thunderchiefs pulling out of bombing runs and the roar of F-4s circling overhead while lighting targets for laser bombs dropped by other F-4s. For the first time in my five years of captivity I was scared, afraid of what I do not know, but I trembled with fear, most nearly incapacitated. I later confessed to our senior ranking officer that I did not think I could have even reacted rationally, had I needed to. Years later the answer came in the form of an explanation of the effects of malaria. Neurological damage by the parasite can induce numerous manifestations of mental health issues including anxieties. It was that, or I just had the "crap" scared out of me. In either case, it was probably the beginning of what we now call Post Traumatic Stress Syndrome (PTSD), an insidious little known demon at that time, and one which returned to haunt the life out of me for years and cut short my career as a military officer.

Wild eyed and fearful, the guards found their way to the outside sills of the large barred windows high up on the walls of the cell. There was one in each of about four windows along the cell wall toward the inside of the prison. Each had a grenade, which looked like a tin can with a handle, in their hand and another on their belt and, of course, an AK-47 slung over their shoulder. There was no casual reason they were there. They were there to make sure that if the Americans were foolish enough to try another Son Tay type raid to rescue us, they would find nothing but a cell full of dead and seriously

Chapter 23 | Big Cells

wounded prisoners. Those hand grenades thrown down into that concrete box of a cell would have been devastating, not to mention the automatic weapons fire that would inevitably follow.

I have never been known to give our captors any credit for much of anything but I will give them credit for keeping their cool at this time, or at least waiting for the order from someone who was keeping their cool. If any of them had panicked and started tossing grenades, then this would very likely be a story untold. I understood clearly the tenuousness of our situation regarding the security of the prison, and the North Vietnamese willingness to sacrifice our lives to prevent any rescue.

Jean Smith, our cell senior ranking officer was a large and impressively statured, red haired, fair skinned, blue eyed and compassionate but very tough Air Force F-105 pilot with uncommon leadership qualities and the rank of Major. After the raid I decided to discreetly confer with him in the event of future raids rather than just passively going before a firing squad by hand grenades should it resort to that. Perhaps our cell should organize a defense response that would at least afford us the morale value of fighting to the very end and taking as many of our intended executioners with us as possible. At best, maybe we could ward off part of an unintended assault until a cease-fire could be called saving the lives of at least some of us. A leadership council discussed the subject and embraced it. Our intention was passed to the other cells and we proceeded with the planning.

Some of the features involved human ladders that would allow our strongest and most athletic to leap to the window sills, yank the hand grenades from the gooks and throw them outside. Then they would either pull our captors relatively small heads through the bars and break their necks, or grab them by their clothing and strangle them against the bars. Once disabled, we would pull their AK-47s inside to be given to those who knew something of its operation for defense of the cell. There were reserves that would remain shielded behind the low concrete pedestal in the center of the room whose job it would be to replace the members of those window attack teams if they were disabled. The eventual outcome of such a plan was not a pleasant thought, but if anything, we felt more like the defenders of the Alamo than sheep in a slaughterhouse and that was good. We were warriors and we liked feeling there was still fight left in us.

CHAPTER 24

BACK TO SCHOOL

In cells of 35, more or less, there was a natural and welcomed expansion of learning from each other. We were a very unique prisoner population; almost all of us were college or military academy graduates, and had a broad range of education, experience, and expertise. We learned a great deal from one another, helping our mutual growth and development, and keeping our minds, as well as our bodies fit, which was paramount to our survival.

Some of our learning was academic, some entertainment, some hobbies, some personal experiences as in travels, some religion, and some literature. Oh, and not to be sold short, we had some who could provide tales of sex and intrigue, especially sex. So, we developed this wealth of knowledge into a full blown academic and social program, including entertainment and religion.

The academic program was extensive. We offered courses in French, advanced French, Spanish, advanced Spanish, German, and Russian. The advanced courses were conversational courses, but as one might expect, having no native speakers of the languages, we ended up developing our own dialect of the languages, not intentionally, but nevertheless we did. Also, offered in our curriculum was algebra, calculus, architectural drawing, art, and music. Other courses were also offered but those mentioned were extensive and usually took several weeks. We broke the day into two academic periods, morning and afternoon. These periods were further broken down into two sections of 45 minutes to an hour. Classes were held three to five times a week just as in a college curriculum.

The Eagle Hunts

Our language program encouraged us to memorize words, conjugate verbs, and choose tenses, excellent exercises in using our minds. Of course, we had an abundant amount of time to develop our foreign language vocabularies. We drew upon the memories of those who had been formally trained in a foreign language and had also studied their English rules of grammar. Some of our group, such as Navy Lieutenant J.G. Paul Galanti, had traveled to France and studied French in a residence program. This experience added a bit of vernacular, and perhaps one might even say saltiness to some of our conversation. In 1970 while at Son Tay, I lived with three other men, one of these being Paul, who at that time started teaching a couple of us an introductory course in French. As previously mentioned, Paul's first challenge was to teach me English, which he did, and much more. I'm not sure why he put up with my ignorance, except what else did he have to do? Plus, there may have been some entertainment value to teaching high school English to this bozo from Missouri. Also, Paul was able to point out the similarities between English and French, and as French vocabulary was a strength of his, it helped us commit to memory a lot of French words and slang.

Later, when we moved in with the larger group, we learned that another one of the men, Air Force First Lieutenant Bill Butler, was also a very good student of French, and his particular forte was grammar. He enabled us to expand and improve our knowledge of grammar and syntax. Bill, as we shall find out, was also very gifted in music.

The four or five of us who started our French lessons early at Son Tay had spent a year building vocabulary and learning grammar by the time we arrived back at the Hilton. So, Paul and Bill continued teaching the basics of French to the other men in the room who so desired. At the same time, the four or five of us who had progressed beyond this stage formed conversational groups and instructed the men who "graduated" from Bill and Paul's basic French course.

I assigned various topics of conversation to utilize the newly learned words from our constantly growing vocabulary. I told my students for the next lesson we would employ those words commonly used about the house and learning them would be their homework.

Chapter 24 | Back to School

When class time came, I asked each student to tell a story about a house, perhaps the house he lived in, or his parent's house. I questioned them about the color of the floor, the ceiling, the walls, or such details as the number of windows in the house. This required the use of previously learned vocabulary and they would, of course, be required to answer in French. I loved doing this, and took lots of poetic license, with dramatic gestures and expressions, as I expected a Frenchman might exhibit. This added some flair and a bit of amusement to the conversation which everyone seemed to enjoy. After having spent quite a bit of time in France, post retirement, I realized I wasn't that far off with the drama in which I took such pleasure in spicing up our conversations.

Along with this stage of our internment that included larger cells came a seemingly more relaxed emphasis by the guards on restricting communication between cells. Even though the gooks seem to be less stringent on their enforcement of "the camp regulations," they did not provide pens, pencils, paper, or any other writing materials so we still had to be innovative in creating these vocabulary lists. Written on small sheets of toilet paper, about two inches by two inches, they were very crude and rough. The pens we used were made out of sharpened bamboo and we discovered that the purple antifungal medicine that they let us keep made excellent ink. This antifungal medicine was our highest quality ink, but we also made ink from cigarette ashes, roof tile dust, coal dust, and anything else that we could crush and mix up with a little water to write on the crude paper.

The words were recorded as best we could remember, and some of them I think, must have been just made up. Paul always said, if in a French conversation you came upon a word which you needed but did not know in French, just say it in English with a French accent and you would be understood a surprising amount of the time. It's true; we are so much closer to the French than most in our unilingual society ever realize. Occasionally, however, we would be inspected and if our materials were discovered by the guards, they were obligated to confiscate our writing supplies and vocabulary lists. So, we started over. When someone new came into the cell, or we were able to talk

The Eagle Hunts

to a member of another cell that had similar language interests to ours, we exchanged lists.

All of the languages we studied were done in a similar way, except Russian. We did not have very much scope or depth in Russian and limited the presentation to just an orientation. I became conversational in French, somewhat less fluent in Spanish, and was able to communicate a few ideas in German. I became familiar with some of the German rules of grammar and knew most of the basic words like numbers and days of the week.

Less involved courses in topics other than language were also offered. One in particular was an outstanding demonstration of ingenuity and originality. Bill Butler, of French fame, whose hobby was music, volunteered a course wherein he explained all of the different tones, harmonics, scales, and chords. To give us some idea of the actual sounds he was talking about, Bill found a way to make those sounds. First, he laid out the outline of a large piano keyboard on the floor in the back of the cell with some white soapstone, which we found in the broken concrete of the courtyard, to represent the white keys. Then, for the black keys, some pieces of coal were likewise acquired.

He directed members of our choir, which he had organized and who were very capable singers, to stand on various keys. Each man would then key off of what Bill thought would be a middle C, and sing the tone for the key on which the choir member stood. Bill hummed the tone for B, or C, or G sharp, or whatever he chose it to be, and ran the scale. He then asked some men to hum at the same time thereby producing a cord. Bill demonstrated how much difference there was in the sound of an augmented, diminished, a minor, a major, and a seventh cord. He did this by having a man move from one key to the next and change his tone, just as if you had moved your finger from one key of an organ to another. He also demonstrated discords and disharmony. It was magnificent. His course of music appreciation lasted approximately three weeks and each class was eagerly anticipated. I could not imagine that the voices of a group of crusty fighter pilots which had been locked up in prison for five years, give or take, tortured, beaten, and

Chapter 24 | Back to School

malnourished could voice such tonal qualities. It's one thing to hear a soloist singing acapella, but yet another to hear a group coordinate their tones with such harmonial accuracy minus the assistance of any apparatus like a piano, and doing so using the tonal memory of only one person.

For his final class, Bill demonstrated that many of the songs popular at the time we were shot down were played with only three or four different cords. To demonstrate this, he asked the choir members to stand on the cord, step to the next note for the next cord, and hum the chords while he sang the words to the song: "Blue suede shoes," "26 miles," and several other songs that we remembered. It was a dynamic and amazing climax to his course.

Our time was also occupied with many other activities. We had starting receiving packages from home and included in some were decks of playing cards and chess pieces. There were games like bridge and chess, both of which attracted several devotees, and considerable experience and expertise existed in both. This naturally led to both bridge and chess tournaments. Since academics were conducted during the week, these diversionary activities were normally held on our "off" days of Saturday and Sunday. Tournaments, of course, lent themselves to betting and wagering. Due to the austerity of our existence and accommodations, there was very little which we had to wager. On occasion, we received a banana and it was considered a delicacy, and a prize to wager. Two excellent chess players loved to wager bananas on who would win a chess match, one being "Chance" Collins of Collins, Mississippi, and yep you guessed it, named after his grandparents. Chance wagered on anything, hence, the nickname Chance. He was the happiest guy in the cell, a consummate optimist, always finding something to smile and chuckle about; the other was Denver Key, a Navy A4 jock from one of the Carolinas. He was also an eternal optimist with more intelligence and common sense than anyone should be allowed to have. Denver came to be known as "Denvers" by Chance and, of course, by the rest of us also. Between the Chance and Denvers wagering on their own skill, and side betting, several bananas changed hands as a result of their games. After our release had been announced by

The Eagle Hunts

our captors and the days of it drew closer it seems that the Chance and Denvers wagers took on an air of substantial margin, that is, betting on bananas that we had not yet received nor could realistically anticipate getting in our remaining time. One could only anticipate the final payoff would have to come after our repatriation and a visit to the grocery store. So, the wagers grew larger, and I do not know what the final tally was, except that I do know that a few months after we were released Denvers arrived at Chance's home bearing a big grin and full stalk of bananas. And so it went among scoundrels.

Supplementing our weekday academic schedule, we had an evening entertainment program. One of us was appointed entertainment chairman, and it was their responsibility to find out what each of the prisoners could share with the group. This sharing was usually informational as well as entertaining. "Show and tell" might be a way of describing it. The topic usually was presented in an hour or two, it wasn't something you could build a whole course with, but a one-time presentation. For example, we had a series on history of sports activities and hobbies. Our hobbyists, athletes, and sports enthusiasts became our teachers, and lectured on subjects like skeet shooting, trapping, literature, camping, skiing, sailing, hot air ballooning, gliding, go-carting, and carpentry among others.

A few years before my departure to Southeast Asia, I had visited the Civil War battlefield at Gettysburg, which seemed a perfect topic for a history lecture. Rolling up our bed and mats, spreading our blankets over them, we simulated the battlefield terrain at Gettysburg. Small pieces of toilet paper ripped in thin strips represented the roads and our chess pieces took the place of troops. Appointed assistants and myself moved them about the hills and fields representing Little Round Top, Big Round Top, the Wheat Field, Devil's Den and various other Gettysburg landmarks. We fought the battle as best we could remember. Our maneuvers probably were wrong but eventually the Blue did defeat the Gray after Pickett's charge, and although I'm sure you won't find our version of the battle of Gettysburg in your history books, everyone got a great deal of enjoyment out of it.

Chapter 24 | Back to School

Every Saturday and Sunday night was "movie" night. It wasn't the movie itself that was as important as the person who told his version of the movie. The presentations ranged from comedy to drama to mystery. One Sunday night we were told "War and Peace" by Russ Temperly. I'm sure you have never heard of the comedy "War and Peace," but Russ was a comic by nature. He did not think so, nor did we, for he was a rough-cut Air Force Captain, F-105 jock who looked as if he would be very comfortable with a minimal amount of camping gear, a large rifle with a scope and some jerky to eat, just by himself, walking through the Rockies on a wild sheep hunting expedition. Russ pantomimed the action, acted out the various parts, both male and female, changed the pitch of his voice, and thoroughly enjoyed his multifaceted role of hero, heroine, antagonists, producer, and director. He absolutely kept us in stitches for a couple of hours. In my estimation, "War and Peace" very definitely was a comedy and it was a great boost for our morale.

"Grand Prix" was another colossal production. At the beginning a man was stationed in each of the four corners of the cell. The narrator and producer asked the audience to close their eyes. Sound effects followed on cue as the story unfolded. These sound effects were supplied by the four men in the cell corners mimicking the sound of a particular sports car. I was pleased to be picked to play the part of a Maserati as one fourth of this quadraphonic production. As I recall, we were also joined in the windows by several nervous guards responding to all the racket of these four high performance engines being fired up, but they soon settled down and remained to enjoy the production.

Our movie productions were not entirely a repeat of the original production; they resembled a building block process. Someone might query, "Is there anyone in the cell who has seen Airport?" Two or three might reply they had. Gathering in the back of the room they would talk out the plot, trying to ascertain how the movie had actually been written. Each of the contributors usually had a different slant on the plot and it fell upon the storyteller to put it together. The result often was a collection of bits and pieces of disconnected action but the producer simply filled in the gaps

The Eagle Hunts

with plot and dialogue of his own creation. Most often the movies didn't come out like their original Hollywood producers had intended, but they were just as entertaining, and sometimes the rewritten version was the better of the two.

Years after my release and return to the States, I delivered a speech on how we POW's spent our time to Air Force ROTC cadets at the University of Missouri School of Mines, at Rolla, Missouri. At the conclusion of my speech I learned that a former Air Force Sergeant, David Arthur, had worn a POW/MIA bracelet with my name and date of capture for over four years. David was 23, self-employed, and a native of Rolla, Missouri. I had not been told beforehand that David would follow my speech to make one of his own. David spoke of how he prayed for my safe return and that I was his adopted prisoner. David spoke with great feeling. He was forced to stop several times because he was overcome with emotion. David presented the bracelet to me as many of those in the audience wiped away tears. I present to you below the speech given on that occasion. I feel it captures so well the emotion of the people who wore these bracelets, and who prayed for us and our families. This is what it's like to be American. Thank you, David, and the many others who gave us so much hope.

> "Good evening, ladies and gentlemen. This evening is one of the greatest evenings of my life, and I would like to share it with you. When the great, good news hit our country that our prisoners of war would soon be coming home, I was happy. I was excited as I'm sure you were also. But I was more excited and thankful when I read the released prisoner list and saw the name that I had been looking for. It was none other than Major John Clark. You see, some four years ago I adopted Major Clark as "my prisoner" in thoughts and prayer. In January of 1971, I was serving in the Air Force, stationed at Vandenberg Air Force Base, California when I heard about "prisoner of war bracelets." A POW/MIA organization was making these bracelets so that we could not forget our prisoners.

Chapter 24 | Back to School

I, along with many others, ordered the bracelet requesting a prisoner from my home state, Missouri. Upon receiving my bracelet, many thoughts raced through my head about this man whose name was inscribed on it. Mainly, was my prisoner alive? How did he become a prisoner? What did he look like? Because I only knew three things about him. He was from Missouri; he was listed as missing March 12, 1967, and his name was Captain John Clark.

At this time, I adopted him as "my prisoner." I slipped that bracelet on my wrist to leave it there until I had heard of my prisoner's release. Shortly after receiving it, I was stationed at Ubon, Thailand to work with communications. Once while on duty in the control tower, another Captain (I'm sorry I don't recall his name) noticed this bracelet and the name on it. He told me that he had known Major Clark when he was listed as missing. He told me he was a graduate from the University of Missouri and he was flying F-4s when listed as missing, to me this was exciting because I had found out a little bit more about "my prisoner."

The longer I wore the bracelet, the more encouraging it became to me. It helped my overseas tour pass more swiftly, as I wanted to do what I could to get him back again, because I saw him is an individual who gave up his freedom trying to save someone else's. Many times, in prayer, I would ask God to strengthen him when he was weak! Lift him up when he was down! Brighten things for him in his darkest hours.

Many times, while working on or around the flight lines area, I would see our beautiful jets taking off for their targets, and my thoughts would be that maybe a bomb would land close enough to Major Clark that he could hear its blast and know that we were still fighting for his release and that it might encourage him to hold on a little longer. Finishing my overseas tour, I was stationed

The Eagle Hunts

at Kirtland Air Force Base, New Mexico, where I finished my enlistment it was there, just two months before I was discharged, that I received a great, happy, exciting news that my prisoner, Major Clark, was coming home. Being thankful and overwhelmed with joy, I knew my prayers have been answered.

I took the bracelet off and put it away knowing that my prisoner was safe. Driving down the highway a week ago yesterday, I heard on the radio where Major Clark was going to be speaking here in Rolla. I feel honored to meet Major Clark and if he would come forward, I would like to present to him his bracelet that I wore."

Sergeant David Arthur.

CHAPTER 25

ONWARD CHRISTIAN SOLDIERS

Church services on Sunday were regular and almost everyone in the room attended. There was a choir, a sermon, and occasionally communion. The services were generally as nondenominational as we could present, and anyone was welcomed to present a service regardless of their beliefs or denomination. All were equally appreciated and respected. After the first service our senior ranking officer, Major Jean Smith, was called out to see the camp commander and told that church services were against camp regulations. In their mind, it too closely resembled the indoctrination gatherings directed by the Communist political leaders of their various Vietnamese governmental, military, and political organizations. However, Jean informed him we were worshiping our God, we believed we had the right to do so, and would continue to do so.

Shortly after we started gathering for our church service the next Sunday, keys clunked in the large iron doors at the end of the cell. Swinging open with the screech of bare rusty metal against bare rusty metal, they revealed a stern looking camp officer and two armed guards both fully equipped with AK-47s and pistols. Looking about, the officer's eyes fell on our SRO, who had taken a prominent position in the front of the cell. The officer signaled, and the guards escorted him out of the room firmly closing the large iron doors with a resounding clunk that seemed to signal an ominous resolve. In our American psyche is the belief that we have the right to believe

The Eagle Hunts

in God, or not, and if we do, to believe however we wish. We may accept another religious mission or not, and we may choose to accept our religious call to mission and expose others to beliefs of our faith, or not. It is our freedom to do so but it is likewise our belief that in doing so we respect the rights of others to reject our mission, and in this we are guided by our Constitution, and the courts. They ensure no specific religion, or lack of, is sanctioned or discriminated against in favor of another, hence, we all respect each other, and our beliefs. It is pervasive and deeply ingrained in our way of life.

And so, the line had been crossed when we were told we could not together worship our Almighty. To this we were willing to stand up and challenge. In refusing to order us to desist in our church service, our SROs were risking isolation, indoctrination, intimidation, and yes, even torture. When I say the plural, SROs, this was happening in each of the several large cells of Americans confined at the Hanoi Hilton. All of the cells were connected together, and all were in contact via the tap code or signing. We all knew the risk and were willing to accept it. Those next higher in rank stepped forward to assume the position of SRO as the individual whose rank of SRO immediately preceding them had stepped forward to refuse the Camp Commanders demands, and been summarily removed from the cell. This was not just a voluntary action, this was included in our military Code of Conduct, to paraphrase, if one is senior, they will take command. It was one reason why the Vietnamese worked so hard to keep us isolated from our senior officers and to force us to break our Code of Conduct. Each man in the large cell had previously compared his rank and "date of rank" with each other to establish a precise man by man seniority within the cell. We were ready and willing, each of us, even the sick, to step forward at their time and be removed. But as we hoped, though reluctant to expect, our captors ran out of individual cells in which to isolate those who were removed and were beginning to realize no matter how many SROs they removed from our cell there would always be another, until there was no one left. So, they conceded to negotiate with us regarding our worship service in exchange for maintaining an acceptable level of security. Two of the demands they made were to present the camp officer, for his approval,

Chapter 25 | Onward Christian Soldiers

the sermon which was to be given and the words to the songs that were to be sung during the service. That was acceptable since it permitted use of a pen and paper by which we would write down the words of the sermons and songs. It could also be used for other writing, like language vocabulary and that was a rare thing indeed. Each of the men who had been removed from the cell after assuming the position of SRO were returned, no worse for the adventure, and the Camp Commander negotiated with the SRO of our entire cell. It was a tacit recognition that we had a military structure which was not approved by the camp regulations. We won once in a while, but they still had the guns and keys.

It was not by luck that the first song we submitted was "Onward Christian Soldiers." If the lyrics of that song are not a part of your religious memory you might enjoy looking them up. I offer the first couple of stanzas below. Within the cell were men who could remember several verses, and any gaps in their memory were filled in by others.

> 1. "**Onward Christian soldiers, marching as to war**
> **With the cross of Jesus going on before.**
> **Christ the royal Master, leads against the flow,**
> **Forward into battle see his banners go!**
>
> **Refrain:**
> **Onward Christian soldiers, marching as to war,**
> **With the cross of Jesus going on before.**
>
> 2. **At the sign of triumph Satan's host doth flee:**
> **On then, Christian soldiers, on to victory!**
> **Hell's foundations quiver at the shout of praise;**
> **Brothers, lift your voices, loud your anthems raise.**
>
> **Refrain:**
> **Onward Christian soldiers, marching as to war,**
> **With the cross of Jesus going on before.**

The Eagle Hunts

And on with the 3rd, 4th, & 5th verses.

The gooks went absolutely ballistic. Here we had the gall to put forth a war song as a religious hymn sung in church. How absolutely perfidious!!

To our captor's vein swelling challenge of the song, Jean responded that all they had to do was consult the numerous Christian hymnals among the many denominations and they would find this song. It was really a church hymn. Flabbergasted and taken aback, they allowed it to be sung but watched from the high windows with AK-47s at the ready, obviously very apprehensive about the possibility of these uncanny Americans springing forth with what resources of war only their imagination could conjure up. So, for this show of solidarity, our Jewish, Mormon, agnostic, atheistic and other non-Christian individuals joined in to add to the demonstration that we were of different beliefs, but all were Americans. It may have been our greatest triumph.

Infrequently, some novel way of passing the time would arise. One of our cellmates had occasion to visit the medical shack and discovered a scale. Stepping on it he saw how much he weighed, then quickly stepped off before the Vietnamese guard realized what he had done. This doesn't seem like a big thing now, but to do something that bold under the circumstances was gutsy to say the least. After returning, he reported the scale and his findings to the rest of us whereupon our curiosity was naturally piqued. The next couple of guys that chanced out that way also stepped on the scale and learned their weight. Unfortunately, the guards eventually caught on and made the scale inaccessible.

Suddenly and very expectedly everyone became curious about their weight. We had been on a very strange and sparse diet for several years and it was obvious that we had lost considerable weight. We expected that the weight loss had been slow enough that we had been accustomed to seeing it and therefore did not realize what our actual weight lost must have been. Comparing our physical selves with one another was just about the only comparison that we had. We remembered the days when we first walked into the cell block, saw the other prisoners and thought, "good grief, these guys look

Chapter 25 | Onward Christian Soldiers

terrible." However, at this point years later, they did not look so bad. One had to assume that you looked almost as bad as they had looked those years before, so how could you not wonder what you really did weigh.

    Denvers and I decided that a way had to be found to weigh those who did not know their weight. As the plan unfolded, Denvers, in addition to everything else having being credited to him, was height challenged but muscular and bold. We needed a balance beam and there were several heavy teak two inches by twelve inches by eight foot beams, normally used as bed boards, stacked up against the cell block wall just outside its door, close to our bathing area. The plan was for me and some others to create a distraction, and while the guards were checking into the distraction, Denvers and another bold one of us would grab one of the boards and whisk it into the cell. Being caught could cause Denvers and several of us to suffer some rather severe consequences because the gooks would most likely decide we wanted the big board for an escape attempt. On the morning this risky event was to take place, and just shortly before our distracting effort began, we heard banging and clunking near the cell block door. Looking over my shoulder I saw Denvers had decided not to wait for the distraction or his designated assistant. Why was never determined, but at that point it was irrelevant. Quickly we began distracting the guards by demonstrating some concern over a large rat. The guards, being interested in what was alarming us, rushed to investigate with guns at the ready. Denvers in his haste had not waited for assistance and as these beams were large and very heavy, he could only carry one end, allowing the other end to drag along behind. As I had positioned myself facing the door, I could not help be amused at seeing Denvers disappearing inside the cell block door with this huge ironwood beam bouncing along behind him and completely unnoticed by our ever alert guards. Go figure. God is ever with us whether we know or not. Shortly after, as we finished describing our alarm to the guards at the fictitious huge rat we had supposedly seen, Denvers emerged from the cell block with his cocky signature smirk. We had acquired our balance beam.

The Eagle Hunts

We placed the beam onto a bamboo rod in the back of the cell where none of the guards could see. We then took water buckets and put them on each end of the balance beam and balanced it with each bucket about half full of water. One of the men whose weight was known stood on one end of the beam and someone else, whose weight we did not know, stood on the opposite end. We then dipped water from one bucket to the other to balance the beam with both men still on it using cans, which we had received in our care packages, as measuring cups. Knowing how much water had been transferred from one side of the balance beam to the other, compensating for the difference in weight of the two-people standing on the beam, allowed us to add or subtract that weight of water to or from the known weight that we had on one end of the beam, giving us the weight of the man on the other end of the beam.

We were able to do this under the watchful eyes of our North Vietnamese guards by performing the process one night while a movie was being told, and the spectators even included the distracted North Vietnamese guards standing at the door and one in the window. While other prisoners screened the back of the room, one man at a time came back and stepped on the improvised scale. We balanced him, he was told his weight and then proceeded back to his place in the audience and sent another man, until we had weighed everyone. This was accomplished all in one evening during the movie.

We were able to determine afterwards that most of us had been weighed accurately, within two or three pounds. Everyone was very interested in the project and it was a welcome relief from our daily routine. It was amusing in its conception and, on top of that, we felt that we had put something over on our captors, yet again. As a matter of interest and to the best of my recollection I weighed in at around 130 pounds standing 6'2". I was a bit lean. I had weighed around 195 when I was shot down.

During this period in our captivity we continued to receive packages from home, as we had earlier, but the packages were now far more complete. We received packages from the Red Cross as well as from home, and according to the Geneva conventions these

Chapter 25 | Onward Christian Soldiers

packages were able to weigh as much as six pounds, but usually were less. Our captors imposed their tax and enjoyed many of the items that came in these packages. But we accepted and welcomed the packages, no matter what the contents, no matter the "tax."

Our SRO assigned one of us the job of being Commissary Officer, who was responsible for the packages of those who wished to donate them to the room community. It was a voluntary act but everyone took pride in doing it, and so those whom were taxed less had more complete packages and could contribute items to those whom the gooks disliked the most. The Commissary Officer compiled lists of the items in the packages such as candy, soups, bouillon, powdered milk, coffee, meat, cheese, peanut butter, honey, and so forth. The packages were then stored by the gooks under our names until we wanted an item. When it was decided to have a party, the Commissary Officer sent out a request for perhaps ham and cheese. The men with ham and cheese in their packages retrieved it from the guards that day and brought it to the cell. Then ham and cheese was pooled and everyone shared.

Dividing the food this way provided everyone a variety because some men didn't get ham and cheese in a package but may have received candy or peanut butter. This act of sharing added to the unity of the room, provided a more even distribution of what extra rations were available, and everyone enjoyed the social aspects of the "parties."

On one occasion, I received in my package a tin can of peanut butter which bore no label except a black stamp labeling it as such. It was a relatively large can for peanut butter, maybe the size of a gallon can of ground coffee. I remind you that at that time pull tabs had not yet been invented nor were we using aluminum cans, so opening a can actually made of tin without a twist can opener was a challenge. Goo-yen, however, decided he wanted to verify the contents, and not having a can opener he set out to open this can of peanut butter with a machete. Yes, an actual jungle chopping machete, and not even a sharp one.

It required several substantial blows with the machete before the tin was even penetrated. It might not have taken quite such a substantial number of blows if he had hit it in the same spot. So, I'm sure you're getting the picture now. When it was finally penetrated, peanut butter sort of "squished" out. Goo-yen, however, was not satisfied and continued hacking at the tin can with ever greater vigor. This gallon tin can of peanut butter was causing considerable loss of face. With every ensuing blow, more and more peanut butter squeezed out of the different ragged gashes and was slung about the room from the machete now covered in peanut butter. Goo-yen persisted in his attack until the object of his violence was an oily, slippery glob of peanut butter covering a tin can. The various small globs and splatters of peanut butter scattered about the room was another amusing attraction. Goo-yen, his loss of face recovered, presented this glob to me with the pride of a conquering toreador.

By sharing food we were also able to take particularly good care of our sick. The Commissary Officer was also given all of the powered milk and protein and vitamin supplements received in the packages. He distributed what was needed among the sick, whether or not they ever received a package, and then redistributed the excess back to the rest of the cell. This gave everyone a good feeling, and I'm happy to say that most all of our sick made it home with us. It was completely voluntary but I know of no one who did not proudly participate.

CHAPTER 26

CELL MATES, SEX, AND SCALAWAGS

Although we were managing to keep our minds occupied, we were hardly living our lives free on a college campus with our families, barbecuing hamburgers and steak, waterskiing and playing with mom and the kids on the weekend. Life was very harsh; torture and death were always close at hand, death by a brutal enemy, slow agonizing death by an untreated sickness, starvation, watching the suffering of a cellmate, and being ignored when requesting help for him.

An F-4 back seater, Dave Raymond, had developed a bad case of asthma and frequently had terrible attacks that constantly brought him close to death. Imagine trying to take a life-sustaining breath and barely being able to do so. There were no inhalers to relieve the constricted trachea and mucus filled lungs and no one who cared, except those who had nothing to offer but encouragement. It was a sign of true strength to not just succumb to death, but to fight for each breath. Dave came home with us.

I could feel the malaria gradually killing me. It manifested itself with heart palpitations, with difficulty breathing like asthma, with an inability to regulate my body temperature, with bouts of anxiety and depression.

Those who had injuries just watched themselves very gradually heal in whatever grotesque form the body found itself. John McCain was badly deformed, but his spirit was not. Whatever medicine was provided was farcical. At some point a couple of us caught pink eye and knowing it's capability to quickly spread among us, the gooks decided to provide some medical assistance. In came the little old gook "doctor" with the white lab coat, escorted by armed guards and an English speaker who told us to line up. He started at the end of the line and proceeded to inspect each one of us by spreading our eyelids with his unsanitized and ungloved hand. Any attempt to remind the "doctor" that this kind of mass examination would only spread it, fell on deaf ears, and was taken as a bad attitude. Any of us who didn't have it soon did. Fortunately, we were given some kind of eyewash that seemed to heal it…eventually.

We all had internal parasites, worms, and no telling what else, so digestive issues were not uncommon, and did not constitute a crisis. However, in at least one situation everyone was exposed to food poisoning and began to vomit and get a roaring case of the diarrhea. It was followed by weakness and what felt like fever for several hours up to a few days while making a recovery. Everyone did not fall ill at the same time, but one at a time. It started off slowly, picked up an alarming pace, and then slowed down over the next hours as more and more fell ill. Those who hadn't fallen tended those who had, until they themselves went down. I went down at about halfway through our cell group and at about four or five hours after the first. I have always used that as a gauge if I thought I might have eaten something toxic. After four or five hours, if I still feel fine, I considered myself home free. Those who were recovering could not help but tease those who hadn't yet gone down that it would soon be their turn. As we approached the end of the episode the few remaining who had not yet taken the dive began to do so with longer intervals between them. By this time, they were so convinced that they would be next, a few were starting to make false declarations, which led to harassing cat calls and remarks. There were even a couple who never did fall and kept wondering when they "could join the club." We could only assume they grew up raiding garbage cans and developing digestive systems that would take on anything. Those of us who did get sick were very grateful for their unselfish continuous aid and assistance.

Notwithstanding the various crises that seemed to occur with regard to our health and security, for which we just rolled the dice,

Chapter 26 | Cell Mates, Sex, and Scalawags

I learned a lot. Dan Glen had helped me to design and draw my "future house" while teaching a class on architectural design including vanishing points. Dan also coached me in drawing a picture of a scantily clad young lady frolicking in the surf, which came out looking surprisingly like my wife. I drew it on the concrete pedestal under my bed mat, and I must say it was amazingly good. Very popular among my cell mates, it drew a lot of attention and numerous comments but fell victim to the scrub brush at the next inspection. I have never tried to draw the human form since.

On a bit of the darker but realistic side, we discussed what we would do if confronted with various marital problems upon our return home. We realized that it had been many years and it would be a lot to expect our wives to still want to continue a marriage with a man who could not possibly be the same person to whom she had said goodbye. This was obvious from the demoralizing and heart breaking "Dear John letters" that a few received from home. Sometimes they came from the wife and sometimes from mom and dad. The letter may have said she had gone to Mexico with some guy, got a Mexican divorce, and then married him and not been seen since. We knew our life upon our return would not be easy after the initial euphoria of freedom and so we were trying to be as realistic as possible in preparation to confront the issues.

Most were willing to accept the fact they might well be required to just walk away and start life over. But most were also willing to pledge long and dedicated understanding and tolerance to those they loved, and who once loved them. We knew in our minds, that even though our lives seemed just as they were when we left, our spouses and sweethearts were living a world of swirling stimulation, challenges, child rearing, temptations, anti-war sentiment, and life in general.

But even with the help of our pessimists, we were unable to conjure up all of that which we actually had to deal with upon our return. On the unbelievably strong and loyal side of some relations, couples who were not even married yet took up almost where they left off, married and are still so, after all these years. Uncle Tom Storey's family was one of these magical ones. So, as it turns out, I learned from the very best, not only how to fly but how to live and love my family and my God.

The family life to which I returned is part of a book not yet written. It was nothing I could have conjured up. So, let's just suffice it to say, my first wife Bonnie, to whom I was married during my six years as a prisoner of war, was not even there to greet me when I walked down the ramp from the airplane and stepped on American soil at Scott AFB in Bellville, Illinois, just east of Saint Louis, and only a three hour drive from where she was living in Columbia. Her very first greeting was informing me my best friend growing up in high school and college, and my fraternity father, Lon Richards, had been killed in the war. So, as one can surmise, though not uncommon, my first marriage did not survive the ordeal of captivity and absence. Now having been married 40 years to my loving second wife, Anne, I can say that blessings are often not recognized at the time.

The peace talks in Paris had broken down again which always seemed to mean another delay of six months before any significant talks regarding the release of POWs would continue. It might be said we had become comfortable in our misery except for the condition of our sick whose illnesses only continued to worsen without competent medical care.

Then the day arrived for another move. Moves were never very welcomed because of their unknown aspect, although the last few seemed to be an improvement. The key to this one would be whether we all stayed together or not. Or not, could be a bad sign. Our pessimists always reminded us of the specter of the past intent of the Vietnamese to put us before tribunals, with verdicts of execution or life in prison.

After we had all completed rolling up our bedroll and dressing in long sleeved shirts and pants, they started issuing us out the large iron doors in single file. That was a good sign because if we were to be split up we would have been taken out one at a time, or in small groups. As I approached the doors, they stopped the file and gestured for me to step out of line and remain in the cell. After I did, they continued to have the rest of my cellmates file out. Then, with no explanation, they slammed the large iron doors leaving me in the cell alone. That

Chapter 26 | Cell Mates, Sex, and Scalawags

was a very sinking feeling. Whatever was to be my fate, I was to go it alone.

The feeling of abandonment was made worse by the sound of the doors to the large adjacent cells also being opened and closed. It indicated to me the departure of those men also. If anything was worse than being left alone, it was being left alone in a cell with no one in adjacent cells to talk to. As things settled down, it appeared I was to be stuck there for a while. I began to offer a prayer for a sign that would boost my strength and resolve to face whatever fate I was to confront.

I had not yet rolled out my bed mat, but sat on the end of the long concrete center pedestal of this now massive cell, which only minutes before had seemed much smaller when it was populated with all of my fellow prisoners. Then I heard keys, the clang and clunk of the large cell doors being opened and the guard stood in front of me. Sensing I was not in much of a mood to be generous with my standing erect and performing a curt head nod to be interpreted by him as a bow, he chose not to antagonize me into a confrontation, and gestured me out. Collecting my bedroll, I preceded as directed into the cell just next door. As I entered, I was greeted by a room full of more American POWs. Where had they come from? I knew none of them, but as they came forward to introduce themselves and shake my hand with some enthusiastic hugs, I realized that I knew these names, these guys were famous for the problems they had caused the gooks over the years. They were held in very high esteem by the lot of us. One of these was Navy Lieutenant Commander John McCain. He looked pretty badly beat up with a broken arm that had healed in a grotesque bent manner, and was dragging a leg that didn't look much better than the arm. But he had a smile and an enthusiastic greeting as if we were long lost friends. I knew who the POW John McCain was, but not the person. I soon learned his father was the Navy Admiral and Commander of the war in the Pacific and Vietnam. Wow, what a catch he must have been!

It was a talkative group as we were apparently gathered together from several different cell and camp groups to be confined in this one cell isolated from any others. Later we realized that we were the only ones in the entire American POW camp that had been comprised of several cells. We were a fresh group, each an individual from which to hear tales and adventures of life, of flying, and the hell that had befallen each of us. How I was ever associated with this group of scalawags was a mystery to me, for my "modus operandi" was to act stupid and stay under the radar. Theirs was not, theirs was just "in your face, go screw yourself!" Nevertheless there I was, and it proved to be a great association.

Bud Flesher, an Air Force Captain flying F-4s who was a declared atheist and one of the happiest pessimists I was ever to know, taught me how to play 21. When Bud felt I was accomplished enough, he started cheating me and then gloating by showing me how I was so easily duped. Well, this did create a bit of a challenge. So, I took him on, and as one might guess we took great pleasure in out cheating each other, then revealing how much of a sucker our opponent was. As we did so we began to gather a few onlookers who grew into a crowd and then who started placing side bets on who would be able to come up with the best cheat. It was no holds barred, and it was fun.

It should not surprise anyone that a collection of twenty to thirty something fighter pilots with little to do, might enjoy comparing sexual conquest adventures. One might also suspect that they would well have some to brag about. It also goes to reason that if they had any to brag about, they would, and they might even brag about some they didn't have. If that offends anyone then I would only say that they haven't been around many fighter pilots!

During my younger years, all those summers I spent on the farm isolated in north Missouri took their toll on me socially. During those summers my friends at home hung around together, guys and gals, but I enjoyed none of that kind of activity. I started dating very late in life and was just a social misfit. As a result, when I went off to war, I was married with one child and had no adventurous sexual conquests.

I did enjoy hearing these adventures from my cellmates, but it wasn't long before they started to press me for some of my stories. I claimed I had none but they weren't convinced and continued to press. After one such gathering, I was sitting on my section of the

Chapter 26 | Cell Mates, Sex, and Scalawags

large concrete center pedestal when John McCain came hobbling down the aisle dragging his one leg and holding the bad arm askew while authoritatively swinging the good one with his eyes sparkling. He said with a bold voice that did not match his diminutive broken up body.

"Clark, you know what your problem is?"

"No, McCain, what is it?"

"These guys are just lying out their ass. Here's what you do. Take your best sex miss and put a big ass lying, scoring end on it and snow 'em!"

You know, he was right. The next time I had a couple of whoppers and there was a lot of: "Clark, we knew you were holding out!"

And that is my John McCain story.

The Eagle Hunts

CHAPTER 27

COLD NIGHTS

Time moved into winter, and winter in North Vietnam could be cold. This winter was colder than the one before, and the one before that, but not as cold as in Missouri. The two could hardly be compared. In Missouri, we have windows with glass and the Hanoi Hilton had huge open windows adorned with iron bars which do very little to keep out the cold. Freezing temperatures become a crisis, especially for anyone with a respiratory illness. The temperature and humidity during winter was similar to the maritime winters we know in England or perhaps Washington state, very damp and low temperatures hovering around freezing with an occasional cold snap.

It was one of those cold snaps with a forecast freezing night that gave me cause to be concerned so I decided to innovate. We were all given two almost useless crude cotton blankets that have been previously described. Knowing a dead airspace was a good insulator from Dr. Scorah's thermodynamics and heat transfer class in college, I set the principal into practice.

Our toilet paper was every bit as crude as our blankets and made by smashing wood up in water until it became a thick mass of soft splinters, then thinly spreading it into sixteen inch squares onto a flat surface, and allowing it to dry. It was even coarse enough one could pick out individual splinters of wood from the sheets. You see I know this because upon returning a free man, I availed myself of the opportunity to visit a Civil War reenactment, whereupon I was privileged to observe the very process being demonstrated by the "enactor toilet paper maker." The upside was we had toilet paper, the downside being it was Civil war vintage. As you might presume, it provided a rather

The Eagle Hunts

harsh ending to one of the most looked forward to activities of the long boring days.

We were given a sparse supply of it so I tore it up into about three inch squares for our daily use. After consulting with various individuals, it seemed no one really cared whether I wanted to sleep under a bunch of toilet paper squares. I placed one blanket over me then one at a time crumpled the little squares into kind of a ball and placed them carefully on top of the blanket as I unrolled the second blanket on top of them keeping the two blankets separated by an inch or two.

The night was cold as expected, the water froze, and there was a lot of colorful language out of my cellmates about the lack of comfort and adequacy of the two crude cotton blankets. I, however, was quite comfortable, surprisingly so, and rather smug I might add. But there was an unintended consequence. It seems I had a stack of three by three inch squares of toilet paper which had to be flattened out. It's one thing to grab a square of wood splinter paper and crumple it up, and another entirely, to flatten them back out. It was very time consuming, but then time was a very plentiful commodity.

CHAPTER 28

LINEBACKER II

Christmas approached and with it came thoughts of home and family and the bustle of buying and wrapping gifts, the cards for friends, the parties, Christmases past, and the prayers for future ones. Propaganda biased news continued to tell us of the breakdown of the Paris peace talks, which had been delayed for months due to the very controversial issue of the table size and shape and how many people should be able to sit around it. Was the table to be round so everyone seemed equally important, or oblong where some could be at the ends and more important, or could they be in the center opposing each other and hence more important, or maybe rectangular where the big dogs sat opposing and the staff in the wings, so to speak? It was mostly delaying tactics so the Communists could strengthen their tactical positions on the ground in Vietnam during the bombing halt and ceasefire, which the American government held out as a carrot to get the North Vietnamese to continue the negotiations. We knew it could go on for months, even years, we had seen it before. I wondered how many more Christmases? Would there even be any more? How much longer would my body keep up the fight? Sadly, the pessimists had a fertile feeding ground on holidays.

It was just a few days until Christmas and Bud Flesher and I were in another cheaters game of 21 seeing who was still the greater cheat. I can't remember if we were still drawing a crowd, however, the victory was not in winning the game, but at the end in showing the opponent how badly he had been cheated, much to the chagrin of his own pride at being beaten in spite of his own especially clever

The Eagle Hunts

cheating tactics. The observers mostly didn't care who won but took great joy in trying to spot the cheats being performed.

Bud's atheist pessimistic side was exhibiting itself. This was their time, so no hope of home by Christmas, breakdown of peace talks and the stark but logical realization that some 350 of us were simply not worth the cost of lives and taxpayer dollars. Then there was the growing division in the country caused by this unpopular non-war. Some might be released eventually, some who had kept their heads down and, though ever resistant, not given to intentionally antagonizing our captors. That, however, would not be anyone in this cell, except perhaps for me. Still I wondered, how I was ever singled out to join this group of "blackest American war criminals," nares-do-well and scalawags, who reveled in their ability to piss off the gooks and had the scars to prove it. As a result of my reconnaissance status I had been called a spy and hence deserving of execution but then I wasn't the only reconnaissance pilot that was shot down and yet here I was.

There was a quiver of the cell floor, as it had not been felt before without the scream of the Eagle and the "bam bam bam" of anti-aircraft guns surrounding the prison. The guns were not intended for our protection, but the North Vietnamese hoped if they were close enough to us they would be inside the no bomb zone around the prison, a zone that our guys religiously observed. This quiver caused several "what the hell' looks among us. It was a "Jell-O" like quiver and no bombs exploding - odd – earthquake maybe? Not in the six to eight years we had been imprisoned there. Curious yes, answers no, speculation rampant. It seemed during the next day the event continued on occasion except the gooks became very nervous and on one such occasion there was distant thunder, a rumble, but a cloudless sky. "BUFFS," B-52s, American strategic bombers of carpet-bombing fame, the holy grail of total destruction, nothing else in the world could do what we were hearing and feeling. We were bombing North Vietnam, Hanoi! President Richard Nixon and Secretary of State Henry Kissinger were fed up with the stalling tactics of the North Vietnamese in Paris.

Chapter 28 | Linebacker II

With the introduction of the Navy's A-6 Intruder, an all-weather day and night tactical operations capability was added that had not previously existed except in some limited numbers of tactical aircraft like the RF-4C Phantom II with its powerful low-level navigation radar. In the early 1970's the Navy started flying night low level high speed tactical bombing raids on targets in the Hanoi area, and almost always they were a surprise; the sirens, the lights go out, there is a whoosh and a roar, the guns start firing but too late, an explosion somewhere and everyone sitting around in the dark with a low rumble fading into the night as the Intruder disappears unscathed. The Eagle now hunted in the dark of night.

The zenith of B-52 attacks in Vietnam was Operation Linebacker II, which consisted of waves of B-52s between 28 and 29 Dec. of 1972 dropping over 15,000 tons of bombs on Hanoi, Haiphong and other targets. In the beginning of the B-52 involvement in Vietnam the B-52s were restricted to bombing in relatively uninhabited areas because their potency approached that of a tactical nuclear weapon. Six B-52s dropping bombs from 30,000 feet could wipe out an area approximately one-half mile wide and two miles long.*

Such was this night that we were awakened by the Intruder or perhaps more correctly the bedlam it created. The 18th of December 1972 was the date, and as more bombs went off and more Intruders

---

* Paraphrased from Wikipedia, the free encyclopedia.

set off the sirens, and an almost continuous blast of guns ensued, it became apparent to us that the Eagle was pissed.

The Grumman A-6 Intruder is an American twinjet all-weather attack aircraft manufactured by Grumman Aerospace. It was flown by U.S. Navy and Marine Corps pilots off of U.S. aircraft carriers operating in the Gulf of Tonkin during the Vietnam war.

An all clear siren and brief calm ensued, and then suddenly the altogether familiar whoosh and boom of several Shrike missiles exploding as they appeared out of the dark of night to strike the radar aimed anti-aircraft artillery positioned just outside the walls of the prison. Here we go again; siren, lights out, but this time the roar and whoosh of surface to air missiles (SAMs) capable of intercepting high-altitude aircraft, the same ones used to down Francis Gary Powers in the previously untouchable U-2 over Russia some years earlier, and the ones used to defend Moscow, were filling the sky. It was clear the Intruders were only a warm up because the Buffs had now joined the fray. Our view only covered about 90 degrees of the sky but it could be presumed that what we were seeing was going on all around us. Hanoi was lit up, the ground and sky above was an inferno. Bright white explosions dotted the sky as the SAMs exploded, arching AAA tracers, with bright white trails of flame from the SAMs streaking overhead and being confused by the electronic counter measures of the B-52s and then crashing back into Hanoi adding to the mayhem

Chapter 28 | Linebacker II

and destruction. We were in the big arched windows looking out, standing on the backs of each other, and standing on tip toes on the concrete center bed pedestal. We cheered and danced and no one told us we couldn't. The ever-present guards who ordered us to not look out the windows and to seek safety behind the massive walls were nowhere to be found. They had come to realize the full wrath of the way we could fight and there was absolutely nothing they could do about it.

Almost as quick as it began, the continual thunder of the exploding bombs ceased but the AAA and SAMs continued sporadically, I assumed due to the weapons triggermen accidently hitting the trigger while trying to change their pants having messed themselves. Hanoi burned furiously with a red glow that lit the night sky, seemingly to the heavens. Finally, the guns went quiet, the sirens blew the all clear and the shaken guards cautiously left the concrete manholes where they had sought refuge. But the night was not over.

While the fires still burned emitting a deeper red glow showing either what had been burning was being consumed by the flames, or perhaps somewhat extinguished, the sirens wailed again! The guns resumed fire and SAMs launched, but this time there was a comparatively small number of explosions, and with them the woosh and roar of what was to become the calling card of the confounding, ever present Intruder. Silent, fast, from where no one was to ever know, with deadly accuracy, and with almost the speed of a bullet, they were gone by the time their bombs exploded. The night owl of the American Navy had again paid a visit. Sometimes the all-clear sirens blew, the previously blacked out lights sporadically turned back on lighting what was left of Hanoi, just to light the target for the lurking Intruders that would some minutes hence attack again. There was no sleep for the Eagles prey!

During the next twelve or so days, except for a 36-hour pause over Christmas, the bombing attacks continued, day and night. During the days, there were tactical attacks by Navy and Air Force appearing quickly and then gone, and by night the more extended constant and defining roar of destruction by the Buffs. The hapless firing of the guns and of unguided barrage fire of the missiles told us the "People's

The Eagle Hunts

Air Defense Forces" had lost control of their skies. After the first night and day much of the radar aiming capability of the SAMs was damaged or destroyed and they were being fired ballistically, which is just being aimed by eye. At some point, they began to realize their supply of SAMs and AAA ammo was running short and the destroyed bridges, railroads and roads, harbors and air fields allowed only a trickle of resupply. Consequently, at times they would just fill the sky with bullets, waiting for some luckless American "air pirate" to run into one. It's what we would refer to as "the silver bullet." It seemed it became the only and very inefficient way to defend their capitol and what was left of its war time capability. A salvo of barrage fire at the nightly waves of Buffs would leave them unarmed for the following unrelenting sudden and low-level attacks of our night flyers. The nightly bombs, explosions, fires, and holocaust outside the prison

This is a photo of the cell that Captain Clark lived in during the Linebacker II raids over Hanoi in December of 1972. This photo was taken after the release of the POWs in 1973 but before the destruction of the main part of the prison. Note the guards are unarmed and are wearing shoes which they were not during the war. In the windows appear to be tourists or official visitors.

walls became commonplace. Our guards stumbled by bleary eyed, clearly gun-shy, and fleeing at the very hint of an Eagle on the hunt, driving them into their manholes dug into the ground of the prison. It was like a field mouse fleeing an airborne predator. It became amusing to watch the gooks get completely rattled with planes

Chapter 28 | Linebacker II

roaring overhead, bombing and disappearing into the distance, the lights going off, the sirens blowing, guns firing at what was unknown because the planes were long gone, then silence, awaiting the rest of the attack that never came. The not so confident blowing of the all clear siren, lights back on, goo-yen looking about cautiously, bleary and bloodshot eyes from total lack of sleep, even more cautiously climbing out of his manhole, standing for a bit while staying within diving distance of the manhole, then slinging his AK-47 over his shoulder and moving off with an unsure gait to issue some gruff orders to the "blackest criminals" who were enjoying American airpower finally taking off the gloves way too much. These captive air pirates apparently had much more confidence in the bombing accuracy of their brothers than the gooks did while crouched down in the manholes outside. It gave me great pleasure upon my return home to talk to some of the "TAC" fighter jocks who made those runs over Hanoi and find out that the prison made a good radar check point. They took great pleasure of making a full afterburner near supersonic low pass over the prison to let us know we had not been forgotten, and to say "hi" in a fighter pilot kind of way. Believe me it was much appreciated. While I'm certain they left more than just a few of those gooks with a good case of PTSD, we loved it and cheered much to the guard's chagrin as they were in no way going to exit their manhole to discipline us. It was the perfect storm.

It became commonplace that just about the time the somewhat tentative guards, having ruffled up their feathers as best they could, approached the cell and swung open the large barred doors, we assumed nonchalant positions of normalcy, awaited the forthcoming chastisement and threats.

If we didn't hear the bombs about the time we heard the jets, we usually hit the deck because we knew, unless it was a reconnaissance run, there had been bombs dropped somewhere. The doors were slammed shut and locked. But on at least one occasion each of the guards thought the other had locked it, and it was not. The superficially blustering guards had shed all modicum of valor and made for the manholes with no regard for bravado. We, however, maintained our cool, and did nothing stupid like make for an unsecured door, because none of us had any misconception that the guards would not have let us get far out of that cell without encountering a hail of AK-47 fire.

After those days and nights, I would have to say that with the exception of occasional outbursts that seemed to be more attributable to delirium and sleep deprivation, the gooks seemed to exhibit a clear attitude adjustment. Having read some intelligence reports after I returned home, I learned that at the time there were no longer any targets in the north that were worthy of such continued mass destruction, except for the civilian population, and we did not want to do that, and I'm glad. The ever-blusterous North Vietnamese did, however, come over the radio and announce that having experienced huge losses at the hands of the "Vietnamese Peoples Air Defense Forces," the "perfidious and obdurate" Americans had shrunk back to the peace talks in Paris to negotiate the end of the bombing campaign. Knowing first hand who was doing the "shrinking," we were more hopeful than we had ever been. I am delighted to say after that my fear of a bombing raid never returned and I was left to enjoy these attacks in all of their devastating aspects. The fear was for the gooks to deal with, ours was only to watch it demoralize and dishearten them.*

"Onward Christian Soldiers."

---

* Authors note: As a parting comment, the North Vietnamese could easily have executed us as a reprisal anytime they wished and although their capability to respond to more B-52 attacks was greatly diminished, they still continued to be a threat to us. This was not to be dismissed.

CHAPTER 29

THE PROCLAMATION

We had heard little about the peace talks, but nothing about them being broken off either. The Eagle was not prowling the skies so things seemed to be returning to normal, which was a bit disappointing. The sound of the large iron gates on the empty cells that had existed around the camp for several months were squeaking open and closing with their characteristic hollow heavy thud. The normally quiet compound was filled by lots of coughing and sneezing revealing the names of the men who had left so many months earlier. Our cell was broken up and I was pulled out and placed back into my old cell with the same group that had left me, with some additions of individuals and a few others having been moved out.

All who had previously departed had returned with the exception of John Fredricks who was a Marine Warrant Officer, F-4 back seater with the scars of being burned when he was shot down, and who could build muscle on pumpkin soup and water. Amazingly strong, and ten years older than most of us, he had contracted an illness and became wracked with fever, was removed from his cell, and never seen or heard of again.

I pause in remembrance of him. He was a solid prince of a guy. In one of my self-defense and physical fitness programs I talked John into demonstrating some hand to hand combat moves. Capable of dispatching me quickly, he always moved with obvious regard for my comparative frailty. It was a sad loss – may God bless him and hold him close.

There was something amiss about the way the cells had been organized upon the return of our compatriots. For years certain camps or groups of prisoners had been established with little movement of prisoners between them. The Vietnamese had learned that moving individuals between camp groups facilitated communications between them. Hence, the individual prisoners in each camp, with a few exceptions, remained the same. Now the different camps, The Plantation, Camp Faith, The Zoo, The Hilton, etc., had been mixed up providing unfettered passing of information among individuals. Of course, as soon as all of the camp groups were returned to the large cells of the Hilton, which were adjacent to each other, communication was regular and extensive. There was no attempt to prevent our open communication between cells. This was a question to be answered, because changes almost always foretold the future if you could figure them out. So, the full resources of our communication types and optimistic thinkers were put into play.

"Holy cow!" We discovered that the cells were now organized by shoot down dates. The POWs that had been shot down the longest were in one cell, then the next longest in another cell, and so forth. We had always declared, as stated by our senior ranking officers, that none of us would return home before anyone who had been shot down before us, excepting of course, the seriously ill and injured. Could it really be that we were organized by cell in the manner that we would be released? What else could it be? It was bad for effective pessimistic behavior, but in order to keep their reputations they conjured up all form of dark alternatives. But their ranks were thinning and if you looked closely, you could see a new life in their eyes. I took on the sense that even they were moving over to the "bright side."

Could this be real? We had experienced similar optimism before and been met with crushing disappointment as it turned out to be only another attempt to play the "see how well we would treat you if you would just realize the way of the Vietnamese people" card. It could just be another dashing on to the cruel rocks of our miserable existence.

In a few days, the word was passed via our now overt communication system that we would all be asked by the camp guards to dress in our long pants and shirts and form up by cell in the court

Chapter 29 | The Proclamation

yard in preparation for the reading of a proclamation by the camp commander.

To put things in perspective, one needs to realize there had been proclamations before. They turned out to be demands for us blackest American criminals to seek the pardon of the Vietnamese people by writing statements about the "good and lenient" treatment we were getting, or be treated as the blackest of criminals and undeserving of the good and forgiving attitude of the Vietnamese people. Hence, we would be "severely bunished," which could be beatings, torture or threats of, or trials and executions that had been threatened for so many years. However, we had never been allowed together with any of the other cells and especially not the whole camp. Clearly something was afoot and our guts were just screaming! Had we made it? Had we survived long enough? Was our country coming to take us home? What would it be like? Even now there are goose bumps.

From the guys who were shot down and captured in the just finished bombing raids over Hanoi at Christmas, word was being sent about what the new world looked like. Of course, girls first, really short skirts, the braless look, free love, full nude centerfolds in Playboy and then the more mundane things like Neil Armstrong's walk on the moon, '73 corvettes, hand held computers and OK, did I mention really short skirts!

All this info was passing quickly because the guards had given up trying to control our communication. Actually, when our SRO was taken out to be informed of the upcoming reading of the proclamation, he asked the Camp Commander to inform the other cells of the plan. The reply was "no you do it, your communication system is faster than ours anyway." We took that acknowledgement as a supreme compliment.

I recall that within a day or so, the word was given by the guards and we suited up in our "longs" and marched out in file behind our cell SROs holding our heads high, stern faced, shoulders back and in step with the man ahead. We were a damn proud bunch for a herd of blackest criminals. We formed up in amazingly straight lines, although some of the pessimists had to be nudged around, as not all had given up on the "deception." The Camp Commander marched

The Eagle Hunts

out, in his smart looking officers dress uniform, unrolled the proclamation and read the terms of **our release!** Composure reined and we received the news stoically, marched back into our cells with stomachs in our throats, and then with amazing decorum we let it all out, hugs, pats, tears, silence, every emotion we had, even disbelief because even at best such an intent by the North Vietnamese could fall through for no particular reason.

We remembered years before many of us had been offered early release to return home and join the peace movement if we would only realize "the way of the Vietnamese people." Yes, most of us would be holding our breath until we were on an American Air Force aircraft with wheels up, "feet wet"[*] and over international waters. There were prayers that should any of it fall through at least the sick and badly disabled would get out. Every cell had some holding on to life day by day.

Our thoughts could not help but churn up our past depressing discussions concerning the enormous cost in equipment and lives it would take to convince our captors to release us. We pondered if we would be worth it to our nation. After all, it seemed it had turned upon us and we were, of course, lead to believe that our countrymen, especially the youth, thought we deserved our imprisonment and would be happy to see us remain so. No one wanted to believe any of this, but it still kept us awake at night with an anxious heart.

---

[*] "Feet Wet" was an expression used by pilots passing over the beach heading out to sea for the safety of the water after missions over the land, perhaps even with a damaged aircraft and needing rescue.

CHAPTER 30

REFUSING TO GO HOME

In a few weeks, the first release group was assembled and departed. Their cell was empty. The first American shot down over North Vietnam eight years earlier in a still undeclared war, Everett Alverez, Jr., was gone. Was he really home or was it a cruel ruse? A week or so later, I was pulled out of my cell, bed roll and all. I do not remember whether I was the only one from my cell or not, but if I wasn't it would have only been two or three of us. I remember the looks from my cell mates, stern questioning faces looking at us walking out, and the guards who were escorting us. In this period of open communication between us and the camp officers this was unusual but had the feel of what we had seen before. Would we be the ones not there when everyone was released and counted? When all the names of known POWs were compared with those released, would we be the ones that just disappeared? It was inwardly crushing and disheartening, but outwardly we were stoic, having walked this morale crushing route so many times before. It was just a matter of survival. I, or we, were joined together with a few others bringing our total number to twenty. We were locked up in a smaller cell away from our previous camp but still within the confines of the Hoa Lo Prison. There was no possibility for communication with our seniors or the cells being released.

One of the camp officers entered our cell with the usual contingent of guards armed with AK-47s and tin can machine guns. He informed us our Secretary of State, Henry Kissinger, was visiting North Vietnam, and we were to be released into his custody as a gesture of good faith. That sounded better than we had feared, but also a bit contrived. Our release would have been out of order, or at least before some who had been shot down before us. Our group SRO, speaking for all of us, replied that we were out of the agreed upon release order and would not go, and that the next twenty men would need to be selected by shoot down date. The camp officer was speechless, and told us to think "deeply and carefully," which was a familiar refrain that we heard when we were first shot down and being tortured for intelligence information. He informed us that we had been selected and must go. We could not believe we were saying no, not as a result of any decision of theirs, but ours. No, we would not accept an "early release." Later, he returned but we stood fast on our collective decision and were told that if we continued to refuse, we would never be released and would be lost for life in the prison system, never to be heard of again. It was not a pleasant thing to contemplate. But, to those who had experienced having a cocked .45 pistol put to their head, and told they were going to be executed, it was just another card in the game. After his departure, we were quiet and solemn, but proud of ourselves and each other, for sticking together and standing on our principles. Not one of us dissented. It was as if there was an American flag in the room and each of us had a hand on the staff holding it proudly and standing tall, **"I am an American fighting man …."**

Our cell SRO had told the Vietnamese Camp Commander that we must receive a personal order from General John Flynn, our American camp Senior Ranking Officer, to take release if we were to violate the "return in order" code, but the line in the sand had been drawn, and any contact with him was extremely unlikely.

I think it was the next morning when a United States Air Force Colonel in full dress blues complete with wheel hat whose bill was adorned in the signature lightning bolts of a full Colonel appeared. Wow! We had not seen one of those in six years. Did we really look that good in uniform? He was accompanied by fully armed Vietnamese guards looking stern and business like. He approached with the full demeanor given him by the Congress of our United States and befitting his senior rank and mission. We "popped to" attention and saluted.

Chapter 30 | Refusing to Go Home

With a crisp return salute, he said something like **"Gentlemen, your release is an act of good faith of the Vietnamese government. To not accept their gesture would be of great embarrassment and loss of face, which could put in jeopardy the rest of the release that is still tenuous. I am here to order you on the command of the highest authority of our government (the President) with the concurrence of General Flynn, your Senior Ranking Officer, to accept this offer and go home without further complications. Congratulations soldiers, let's go home; your country awaits you."**

Photo of a U.S. Air Force C-141 transport aircraft on final approach to landing. This is exactly a view like Captain Clark saw as he passed along a Red River dike heading to the Hanoi airport to board that airplane, which would take him home. At that time, he felt like he might really be going home.

Finally, we accepted the reality of going home. Even now after all these years I choke up and tears make it difficult to see the page.

Shortly after, we were issued new blue long sleeve shirts and trousers with black shoes and a carry-on bag with miscellaneous items like soap, a tooth brush and tooth paste for our trip home.

That afternoon we boarded what looked like a camouflaged VW minivan and started driving through Hanoi to the airport. We were no longer blindfolded and were free to talk but I can't remember that much was said. As we approached the airport a single C-141 U.S. Air Force cargo jet, just like the one that I rode on into this conflict,

The Eagle Hunts

could be seen approaching the runway with gear and flaps down, the sun glinting off of the bright Red Cross on the tail. There is a large picture that so much reminds me of that moment hanging on my wall to this day.

And so, on that day, February 18, 1973, the Eagle gathered her twenty wayward chicks and with angels flying escort on her wings took them home.

A photo that was taken of Captain Clark's release just before he was escorted to the C-141 Loadmaster called the 'Hanoi Taxi' that would fly him and the rest of the 'Kissinger- 20' to Clark Air Base in the Philippines beginning their trip home. Captain Clark is the 4th POW in line from the front whose face is partially obscured by a POW to his right.

Chapter 30 | Refusing to Go Home

The Kissinger-20 after debriefings, being deloused, dewormed, outrageously overfed, fitted for uniforms, talking to their families and pampered more than deserved are preparing to head home from their first stop at Clark Air Base in the Philippines.

Captain Clark says goodbye to well-wishers at Clark Air Base as he prepares to board the C-141 that will fly him and the rest of the group back to the military hospitals closest to their homes in the United States.

Colonel Clark shortly after he retired from the Missouri Air National Guard in 1992.

The Eagle Hunts

EPILOGUE

Written by
"Uncle" Tom Storey
Lt. Col. USAF (Ret)

The Eagle Hunts

When circumstances place you in a situation where literally ALL your God-given rights are stripped from you in an instant, and you are left with nothing more than the ability to exist…you find you will begin a journey of the mind and soul that few ever encounter. It is a journey that you could never truly be prepared to experience, a journey where you will try to make sense of the senseless, logic from the illogical, and determine truth from falsehood. A journey that will ultimately determine whether you will live…or die. Where the mind goes, the body will follow.

After years of solitary confinement after my initial shoot down and capture, the first American that I was thrown in a cell to live with was my old squadron mate, John Clark. What a glorious day that was! Finally, I was able to share this journey with another brother and most importantly be able to lean on each other…and not be alone. Living inside only one's thoughts can be so lonely.

John and I shared absolutely everything about our lives. We tore down our lives backwards and forwards over those many first months together to the point where we thought we would run out of things to talk about. We never did. We went through the hell of torture, malnutrition, disease, and depression, but we had each other! Man is a social animal and as sure as the air we breathe…we needed each other. Our captors knew how to break us…and that isolation was the key.

After years together we finally had to just 'boil it all down'… down to what it takes to survive the journey… down to what the simple truths were that we had so tightly embraced to go beyond just to breathe. Those truths became…'The Fabulous Five Fs'.

After being repatriated in 1973, many of us travelled around the country speaking to other Americans. The country had been so fractured by the Vietnam War and we POWs seemed to be the only thing that most of the American people seemed to rally around. So, we headed out, so eager to pass on lessons from the cauldron of captivity. We had hoped that teaching about dealing with the hopelessness and despair, but most importantly, 'how we survived and bounced back' would help this country to do the same.

Epilogue

The 'Fabulous Five Fs'

The following 'Fabulous Five Fs' was the winner of the 1973 Freedoms Foundations letter writing contest. It was submitted by Major Robert E. Miller, ARNGUS. He was in attendance at the Galesburg, Illinois High school when I spoke to the graduating class of 1973. I have always liked how he captured the essence of our five truths…simple and straight forward. It says it all. Everyone who appreciates the 'Fabulous Five' should think about their own meanings and how they apply to them and their families.

"Maj. Thomas Gordon Storey returned to speak to his hometown (Galesburg, IL) high school commencement class in June of 1973 after more than six years as a prisoner of the North Vietnamese. During years of isolation and captivity this man's values, his goals were in his words "these Fabulous Five": Faith, Family, Friends, Future and Freedom. I believe this best summarizes Major Storey's thoughts as he awaited to return to his homeland – our beloved America.

Faith

Our faith to pray: To pray for strength to endure whatever life requires. Faith to believe in answered prayer and strength from an Almighty God. Faith to overcome human failings and to forgive one's fellowman.

Family

The blessing of family ties. The strength, determination and love of a wife. The patience and dedication of a mother. The sacrifice of a father. The adoration of a son and a daughter. The inner "Fortress" of belonging and having your own family and being a part of God's family.

Friends

Having friends: Friends from childhood, from school, from within your church, from work. Friends who help and who need help. The neighbor, doctor, pastor and the paperboy. The multitude of daily incidents where lives touch to communicate our human needs for ourselves and for our offering to other.

Future
Our future hopes, plans, desires for personal achievement. Our jobs, education, family, security for our children and their children. Our happiness and freedom to pursue our personal goals. The future of our community, our state and our nation.

Freedom
Yes, freedom to believe in justice, dignity, law and order and human rights. Freedom to think. Freedom to choose. Freedom to elect. Freedom to pray. Freedom to work. Freedom to discuss and freedom to act within the boundaries of just laws.

Major Storey's "Fabulous Five" are ageless and timeless. They fit any calendar in American history. On what better foundation could we build the peace for future generations?"
(Major Robert E. Miller, 1973)

A few weeks after the Galesburg address, I gave the graduation address at Millikin University in Decatur, Illinois. I had taught at Millikin as a professor prior to being recalled to full-time active duty and a regular commission in 1961 during the Berlin Crisis. After I finished my talk and was handing out the diplomas, one of the graduates whispered in my ear. "Sir, you forgot one 'F'… what about forever?" Kids are thinking all the time. Maybe she was right and it should be the Fab Six!

Faith is at the top of the list for the principles that John and I used to survive. It is the mortar that binds the foundation for the 'Fab Five'. This wonderful read reveals truly how even 'the faith of a mustard seed' can unchain a captive soul to fly free. I know I would not have survived my journey without my friend, my 'Brother in Christ'… John Clark.

Thank you, John, for saving my life.

"Uncle Tom"

ABOUT THE AUTHOR

Colonel John W. Clark, USAF (Ret.) spoke to the International Club of Atlanta, on Feb 6, 2021 and then, as shown above, spoke to the Atlanta Council on International Relations on Feb 7, 2019 in Atlanta Georgia.

John W. Clark is a retired Professional Engineer and Colonel in the United States Air Force retiring from the Missouri Air National Guard as commander of a "highly trained and very selective, engineering, Command staff Augmentation Flight."

He graduated from the University of Missouri's College of Engineering and Air Force ROTC in 1962 with a Bachelor of Science in Mechanical Engineering and as a **Distinguished Military Graduate** and was awarded a **Regular Air Force commission**, which only highly esteemed and Air Force Academy graduates were privileged to receive.

As a **Distinguished Flying Graduate** from Air Force pilot training, he began flying the C-131 for Aeromedical Evacuation missions and then after Combat Crew Training in the RF-4C Phantom II, flew tactical reconnaissance missions in Europe.

After flying approximately 80 combat reconnaissance missions over Vietnam, on one of which he was awarded the **Distinguished Flying Cross**, he was shot down, captured and released six years later.

He then attended the University of Missouri in Columbia where he obtained a **Master of Business Administration degree**. After returning to the cockpit and earning a **Certificate of Graduation as an Instructor Pilot** he trained student pilots in the T-38 while holding the positions of Flight Commander and Chief of Academics.

In 1979 he joined the 131st Tactical Fighter Wing of the Missouri Air National Guard as a War Plans, and Command and Control Specialist. He progressed through the ranks holding the positions of Commander of the 131st Civil Engineering Squadron, Missouri State Director of Operations for Air, and State Plans and Programs Officer. After being **promoted to Colonel** he assumed **Command of the 231st Civil Engineering Flight** and was awarded his **2nd Legion of Merit**.

Colonel Clark retired as the Water Engineer from the City of Columbia, MO, where both his wife, Anne, and he now live.

Colonel Clark is a lifetime member of the University of Missouri's Alumni Association and continues his contribution to the University of Missouri and the community through his ability to speak of his experiences and how those lessons can impact the lives of our youth. He is a 2021 recipient of the prestigious **University of Missouri Faculty-Alumni Award**, which was presented to him by University President Mun Choi.

Colonel Clark has served as treasurer of both the **Mayor's Task Force and the Committee of the Friends of the USS Columbia** fast attack nuclear submarine of which he and wife Anne were appointed Co-Chair of the original committee by the Columbia, MO Mayor in 1994.

Having been active in the national organization of The American Ex-Prisoners of War he has held the positions of **Missouri State**

About the Author

Department Commander and the National Director of the North Central Region.

He has served on the **Board of Advisors of the Jefferson Barracks Prisoner of War/Missing in Action Museum** from its inception until April of 2021.

He continues as a member of **Congresswoman Vicky Hartzler's Military Advisory Council** and has spoken to her youth Leadership Summit.

"For the sacrifice made for freedom" he has **twice** been awarded the **Silver Star Banner by the Silver Star Families of America**.

Colonel Clark also holds an **Outstanding Graduate Diploma** from the National Management Security Course, of **the National Defense University, in Washington D.C.**

His military decorations and awards include among others the **Silver Star, two Legions of Merit, the Distinguished Flying Cross, two Purple Hearts, the Meritorious Service Medal, six Air Medals, the Air Force Commendation Medal, the Prisoner of War Medal and two Republic of Vietnam Gallantry Crosses.**